The Classic Slum

By the same author
Imprisoned Tongues

Corner shop

Robert Roberts

The Classic Slum

*Salford life in the first quarter
of the century*

*Manchester
University Press*

© 1971 ROBERT ROBERTS

Published by the University of Manchester at
THE UNIVERSITY PRESS
316–324 Oxford Road, Manchester M13 9NR

ISBN 0 7190 0453 5

First published 1971
Second impression 1972

Printed in Great Britain by
Butler & Tanner Ltd, Frome and London

Contents

Illustrations

The photographs, which have not been published before, were taken around the early 1900's by a Worsley man, Samuel Coulthurst, who went about Salford dressed as a rag and bone merchant with his camera concealed on a handcart.

To E. and A.,
who left early

Preface

Many writers of modern social history have described with sympathy, and with passion even, the plight of the undermass in pre-1914 industrial Britain, when the rich seemed never so wealthy nor the poor so poor. But such description has naturally lacked the factuality that first-hand experience might have given it; few historians are the sons of labourers. Young myself, and a dweller in that world of want when the century was new, I have written down some of what I saw, heard and experienced and set it in the context of the times, hopeful, in standing so close to the common scene, not to have distorted too much.

This is a book made much from talk, the talk first of men and women, fifty or more years ago, of ideas and views repeated in family, street, factory and shop, and borne in mind with intent! The corner shop, my first home, was a perfect spot for young intelligence to eavesdrop on life. Here, back and forth across the counters, slid the comedy, tragedy, hopes, fears and fancies of a whole community: here was market place and village well combined. Only a fool could have failed to learn in it. Then, and for long afterwards, I mixed with people, adult in Edwardian and Georgian days, who had lived out their time in ghettos spawned by the industrial revolution. Many among them, shrewd and thoughtful, could not only recapitulate experience, they knew how to assess its value in relation to their lives. Men discussed, argued, reminisced: I listened and remembered. To them all, many long gone now, I am indeed grateful for what they taught.

'They're knocking our life and times away!' said an elderly Mancunian. We stood together gazing over a wilderness on which still another vast slum had been razed, and he spoke in grief. A kind of culture unlikely to rise again had gone in the rubble, and he knew it. But most of the young who left such places had no such regrets: the old ways their fathers had accepted had long grown insupportable; better by far the 'cliff' dwellings of modern Manchester. How life appeared in the slums which beset that great city during the early decades of the twentieth century I have tried in this book to show.

Thanks are due and recorded with gratitude to Mr Frank Mullineux, Keeper of the Monks Hall Museum, Eccles, for his kindness in allowing me to use photographs from his private collection and to Salford corporation for permission to reproduce the drawing by L. S. Lowry on the jacket.

R. R.

The Edwardian poor have attracted little attention in imaginative literature and play almost no part in commonly held images of Edwardian England. But to look at the domestic lives of the poor, both urban and rural, is to shadow our picture of upper and middle-class life with horror and dismay.

H. Laski

Chapter 1

Class Structure

We are the mob, the working class, the proletariat
Song

No view of the English working class in the first quarter of this century would be accurate if that class were shown merely as a great amalgam of artisan and labouring groups united by a common aim and culture. Life in reality was much more complex. Socially the unskilled workers and their families, who made up about 50 per cent of the population in our industrial cities, varied as much from the manual élite as did people in middle station from the aristocracy. Before 1914 skilled workers generally did not strive to join a higher rank; they were only too concerned to maintain position within their own stratum. Inside the working class as a whole there existed, I believe, a stratified form of society whose implications and consequences have hardly yet been fully explored. Born behind a general shop in an area which, sixty years before, Frederich Engels had called the 'classic slum', I grew up in what was perhaps an ideal position for viewing the English proletarian caste system in all its late flower.

All Salford [wrote Engels in 1844] is built in courts or narrow lanes, so narrow that they remind me of the narrowest I have ever seen, in the little lanes of Genoa. The average construction of Salford is, in this respect, much worse than that of Manchester and, so, too, in respect of cleanliness. If, in Manchester, the police, from time to time, every six or ten years, makes a raid upon the working-people's district, closes the worst dwellings, and causes the filthiest spots in these Augean stables to be cleansed, in Salford it seems to have done absolutely nothing.

For twenty years from 1850 Engels held interests in cotton mills on the western side of Manchester. This meant that on journeys between town and factory he had to pass through Salford; our 'village' lay the greatest slum *en route*. One of his early mills

(Ermen and Engels) stood in Liverpool Street, which ran through the heart of it. This is how Engels described our area in 1844:

> The working-men's dwellings between Oldfield Road and Cross Lane (Salford), where a mass of courts and alleys are to be found in the worst possible state, vie with the dwellings of the Old Town in filth and overcrowding. In this district I found a man, apparently sixty years old, living in a cow-stable. He had constructed a sort of chimney for his square pen, which had neither windows, floor nor ceiling, had obtained a bedstead and lived there, though the rain dripped through his rotten roof. This man was too old and weak for regular work, and supported himself by removing manure with a hand-cart; the dung heaps lay next door to his palace.

Through a familiarity so long and close, this district must have become for Engels the very epitome of all industrial ghettos, the 'classic slum' itself. He died in 1895 having seen that little world change, develop, 'prosper' even, yet stay in essence the same awful paradigm of what a free capitalist society could produce. By 1900 the area showed some improvement; his 'cow-stable' had doubtless been demolished together with many another noisome den, but much that was vile remained.

Our own family was in the slum but not, they felt, of it: we had 'connections'. Father, besides, was a skilled mechanic. During the '60's of the last century his mother, widowed early with four children, had had the foresight to bypass a mission hall near the alley where she lived and send her three good-looking daughters to a Wesleyan chapel on the edge of a middle-class suburb. Intelligent girls, they did their duty by God and mother, all becoming Sunday school teachers and each in turn marrying well above her station, one a journalist, another a traveller in sugar and a third a police inspector—an ill-favoured lot, the old lady grumbled, but 'you can't have everything'. The girls adapted themselves smoothly to their new milieu, paid mother a weekly danegeld and Carter's Court knew them no more. My father, years their junior, stayed working-class; it was, in fact, always harder for a man to break into the higher echelons. At the age of eight he took up education and, twelve months later, put it down, despite the new-fangled 'Compulsion' Act, to find, his mother[1] said,

---

[1] Grandma indeed seemed a realist all round. When, for instance, her husband, like Charles II, stayed lingering over his demise, solicitous

'summat a sight better to do at the blacksmith's'. At twenty-one Father married a girl from a cotton mill.

As a child my mother had been something of a prodigy and was hawked from one local school to another to display her talents; but, her father dying, she got work, at nine, helping in a weaving shed. Happily her family had 'expectations'. When the £900 legacy arrived it was laid out with skill and duly improved status: one sister married a clerk, and two elder brothers opened little shops, which prospered. They were on the way up! My father, a man given to envy, felt the call of commerce too and came home one evening twelve months after marriage to announce in tipsy triumph that he had, on borrowed money, just bought a grocery store for £40. Horrified, my mother inspected his 'gold mine'—in the heart of a slum—and refused point blank to go. But he cajoled and persuaded. In two or three years, he said, they could build it up, sell it for hundreds of pounds and buy a nice place in the country. She looked at the dank little premises and the grim kitchen behind. 'Two years,' she told him, 'and no more! This is no place to bring up a family.' Solemnly he promised. In the little bedroom above the kitchen she bore him seven children and stayed thirty-two years—a life sentence.

Every industrial city, of course, folds within itself a clutter of loosely defined overlapping 'villages'. Those in the Great Britain of seventy years ago were almost self-contained communities. Our own consisted of some thirty streets and alleys locked along the north and south by two railway systems a furlong apart. About twice that distance to the east lay another slum which turned on its farther side into a land of bonded warehouses and the city proper. West of us, well beyond the tramlines, lay the middle classes, bay-windowed and begardened. We knew them not.

In the city as a whole our village rated indubitably low. 'The children of this school', wrote one of King Edward VII's inspectors, commenting on our only seat of learning, 'are of the poorest class; so, too, is the teaching.' With cash, or on tick, our villagers, about three thousand in all, patronised fifteen beer-houses, a hotel

---

neighbours were met with a cool 'I don't care how soon he's either better or worse'! She herself reached the age of ninety-three and died only moderately lamented.

and two off-licences, nine grocery and general shops, three green-grocers (for ever struggling to survive against the street hawker), two tripe shops, three barbers, three cloggers, two cook shops, one fish and chip shop (*déclassé*), an old clothes store, a couple of pawnbrokers and two loan offices.

Religion was served by two chapels (Primitive Methodist and Congregationalist), one 'tin' mission (Church of England) and one sinister character who held spiritualist seances in his parlour and claimed from the window to cure 'Female Bad Legs'. (Through overwork innumerable women suffered from burst varicose veins.) Culture, pleasure and need found outlet through one theatre (and, later, three cinemas), a dancing room ('low'), two coy brothels, eight bookmakers and a private moneylender.

The first of our public buildings reared its dark bulk near the railway wall. Hyndman Hall, home of the Social Democratic Federation (SDF), remained for us mysteriously aloof and through the years had, in fact, about as much political impact on the neighbourhood as the nearby gasworks. The second establish-ment, our Conservative Club, except for a few days at election times, didn't appear to meddle with politics at all. It was notable usually for a union jack in the window and a brewer's dray at the door.

Over one quarter of a mile industry stood represented by a dying brickworks and an iron foundry. Several gasholders on the south side polluted the air, sometimes for days together. Little would grow; even the valiant aspidistra pined.[2] We possessed besides two coal yards, a corn store, a cattle wharf and perhaps as closed an urban society as any in Europe.

In our community, as in every other of its kind, each street[3] had the usual social rating; one side or one end of that street might be classed higher than another. Weekly rents varied from

[2] To encourage the Adam in us our local park sold 'garden soil' at a penny a bucket. At home, expending twopence, we once tried a window box 'for flowers' in the back-yard. A few blooms struggled up then collapsed. 'So!' said my mother, loud in her husband's hearing, 'you can rear a child, it seems, on coal gas, but it does for geraniums!'

[3] The railway company which owned most of our streets kept its houses in a moderate state of disrepair. Two workmen haunted the properties, a crabby joiner and, trailing behind him with the hand-cart, his mate, a tall, frail consumptive. This pair were known to the neighbourhood unkindly as 'Scrooge' and 'Marley's Ghost'.

2*s* 6*d* for the back-to-back to 4*s* 6*d* for a 'two up and two down'. End houses often had special status. Every family, too, had a tacit ranking, and even individual members within it; neighbours would consider a daughter in one household as 'dead common' while registering her sister as 'refined', a word much in vogue. (Young women with incipient consumption were often thought 'refined'.) Class divisions were of the greatest consequence, though their implications remained unrealised: the many looked upon social and economic inequality as the law of nature. Division in our own society ranged from an élite at the peak, composed of the leading families, through recognised strata to a social base whose members one damned as the 'lowest of the low', or simply 'no class'. Shopkeepers, publicans and skilled tradesmen occupied the premier positions, each family having its own sphere of influence. A few of these aristocrats, whilst sharing working-class culture, had aspirations. From their ranks the lower middle class, then clearly defined, drew most of its recruits—clerks and, in particular, schoolteachers (struggling hard at that time for social position). Well before translation those striving to 'get on' tried to ape what they believed were 'real' middle-class manners and customs. Publicans' and shopkeepers' daughters, for instance, set the fashion in clothes for a district. Some went to private commercial colleges[4] in the city, took music lessons or perhaps studied elocution—that short cut, it was felt, to 'culture'—at two shillings an hour, their new 'twang', tried out later over the bar and counter, earning them a deal of covert ridicule. Top families generally stood ever on the look-out for any activity or 'nice' connection which might edge them, or at least their children,

[4] Since the State educational system was doing little to train the mass of cheap female labour that commerce and the civil service drew upon after 1900, private 'colleges' sprang up in all the larger towns teaching shorthand, typing, book-keeping and foreign languages. One of these in the city, typical of many, opened in two small rooms, soared to prosperity through the inter-war years with more than a thousand students annually ('20 lessons, 20 shillings!'), then collapsed in the '60's when the State finally got round to providing commercial education for all who needed it.

In the years of mass unemployment after the first world war some of these private establishments used to 'guarantee' their students a post after training. Many, desperate for work, borrowed or used savings to pay fees, only to be offered in the end one of those numberless jobs in commerce always to be had at starvation salaries.

into a higher social ambience. But despite all endeavour, mobility between manual workers, small tradesmen and the genuine middle class remained slight, and no one needed to wonder why; before the masses rose an economic barrier that few men could ever hope to scale. At the end of the Edwardian period an adult male industrial worker earned £75 a year; the average annual salary of a man in the middle classes proper was £340.

That wide section beyond the purely manual castes where incomes ranged between the two norms mentioned was considered by many to be no more than 'jumped-up working class', not to be confused with the true order above: but the striving sought it nevertheless, if not for themselves, at least for their children. The real social divide existed between those who, in earning daily bread, dirtied hands and face and those who did not.

The less ambitious among skilled workers had aims that seldom rose above saving enough to buy the ingoing of a beer-house, open a corner shop or get a boarding house at the seaside. By entering into any business at all a man and his family grew at once in economic status, though social prestige accrued much more slowly. Fiascos were common; again and again one noticed in the district pathetic attempts[5] to set up shops in private houses by people who possessed only a few shillings' capital and no experience. After perhaps only three weeks one saw their hopes collapse, often to the secret satisfaction of certain neighbours who, in the phrase of the times, 'hated to see folk trying to get on'.

On the social ladder after tradesmen and artisans came the semi-skilled workers (still a small section) in regular employment, and then the various grades of unskilled labourers. These divisions could be marked in many public houses, where workers other than craftsmen would be frozen or flatly ordered out of those rooms in which journeymen forgathered. Each part of the tavern had its status rating; indeed, 'he's only a tap-room man' stood as a common slur. Nevertheless, whatever the job the known probity of a person conferred at once some social standing. 'She was poor but she was honest' we sang first in praise, not derision. I remember neighbours speaking highly of an old

---

[5] 'CURRAN CAKES! 3 FOR 2*d*' advertised one neighbour on a little pile of grey lumps in her house window. Nobody bought. We children watched them growing staler each day until the kitchen curtain fell again on the venture like a shroud.

drudge, 'poor but honest', who had sought charing work with a flash publican new to the district. 'I dunno,' he told her, 'but come tomorrer and fetch a "character".' She returned the next day. 'Well, yer brought it?' he asked. 'No,' she said, 'I got yours an' I won't be startin'!'

Many women and girls in the district worked in some branch of the textile industry. Of these, we accepted weavers as 'top' in their class, followed by winders and drawers-in. Then came spinners. They lacked standing on several counts: first, the trade contained a strong Irish Catholic element, and wages generally were lower than in other sections. Again, because of the heat and slippery floors, women worked barefoot, dressed in little more than calico shifts. These garments, the respectable believed, induced in female spinners a certain moral carelessness. They came home, too, covered in dust and fluff; all things which combined to depress their social prestige. Women employees of dye works, however, filled the lowest bracket: their work was dirty, wet and heavy and they paid due penalty for it. Clogs and shawls were, of course, standard wear for all. The girl who first defied this tradition in one of Lancashire's largest mills remembered the 'stares, skits and sneers' of fellow workers sixty years afterwards. Her parents, urgently in need of money, had put her to weaving, where earnings for girls were comparatively good. They lived, however, in one of the newer suburbs with its parloured houses and small back gardens. To be seen in such a district returning from a mill in clogs and shawl would have meant instant social demotion for the whole family. She was sent to the weaving shed wearing coat and shoes and thereby shocked a whole establishment. Here was a 'forward little bitch', getting above herself. So clearly, in fact, did headwear denote class that, in Glasgow, separate clubs existed for 'hat' girls and 'shawl' girls. Nevertheless, before 1914 even, continued good wages in weaving and the consequent urge to bolster status had persuaded not a few to follow the lone teenager's example. By the end of the war, in the big town cotton mills at least, coats and shoes could be worn without comment.

Unskilled workers split into plainly defined groups according to occupation, possessions and family connection, scavengers and night-soil men rating low indeed. Following these came a series of castes, some unknown and others, it seems, already withered into insignificance in Professor Hoggart's Hunslet of the 1930's:[6] first, the casual workers of all kinds—dockers in particular (who lacked prestige through the uncertainty of their calling), then the local street sellers of coal, lamp oil, tripe, crumpets, muffins and pikelets, fruit, vegetables and small-ware. Finally came the firewood choppers, bundlers and sellers and the rag and boners, often whole families. These people for some reason ranked rockbottom among the genuine workers. It may have been that firewood sellers rated so very low socially because they competed in some districts with small teams of paupers who went about in charge of a uniformed attendant hawking firewood, chopped and bundled at the Union. Workhouse paupers hardly registered as human beings at all. Even late in the nineteenth century ablebodied men from some Northern poorhouses worked in public with a large P stamped on the seat of their trousers. This not only humiliated the wearer but prevented his absconding to a street market where he could have exchanged his good pants for a cheap pair—with cash adjustment. The theft of 'workhouse property' was a very common offence among the destitute.

Forming the base of the social pyramid we had bookies' runners, idlers, part-time beggars and petty thieves, together with all those known to have been in prison[7] whatever might be their ostensible economic or social standing. Into this group the community lumped any harlots, odd homosexuals, kept men and brothel keepers. Hunslet's sympathy with a prostitute, mentioned in *The Uses of Literacy*, seems unusual even during the '30's. In the proletarian world of my youth, and long after, the active drab was generally condemned out of hand, certainly by 'respectable' women. Their menfolk agreed or remained uneasily silent. Nor did retirement lead to social acceptance. I recall one street walker, ten years after ceasing her trade, blamelessly married, with a 'clean doorstep and a beautiful house of furniture', who was still cold-shouldered by her neighbours. Drunk one day, she could stand it no longer and burst in a passion through her doorway, half pleading, half enraged. 'It's not what I was!' she screamed again and again, 'it's what I am now—a decent, clean-living woman.' This, over a knot of

---

[6] *The Uses of Literacy.*

[7] Who, among the lowest orders, had just gone into or come out of Strangeways was of course a common topic of shop and beer-house.

startled children playing in the street, to rows of closed, condemnatory doors. The moralists found it hard to forgive and they never forgot. 'I wonder,' sniffed one old neighbour to another, after hearing of the outbreak of the second world war, 'I wonder if Mrs J., with her husband away, will go on the game again, like what she did last time?'

I don't recall, though, that any 'lost women' ever threw themselves off bridges in despair; as they grew older most found a complaisant male to marry or live with and dwelt, if not accepted, at least tolerated by most neighbours.

Drunkenness, rowing or fighting in the streets, except perhaps at weddings and funerals (when old scores were often paid off), Christmas or bank holidays could leave a stigma on a family already registered as 'decent' for a long time afterwards. Another household, for all its clean curtains and impeccable conduct, would remain uneasily aware that its rating had slumped since Grandma died in the workhouse or Cousin Alf did time. Still another family would be scorned loudly in a drunken tiff for marrying off its daughter to some 'low Mick from the Bog'. With us, of course, as with many cities in the North, until the coming of the coloured people Irish Roman Catholic immigrants, mostly illiterate, formed the lowest socio-economic stratum. A slum Protestant marrying into the milieu suffered a severe loss of face. Such unions seldom occurred.[8]

At all times there were naturally many unsnobbish people in the working class who remained indifferent to the social effects of affluence or poverty on those about them and who judged others not at all by their place and possessions. On the whole, though, most families were well aware of their position within the community, and that without any explicit analyses. Many households strove by word, conduct and the acquisition of objects to enhance the family image and in so doing often overgraded themselves. Meanwhile their neighbours (acting in the same

[8] Engels pointed out how, in the 1840's, the million or more brutalised Irish immigrants pouring into English slums were depressing native social and economic standards. Little integration, however, seems to have followed upon the influx. Even up to the outbreak of the first world war differences in race, religion, culture and status kept English and Irish apart. The Irish poor, already of course deeply deferential to the Church, remained, in sobriety, even more than their English counterparts, respectful to the point of obsequiousness to any they considered their social superiors.

manner on their own behalf) tended to depreciate the pretensions of families around, allotting them a place in the register lower than that which, their rivals felt, connections, calling or possessions merited. In this lay much envy (envy was the besetting sin), bitterness and bad blood which, stored up and brooded over, burst on the community in drunken Saturday night brawls. Tiffs over children usually provided the opening skirmishes, but before the fighting proper began between the males, housewives shrieked abuse at one another, interspersed with 'case history' examples aiming to prove to the world that the other party and its kindred were 'low class' or no class at all. One waved, for instance, a 'clean' rent book (that great status symbol of the times) in the air, knowing the indicted had fallen in arrears. Now manners and morals were arraigned before a massed public tribunal; innuendos long hinted at found blatant proof, and shame fought with outraged honour screaming in the gutter: a class struggle indeed! Purse-lipped and censorious, the matriarchs surveyed the scene, soaking it all in, shocked by the vulgarity of it all, unless, of course, their own family was engaged. Then later, heads together and from evidence submitted, they made grim readjustments on the social ladder.

As a child before the first world war I hardly knew a weekend free from the sight of brawling adults and inter-family dispute. It was then one saw demonstrated how deeply many manual workers and their wives were possessed with ideas about class; with some, involvement almost reached obsession. Yet in examining the standards of the Edwardian lower orders one has always to bear in mind that street disturbers, gutter fighters and general destroyers of the peace came from a comparatively small section of the community. Nevertheless, in the 'dialogue' of street dissension one saw exposed all the social inhibitions of the more respectable.

One or two proletarian authors, writing about these times and of the slump between the wars, appear to me to sentimentalise the working class: even worse, by too often depicting its cruder and more moronic members they end by caricaturing the class as a whole. In general, women in the slums were far from being foul-mouthed sluts and harridans, sitting in semi-starvation at home in between trips to the pub and pawnshop, nor were most men boors and drunken braggarts. People *en masse*, it is true, had little education but the discerning of the time saw abundant evidence of intelligence, shrewdness, restraint and maturity. Of course, we had low 'characters' by the score, funny or revolting: so did every slum in Britain. Such types set no standards. In sobriety they knew their 'place' well enough. Very many families even in our 'low' district remained awesomely respectable over a lifetime. Despite poverty and appalling surroundings parents brought up their children to be decent, kindly and honourable and often lived long enough to see them occupy a higher place socially than they had ever known themselves: the greatest satisfaction of all. It is such people[9] and their children now who deny indignantly (and I believe rightly) that the slum life of the industrial North in this century, for all its horrors, was ever so mindless and uncouth as superficial play and novel would have a later generation believe.

Position in our Edwardian community was judged not only by what one possessed but also by what one pawned. Through agreement with the local broker the back room of our corner shop served as a depot for those goods pledged by the week which owners had been unable to redeem before nine o'clock on Saturday, when the local pawnshop closed. Our service gave women waiting on drunken or late-working husbands a few hours' grace in which to redeem shoes and clothing before the Sabbath, and so maintain their social stake in the English Sunday. Towards our closing time there was always a great scurrying shopwards to get the 'bundle'. Housewives after washday on Monday pledged what clean clothes could be spared until weekend and returned with cash to buy food. Often they stood in the shop and thanked God that *they* were not as certain others who, having no clothes but what they stood in, had sunk low enough to pawn ashpans, hearth rugs or even the 'pots off the table'. Other customers tut-tutted in disgust. News of domestic

[9] Some professional inquirers into the past have persuaded the elderly both to reminisce and to complete lengthy questionnaires covering aspects of their lives in youth. This can of course yield valuable information, social and historical. But a certain caution is needed. During the '30's and '40's I often talked with people who were already mature by 1914. They criticised the then fairly recent past, faculties alert, with what seemed some objectivity. But by the '60's myths had developed, prejudices about the present had set hard; these same critics, in ripe old age, now saw the Edwardian era through a golden haze!

distress soon got around. Inability to redeem basic goods was a sure sign of a family's approaching destitution, and credit dried up fast in local tick shops. Naturally, the gulf between those households who patronised 'Uncle', even if only occasionally, and those who did not gaped wide. Some families would go hungry rather than pledge their belongings.

The interest charged on articles pawned was usually a penny in the shilling per week, one half being paid at pledging time (Monday) and the other on redemption of the goods (Saturday). Much trucking went on among neighbours, and this often led to dispute. One woman, as a favour, would make up a bundle of her clothing for another to pawn. The pledger would then gradually gear her household economy to the certainty of hocking the same bundle every Monday morning. But the boon would be withdrawn with 'I don't know whose clothes they are—mine or hers!' Then came bitterness, recrimination and even a 'stack-up' street fight.

The great bulk of pledged goods consisted of 'Sunday best' suits, boots and clean clothing. Their lying with Uncle provided not only cash but also convenient storage for households with next to no cupboards and where the word 'wardrobe' was yet unknown. Among that body of 'white slaves', the washerwomen, there was always one notorious for pledging the clothes she had laundered professionally. Bold with booze from the proceeds of her crime, she would then send her client (usually a publican or shopkeeper) the pawn ticket and a rude verbal message ending her contract for ever. But even in those days washerwomen were hard to come by and the good one, though occasionally dishonest, could always find labour at two shillings *per diem*.

Behind his cold eye and tight lip our local broker, it was said, had a heart of stone. Only one customer, he boasted, had ever 'bested' him. An Irish woman he knew as a 'good Catholic' had presented him with a large bundle containing exactly the same washing week after week for months on end. At last he ceased to open it and paid her 'on sight'. Suddenly she disappeared and left the goods unredeemed. Weeks after a revolting smell from the store room forced him to open her pledge. He found, rotting gently among rags, an outsize savoy cabbage.

Few shopkeepers indeed would lend cash. Women customers at our shop very seldom asked for a loan but their husbands, banking on a wife's good name, would send children from time to time—'Can yer lend me father a shilling, an' he'll give yer one an' three at the week end?'

'Tell him this is a shop,' my mother would snap, 'not a loan office.'

This usually happened on the day of some big race. If the would-be punter's fancy won, he blamed Mother bitterly for robbing him of his gains.

Only those in dire straits, and with a certainty of cash cover to come, patronised the local blood sucker; he charged threepence in the shilling per week. To be known to be in his clutches was to lose caste altogether. Women would pawn to the limit, leaving the home utterly comfortless, rather than fall to that level.

Though the senior members of a household would try to uphold its prestige in every way, children in the streets had the reprehensible habit of making friends with anyone about their own age who happened to be around, in spite of the fact that parents, ever on the watch, had already announced what company they should keep. One would be warned off certain boys altogether. Several of us, for instance, had been strictly forbidden ever to be seen consorting with a lad whose mother, known elegantly as the She Nigger, was a woman of the lowest repute. Unfortunately we could find nothing 'low' in her son. A natural athlete (he modelled his conduct on Harry Wharton of the *Magnet*), a powerful whistler through his teeth, generous, unquarrelsome, Bill seemed the kind of friend any sensible lad would pick. We sought him out at every opportunity but took very good care to drop him well away from home base. He accepted our brush-off meekly, but in the end protested with a dignity which left the other three of us in the group deeply embarrassed. 'Why', he asked, 'won't you be seen with me in the street?'

We looked at one another: 'It's—it's your old lady,' I mumbled at last—'You know!'

'I can't help what the old lady does, can I?' he asked.

'It's not us,' we explained lamely. 'It's them—you know—them at home . . .'

He turned and walked away.

All of us were then within a few weeks of leaving school; no longer children. We went again to our common haunts but he came no more; the friendship was over.

Through our teens we saw him pass often, but he ignored us. The break would have come in any case, I told myself uneasily. He got a job after school as a mere chain horse lad; we had become apprentices of a sort; but a social barrier had risen for good.

The class struggle, as manual workers in general knew it, was apolitical and had place entirely within their own society. They looked upon it not in any way as a war against the employers but as a perpetual series of engagements in the battle of life itself. One family might be 'getting on'—two or three children out to work and the dream of early marriage days fulfilled at last. The neighbours noted it as they noted everything, with pleasure or envy. A second household would begin a slip downhill as father aged or children married. They watched, sympathetically perhaps, or with a touch of *schadenfreude*. All in all it was a struggle against the fates, and each family fought it out as best it could. Marxist 'ranters' from the Hall who paid fleeting visits to our street end insisted that we, the proletariat, stood locked in titanic struggle with some wicked master class. We were battling, they told us (from a vinegar barrel borrowed from our corner shop), to cast off our chains and win a whole world. Most people passed by; a few stood to listen, but not for long: the problems of the 'proletariat', they felt, had little to do with them.

Before 1914 the great majority in the lower working class were ignorant of Socialist doctrine in any form, whether 'Christian' or Marxist. Generally, those who did come into contact with such ideas showed either indifference or, more often, hostility. Had they been able to read a *Times* stricture of the day, most would have agreed heartily that 'Socialist is a title which carries in many minds summary and contemptuous condemnation'. They would have echoed too its pained protests on the iniquities of the doctrine. 'To take from the rich', said a leader in 1903, *à propos* a mild tax proposal, 'is all very well if they are to make some more money, but to take from the rich by methods that prevent them replacing what is taken is the way to national impoverishment from which the poor, in spite of all doles and Socialist theories, will be the greatest sufferers.'

Meanwhile, though the millennium for a socialist few might seem just around the corner, many gave up struggling. The suicide rate among us remained pretty high. There was Joe Kane, for instance, an unemployed labourer who was found by a neighbour blue in the face with a muffler tied about his neck. Some time previously he had taken carbolic acid and bungled that attempt too. But the magistrate didn't think much of Joe's efforts.

'If the prisoner', he said, 'is anxious to go to heaven, one would have thought he could have managed it by some better means than that. He could, now, have thrown himself into the river, or something else.'

The prisoner was discharged. But several months later Joe took up the magistrate's thoughtful suggestion and drowned himself in the canal.

Throughout a quarter of a century the population of our village remained generally immobile: the constant shifts of nearby country folk into industrial towns, so common during the previous century, had almost ceased; though our borough was still growing at a diminished rate. A man's work, of course, usually fixed the place where his family dwelt; but lesser factors were involved too: his links, for instance, with local kith and kin. Then again, he commonly held a certain social position at the nearby pub, modest, perhaps, but recognised, and a credit connection with the corner shop. Such relationships, once relinquished, might not easily be re-established. All these things, together with fear of change, combined to keep poor families, if not in the same street, at least in the same neighbourhood for generations. There was of course some movement in and out, and naturally we had the odd 'moonlight' flitting when a whole household, to dodge its debts, would vanish overnight. Everybody laughed about it except the creditors. What newcomers we got were never the 'country gorbies' whom my grandfather remembered as the 'butt of the workshops' in his youth, but families on the way up or down from other slums of the city: yet new neighbours or old, all shared a common poverty.

Even with rapidly increasing literacy during the second half of the nineteenth century, years were needed, sometimes decades, before certain ideas common to the educated filtered through to the very poor. By 1900, however, those cherished principles about class, order, work, thrift and self-help, epitomised by Samuel Smiles and long taught and practised by the Victorian bourgeoisie, had moulded the minds of even the humblest. And slow to learn, they were slow to change. Whatever new urges might have roved abroad in early Edwardian England, millions among the poor still retained the outlook and thought patterns imposed by their Victorian mentors. For them the twentieth century had not begun. Docilely they accepted a steady decline in living standards and went on wishing for nothing more than to be 'respectful[10] and respected' in the eyes of men. For them the working-class caste structure stood natural, complete and inviolate.

[10] Harry Quelch, proletarian leader in the SDF, who knew the common people if ever a man did, called the English working class of that day the 'most reverential to the master class' of any in Europe. In London in 1889 at the time of the dockers' and gasworkers' strikes Engels wrote: 'The most repulsive thing here is the bourgeoise "respectability" which has grown deep into the bones of the workers. The division of society into innumerable strata, each recognised without question, each with its own pride, but also inborn respect for its "betters" and "superiors", is so old and firmly established that the bourgeoisie find it fairly easy to get their bait accepted.'

Engels seemed to find the workers' leaders little better. 'Even Tom Mann,' he complained, 'whom I regard as the best of the lot, is fond of mentioning that he will be lunching with the Lord Mayor.'—V. I. Lenin, *On Britain*.

Chapter 2

Possessions

Them as 'as nowt is nowt
Northern saw

The social standing of every person within the community was constantly affected by material pressures, some of the slightest, and the struggle for the acquisition and display of objects seemed fiercer than any known in Britain now for cars, boats or similar prestige symbols. For many in the lowest group the spectre of destitution stood close; any new possession helped to stifle fear.

Family ambitions in the pre-1914 era appear to us now pathetically modest. One scrimped and saved to get a new piece of oilcloth, a rag rug, the day at Southport, a pair of framed pictures—'Her First Singing Lesson' perhaps, with 'Her First Dancing Lesson'. Pictures, in a society far from wholly literate, were especially esteemed. Luxury articles most longed for were pianos, of course, but one would settle happily for a banjo,[1] sewing machines (drop heads if possible), bicycles, gramophones, gold lockets and watches and chains. Fireside objects in brass and copper instead of plain steel gave a kitchen special tone, the more so if one dispensed with the 'blue-moulded' hearth stone for a metal plate painted with tiles. Bedding and underclothes in good condition were anxiously sought after, since on washing day they would have to be hung to dry across the street: a poverty-stricken display could do one much social damage. All goods one saved for, of course, and bought on the nail, or at worst through weekly clubs run by local shops—a method much frowned on. One young married woman, I remember, bewitched by a strip of carpet, got it on hire-purchase, 'feeling like a criminal', but only after the family had sworn to keep the deed

[1] Except for humble mouth organs the melodeon was the most popular among musical instruments. It cost from 2s 11d to 14s 6d.

from her parents, who would have been horrified to hear of it. Clothing clubs existed but respectable folk eschewed them altogether. Not so many of the needy, who would get a check, buy clothes at once to cover nakedness and pay for them by weekly instalments; a boon indeed. More improvident people exploited this system to gain themselves a little spot cash; taking out a thirty-shilling check, say, they would sell it immediately to a neighbour for a third to half its face value and, often enough, get drunk on the proceeds without delay.

'Draw' clubs were very popular in mill, factory and street, particularly among the women, as a means of providing goods or ready cash. By arrangement with a local household store twenty people would agree to subscribe sixpence a week for twenty weeks. The numbers 1–20 would then be drawn at random and each member would be given the date on which she could go and take possession of her goods. To help an honest neighbour fallen suddenly into debt, a street money 'draw' would be run along the same lines, the unfortunate one, on payment of her sixpence, being allowed to take the first week's total subscription.

Window curtaining with us had high significance; the full drape, if possible in lace, being a necessity for any family with pretensions to class. No one scorned the clean modest half curtain, but a newspaper across the panes showed all too clearly that still another household had been forced to hoist the grey flag of poverty. Doors were painted brown and roughly grained: any tenants daring to use a colour gaily different would have been damned as playing 'baby house', a serious indictment in a world where the activities of childhood and maturity were strictly separated.

There was a marked division between those houses which had an overmantel and those possessing no more than a plain shelf above the fireplace. The overmantel, mirrored, and laddered with brackets, displayed a mass of tawdry ornaments, the more the better. Our own specimen the neighbours classed as 'a work of art'. Every Christmas my father invited favoured tick customers in turn into the kitchen and gave each a tot of Dumville's Special. The guest, much honoured, sat on the edge of her chair, sipped whisky and eyed all about her in humble admiration. First the brass chandelier, a mass of twirled metal and variegated knobs (this my father had made himself). He would demonstrate how its three upright gas mantles (classier than the inverted type) could be raised almost to the ceiling or lowered by means of three large pear-shaped weights. Then his guest would eye in wonder a repulsive, three-foot-square print of the 'Battle of Quatre Bras',[2] and after that, the piano with its gilded candlesticks; but most of all the opulent show of bric à brac on the overmantel.[3] This homage to our family possessions seemed to give the old man much satisfaction.

When in 1910, on my mother's insistence, the landlord installed a cast iron bath (one shilling a week on the rent), several customers asked to be allowed to inspect it. My father took them on a conducted tour, pointing out the hot and cold taps and the purposes of plug, chain and overflow pipe. Till then some had never seen a bath, much less used one.

Oilcloth was much in demand, even if one could only afford enough to cover a kitchen floor as far as the furniture. More than anything it gave that 'lived in' look, especially if the home ran to a bob-fringed plush table cloth that could be laid in the evening after tea. Most families had a rag hearth rug. With such comforts, a ramp of hot coals blazing beyond the fire-irons, and the door shut against the world, drowsy cosiness spread over all. Those establishments without floor covering, except perhaps a sack or two, and rubbed stone colouring on bare flags, and those who used newspapers as tablecloths, were marked and duly 'registered'—not, it should be said, with malice; it was merely that, in the social appraisal of the times, one needed to be aware of such facts.

From some shops you could buy the 'basic' 'House of Furniture' complete, designed to fill the 'one up and one down' home. This cost twelve guineas, with £1 8s 0d added if you were feckless

---

[2] This, he used to boast, was 'an heirloom—in the family two hundred years!' And unique in that we had had it for more than a century before the battle took place.

[3] Once, in drunken rage, father took a haymaker with a beer bottle at its lower magnificence—the gondolas, the two massive dogs (with pup) hugging a hollow bust of William Gladstone, the bowl of china cherries! Cheap glazed pot burst on the air like, my brother said later, an explosion in a public convenience. Stunned sober, the old man gazed at his mantelboard. 'Well,' said my mother, coldly unafraid at such antics, 'you've improved the look of it at last!'

c

enough to buy on credit. For £12 12s 0d you received immediate delivery of:

	£	s	d
One leather couch or sofa	1	6	0
One hardwood armchair		9	6
One hardwood rocking chair		9	6
Four best kitchen chairs		15	6
One square table		10	6
3½ × 4 yards oilcloth		14	0
One cloth hearth rug		4	9
One kitchen fender		6	6
One set kitchen fire-irons		4	6
One ashpan		2	11
One full-size brass-mounted bedstead	1	12	6
One double woven wire mattress		14	6
One flock bed bolster and pillows		16	6
3 ft 6 in. enclosed dressing table with fixed glass	1	15	0
Ditto washstand with tile back	1	9	0
Two cane seat chairs		7	0
2½ × 4 yards oilcloth		10	0
Two bedside rugs		3	10
	12	12s	0d

Four-roomed houses could be furnished for £25. But only the most fortunate started with their dream home complete in this way.

Since privies were in the back yard, most households early after setting up would try to add a 'Toilet Set' to basic requirements. The standard combination, costing eight shillings, consisted of 'ewer and basin, chamber pots (2), brush, vase and soap dish'. The very poor compromised and bought a galvanised bucket.

Among objects of personal adornment the watch held peculiar eminence. Prized by princes of previous ages, much sought after in the seventeenth and eighteenth centuries by the rising middle classes, it lay now through mass production within the buying power of millions. Lewis's Five Shilling Watch and the like finally put time into the pockets of all but the poorest. With the publican, until well into the '30's, a gold watch and guard, much befobbed, dangling over a bulging waistcoat acted almost as badge of office; a rich display brought both respect and admiration. But the best proof of domestic solidity stood enshrined in the chiffonier. This article of furniture, placed where it could be seen through the open street door and loaded with glass drops and other discards of middle-class fashion, shone like today's new Jaguar (except that it was paid for), a symbol of prosperity.

Prestige, however, was not automatically increased by such proofs of affluence. One needed to know how wealth had been acquired. The fruits of prostitution we condemned. Nelly, for all her fancy boa, frocks and jewellery stayed 'ruined', while the temporary 'flushes' of thieves served only to lower their status further. Much delinquency, it should be said, by modern standards was astonishingly trivial, yet the stigma for filching even the smallest objects remained real. Through their known affluence bookmakers held positions of importance among us, though many among our upper classes treated them with reserve. We secretly enjoyed their picaresque calling, the feeling of suppressed excitement about on big race days and the hope amongst youngsters of still another police raid: but their 'morals', flash suits and bedecked wives (*they* never wore shawls and clogs) usually put them beyond the pale of proper respectability.

Most people kept what they possessed clean in spite of squalor and ever-invading dirt. Some houses sparkled. Few who were young then will forget the great Friday night scouring ritual in which all the females of a house took part. (Dance halls closed on Friday evenings for lack of girls.) Women wore their lives away washing clothes in heavy, iron-hooped tubs, scrubbing wood and stone, polishing furniture and fire-irons. There were housewives who finally lost real interest in anything save dirt removing. Almost every working hour of the week they devoted to cleaning and re-cleaning the same objects so that their family, drilled into slavish tidiness, could sit in state, newspaper covers removed, for a few hours each Sunday evening. On Monday purification began all over again. Two of these compulsives left us for the 'lunatic asylum', one of them, I remember vividly, passing with a man in uniform through a group of us watching children to a van, still washing her hands like a poor Lady Macbeth.

Only too well known was the Saturday morning custom common then and for long after of cleaning and colour-stoning the doorstep and then the pavement across a width that took in one's frontage. This chore helped to project the image of a spotless

household into the world at large. In a street of coloured flagstones the non-conforming housewife stood branded each week
end by the dirty gap before her premises. At the shop, for this
kind of cleaning, we sold large quantities of brown stone and a
chalky substance called blue mould in competition with hawkers
known not as 'rag and bone' but as 'sand bone' men, a name that
lingered through Edwardian days, presumably from the times
when they sold sand for floor covering.

In the Edwardian age clothes denoted status as plainly as any
military uniform. On weekdays among us our few artisans wore
rough, hard-wearing jackets and pants, and worked at lathe or
bench, sleeves of their union shirts rolled, in white aprons, over-
alls as yet being hardly known. 'Turpin's 10/6 Trousers Astonish
the World!' advertised the local store. Unamazed, we bought
them—heavy, rebarbative garments that would stand erect even
without a tenant. A few coppers extra bought a double-seated
pair. All clothes, of course, were made to last and many were
designed to allow adaptation later to meet the needs of successive
younger members in a family. Men's outerwear was brushed but
never really cleaned. One dabbed a best coat or suit with pungent
patent liquids bought in twopenny bottles from the corner shop,
but only the well-to-do sent the more expensive of their garments
to what few 'dyers and cleaners' existed. Some men working in
the many offensive trades of the day smelled abominably, and
people would avoid the public houses where they forgathered.

'Low quarter' shoes were, of course, derided by all proper
males, but for week-end wear the artisan would go as far as a pair
of 'light business boots', price 10s 6d, and make a dignified if
squeaky way to the pub, smoking, perhaps, one of his five-for-a-
shilling whiffs. When the boots needed repair he would often do
this himself, buying leather at 'threepence per shoe'.

Tradesmen took pride in wearing stiff collars even in the
'workshop' (a 'factory' was where the unskilled laboured). A
child's weekly chore was to have this neckwear at the laundry
and returned in time for father to choose the best out of a frayed
collection and go off, 'dressed up to the nines', on his Saturday
evening booze.

No artisan, except in jobs which demanded them, would have
been seen in clogs. These, women and children wore on weekdays; but to disturb the Sabbath with their clatter was both vulgar

and a sure sign of the wearer's poverty. Some parents once affluent enough to provide 'best' clothes for the family, then falling on hard times, would on no account allow their children to go out on Sunday in their weekday wear. No matter how fine the weather, they were kept cooped up all day in kitchen or bedroom so that face might be maintained before the neighbours. Cheap Sunday boots for children were the bane of young lives. Hard and ill-fitting, they rubbed the skin off heels and toes without one's getting much sympathy from adults who often enough were plagued themselves with corns, callouses, 'segs' and bunions. In any crowd of workers on the move a sizeable number would have been seen walking badly. At week end boys smeared sharp-odoured blacking from a paper pack onto leather vamps and polished all the footwear. One wore shining boots and clogs as a blazon of family respectability.

On Sundays the artisan in his best suit looked like the artisan in his best suit: no one could ever mistake him for a member of the middle classes. But any day at all the poor looked poor. With us they wore, irrespective of fit, whatever would hide indecency: clogs or bluchers on the feet and about the neck a muffler—white, if possible, for the Lord's day. Those in greatest need found even the old brokers' shops too expensive: they bought everything from the local Flatiron Market. Some writers since have found a certain romance about the place; it is hard to see why. The 'Flatiron' differed little from any other street mart in our industrial cities, except perhaps that, established close by a ganglion of railway lines, it lay constantly under the thickest smoke pall in Britain. Its frequenters, then, could have looked sleazier and the pathetic wares on sale even more grimy than most. In such places poverty busied itself.

For men with any claim at all to standing the bowler hat, or 'billy pot', was compulsory wear. Only the lower types wore caps. Even the most indigent tried to get head covering of some sort.[4] A man or woman walking the streets hatless struck one as

[4] More than half a century earlier Engels had noted the same need. 'Hats', he wrote, 'are the universal head-covering in England, even for working men, hats of the most divers forms, round, high, broad-brimmed, narrow brimmed, or without brims—only the younger men in factory towns wearing caps. Any one who does not own a hat folds himself a low, square paper cap.' This last custom was still in vogue among the elderly poor even after 1900.

either 'low', wretchedly poor, just plain eccentric or even faintly
obscene. Those brave spirits who in the years before the first
world war dared to stroll bare-headed in the open gave rise to a
jeering urchin cry that swept the land—'No 'at brigade!' All
boys save the poorest wore celluloid Eton collars that curled with
age, turned yellow and exuded a peculiar smell. Corduroy
breeches,[5] odorous too, covered the tops of stockings, held in
place by garters of rubber that left livid circles round the thick
of one's legs. Knees could on no account be bare. When a ten-
year-old, son of an actor visiting the local theatre, appeared on
the street in short pants we drove him, screaming ridicule, back
into his lodgings.

When they could get them, the very poor frequently wore
more, not fewer clothes than the rest—two old shirts, three waist-
coats of varying sizes, or even a second pair of trousers. In this
way they kept warm, guarded their property and had extra
pockets available to secure anything picked up. Layers of clothing
served as a physical and psychological defence against the buffet-
ings of the hard world. In school yard and street one grew used
to seeing some poor soul under verbal or bodily assault cower
into his clothing like a tortoise into its shell.

Flannel cloth, long esteemed, as Frederich Engels pointed out,
by the bourgeoisie, was much valued too among the working
class. Most men tried to come by at least one flannel vest, and
women a petticoat of the same material. A piece of flannel, pre-
ferably red, placed on the chest was supposed to have therapeutic
properties. Often enough, though, one made do with cheap, all-
purpose 'flannelette', a cotton substitute.

A working-class woman, if she went even a short distance from
her own door, would slip on a shawl. In public without it she was
said to be 'in her figure', and to be seen that way too often caused
comment. With their graceful hair styles, sweeping gowns,
narrow waists and curving forms, women seem to have held
more feminine allure then than at any time since. But realists
among the old working class today remember, and with sadness,
not King Edward's 'lovely ladies' and tea on the lawn at Hurling-
ham, but the many women broken and aged with child bearing
well before their own youth was done. They remember the

---

[5] The commonest sight was a boy with his shirt showing through the
seat of his trousers. He was said to be 'selling calico'.

spoiled complexions, the mouths full of rotten teeth, the varicose veins, the ignorance of simple hygiene, the intelligence stifled and the endless battle merely to keep clean. Unlike many in the middle and upper classes, fondly looking back, they see no 'glory gleaming'. They weep no tears for the past. What things the poor did own then, most made gallant use of. The tragedy was that in the most opulent country in the world so many possessed so little.

Chapter 3

Manners and Morals

Masks do not hide, they shape the human heart
C. A. Trypanis

Over our community the matriarchs stood guardians, but not
creators, of the group conscience and as such possessed a sense of
social propriety as developed and unerring as any clique of
Edwardian dowagers. Behind the counters of a corner shop one
learned to realise their power. In and out they trailed from early
morning to an hour before midnight, little groups that formed
and faded, trading with goodwill, candour or cattishness the
detailed gossip of a closed society. Over a period the health,
honesty, conduct, history and connections of everyone in the
neighbourhood would be examined. Each would be criticised,
praised, censured openly or by hint and finally allotted by tacit
consent a position on the social scale. Misdeeds of mean, cruel or
dissolute neighbours were mulled over and penalties unconsciously fixed. These could range from the matronly snub to the
smashing of the guilty party's windows, or even a public beating.
The plight of the aged, those without shelter or reaching near-
starvation would be considered and their travail eased at least
temporarily by some individual or combined act of charity.

The poor certainly helped the poor. Many kindly families little
better off than most came to the aid of neighbours in need without thought of reward, here or hereafter. They were the salt of
the earth. We knew others, too, who in return for help exacted
payment in fulsome gratitude.[1] Again, not all assistance sprang
from the heart: in a hard world one never knew what blows fate
would deal; a little generosity among the distressed now could
act as a form of social insurance against the future.

The matriarchal group held within itself a powerful inner ring

[1] 'I gave her a bag of coal,' said one Samaritan, 'and she only thanked me
once. I asked her not to tell anybody and', he added bitterly, 'I don't suppose
she will!'

of grandmothers marked enough to be known among our irreverent youth as the 'old queens'. Wielding great influence behind the scene, they of course represented an ultra-conservative bloc in the community. As long as a grandmother kept up her home to which children and grandchildren could regularly go for material help and counsel she reigned supreme. But as soon as illness or need forced her to give up house and live with son or daughter her influence in both clan and street generally diminished, though affection remained. On the whole, grandmothers were more illiterate, narrower in outlook and less self-aware than their daughters. At the corner shop many a mother with a problem, after a chat with my own mother or a knowledgeable customer, would modify her attitude towards a family ailment, perhaps, or the disciplining of a child, or the treatment of some erring neighbour. Thus was instilled habit undermined.

Gossip, that prime leisure activity of the time, played a vital role in a milieu where many, through lack of education, relied entirely on the spoken word. As a boy in the shop, I remember, much of the talk among customers was both kind and helpful. Some women, to be sure, were renowned as mines of misinformation; others as evil-tongued and malicious. Nevertheless, that daily feature of the slum scene, the 'hen party', did not function, as many thought, merely to peddle scandal; matrons in converse were both storing and redistributing information that could be important economically to themselves and their neighbours.

Whenever status was being assessed in shop or street group, one marked with puzzlement that one or two households were dismissed with ominous brevity, and this not for any obvious reason, social or economic. Only in late teenage did we discover that the closed community, like the family, could hold skeletons in its cupboard. The damned houses were those where, neighbours knew, incestuous relationship had borne a fruit which walked the streets before their very eyes. Here stood a hazard that faced all poor parents of large adolescent families sleeping together, perhaps with older relatives, in two small bedrooms. In their hearts they harboured a dread of what seemed to a respectable household the ultimate disgrace. Such sin, of course, had to be recognised in whispered *tête à tête*; but I don't recall a single prosecution: strict public silence saved miscreants from the rigours of the law.

The matriarchy presided in judgment over the public behaviour of both children and young teenagers. Mothers round washing lines or going to the shop half a dozen times a day would inevitably hear of the peccadilloes of their offspring. Punishment followed, often unjustly, since the word of an adult was accepted almost always against that of a child. With some people a child had no 'word'; only too often he was looked upon as an incomplete human being whose opinions and feelings were of little or no account—until he began to earn money! It is true that a much more indulgent attitude towards the young had already developed among the middle classes, but it had not yet spread far down the social scale. In the lower working class 'manners' were imposed upon children with the firmest hand: adults recognised that if anything was to be got from 'above' one should learn early to ask for it with a proper measure of humble politeness. There was besides, of course, the desire to imitate one's betters.

Two generations afterwards, when I taught, in prison, the grandsons of some of my Edwardian contemporaries, the same attitude persisted. In hundreds of essays on 'Bringing up children' students cited 'good manners' above all else as a virtue required from the young, followed by 'kindness'. Honesty and truthfulness remained almost completely unmentioned. And this, not because they felt that to demand probity from others whilst eschewing it themselves smacked of cant; in discussion, one discovered, manners and kindness received top rating on merit.

In his book *Exploring English Character* Geoffrey Gorer shows with an abundance of statistical detail how, even in the 1950's, the corporal punishment of children still figured largely in English working-class homes. It seems certain that during the early years of this century the practice was much more widespread and severe. Because of it many children went in awe and fear, first of their parents, then of adults generally. Naturally, across the gulf, even in the strictest households, there could be much love and understanding for the young, and parents who rejected beating altogether. But no one who spent his childhood in the slums during those years will easily forget the regular and often brutal assaults on some children perpetrated in the name of discipline and often for the most venial offences. Among the fathers administering such punishment were men who in childhood had themselves received forty-eight strokes of the birch—

a common sentence—at the local prison, for small misdemeanours. Whenever my mother heard of a heinous case, as with the woman who boasted in the shop, 'My master [husband] allus flogs 'em till the blood runs down their back!' she quietly 'put the Cruelty man on'. In its city windows the NSPCC displayed photographs of beaten children and rows of confiscated belts and canes. Gallantly as it worked, the Society hardly touched the fringe of the problem.

Parents of the most respectable and conformist families were the staunchest upholders of 'discipline', though adults whose social standing was suspect or who had in any way transgressed against accepted conduct would often brag about the severity of the chastisement meted out to their erring young, in an effort to restore tarnished prestige. Often, we knew, it was merely sound and fury; but there were those who spoke in earnest. Ex-regulars from the army or navy often had a bad reputation for the treatment of their children.

The lowest ranks of the community, however, were known and condemned for the latitude they showed, whether through indulgence or indifference, to their offspring. Children were not slow to recognise this dereliction of duty, this contempt for one of the safeguards of the good society, and they delighted in it. Time and again, in their hearing, elders of the family had discussed the 'scum', dismissing them as idle, dirty, worthless, dishonest. Taught to accept the inerrancy of adults, the child too should have felt similar disgust. Yet often enough what he remembered, and with gratitude, was the generosity of some drunken 'no-good', the genial smile and the friendly word, given on level terms, without a hint of adult superiority. Suppressed himself, he felt some strange affinity with these, the underdogs. Many of the children of such 'riff-raff' were notorious for their impudence, their swagger and the bold unswerving eye before a grown-up, sure sign of the unchastened. From the cheerful urchin mass in general one could pick out, too, a boy or girl, sometimes a whole group of brothers and sisters, who in any company stood cowed and silent. Here a 'strict' family discipline had been imposed to ensure permanent conformist behaviour. Caned in school for any fault, these children were often severely beaten again at home for having been punished at all. A certain joy died early in them. Broken in spirit, scurryingly obedient, bleak in personality, they would be the slaves now of any who cared to command them. Conformity had been bought at a price indeed. On maturity and marriage to perhaps a less inhibited partner some, in order to compensate for a bitter childhood, became over-indulgent parents; others, admirers now of past disciplines, went on to damage the lives and personalities of their own children. The authoritarian society had much to answer for.

Women having babies at home were always 'confined', a word that developed most peculiar connotations in the minds of children. Any neighbourhood had half a dozen middle-aged women with special skills who could be booked for the lying-in. Ours, I remember, was kindly but totally illiterate. The district had besides two midwives, one loved by all, the other displaying such queenly hauteur to her poorer patients that even the doctors rebuked her sharply.

If a single girl had a baby she lowered of course not only the social standing of her family but, in some degree, that of all her relations, in a chain reaction of shame. Strangely enough, those who dwelt together unmarried—'livin' tally' or 'over t' brush', as the sayings went—came in for little criticism, though naturally everybody knew who was or who was not legitimate.

In our day some sociologists have been apt to write fondly about the cosy gregariousness of the old slum dwellers. Their picture, I think, has been overdrawn. Close propinquity, together with cultural poverty, led as much to enmity as it did to friendship. There could be much personal unhappiness and fear of one neighbour by another, especially if a bullying woman was a member of a large family group in the district. People deprived of social outlets only too easily gave over their minds to the affairs of others. A petty curiosity could soon turn into active inter-ference. One recurrent feature of the scene was the burgeoning of goodwill between any pair of families on the same socio-economic level—an activity, condemned by the respectable, known as 'neighbouring'. For weeks together one would notice the members of two households constantly in and out of each other's home, often bearing small gifts. This intimacy, watching cynics knew, was far too fervid to last. And sure enough, one Saturday night shrieks, screams, scuffles and breaking glass would herald the end of another lovely friendship. Confidences foolishly bestowed were now for bruiting loud on the common air, much to the neighbourhood's pleasure. In the days which followed, the matrons, according to their own liaisons, would 'polarise' about each disputant, partly in sympathy, partly to fish in troubled waters. From such contacts new buds of amity would spring and flower, only to wither in some later social blast.

Friendships with people outside the village were generally few, but those who had them gained points in prestige. Some neighbours mentioned or still held a tenuous contact with relatives in Cheshire, Derbyshire and Yorkshire villages, thus showing that they were likely descendants of those who had migrated to the city in an earlier phase of the industrial revolution. With any visitors due at all, children would announce the event proudly in the street—'We're 'avin' comp'ny.' By the curtain edge, neighbours carefully 'weighed up' the strangers and forbade their own children to stand staring in at the honoured doorway. Company arriving stiff and staid did, however, receive its meed of awe from gaping youngsters. This respect, though, could receive a setback when perhaps only a few hours, and six jugs of ale, later one saw the dignitaries staggering home again 'palatic' (paralytic) drunk. One lady, I remember, who minced into our world (where all women wore shawls) in a magnificent hat, left kicking it along the pavement. Thus were social gains wantonly squandered.

Since most families were closely knit, members had often to sacrifice personal needs and desires to the will of the whole or to powerful leaders within it. No! one couldn't learn to dance, or go roller skating! What would Uncle Eli (the lay preacher) think! This led to much heartburning. So too did any wide social or economic disparity between the lives of individuals within the group. A great-uncle of mine, I remember, reputed at thirty to be earning the colossal salary of £300 a year, scandalised his tribe by marrying a 'flashy, ignorant, brazen' (i.e. sexually attractive) 'faggot', of 'no class at all!' Humbly she accepted her icy induction into the family and for the next thirty years paid 'duty' visits to its separate branches, 'done up', as her sisters-in-law observed, in 'dead rabbit skins'. 'And how,' she would ask them anxiously, always deferring, and laying a jewelled hand on her new stole, 'how d'y like this? It cost George twenty guineas!' Unfortunately she was nearly illiterate and never made the social strides commensurate with her wealth, which gave the family some consolation. But after any of her visits it was dangerously easy for small fry to get slapped: over-generous as she was with her laughter and small silver, they had too obviously admired her.

Among women in shop talk the confinement of daily life was often a subject for bitter complaint. Some did manage an occasional visit to the cemetery, or an hour in a balding park on the edge of the village, but many were denied even this. One, I recall, spoke wearily of never having been more than five minutes' walk from her home in eighteen years of married life. Husbands were luckier: at least once a year a beer-house picnic would take them for a long boozing day in the country. Children too got intense pleasure from the outings that charity or the Sunday school provided. Our top people paid annual visits to Blackpool, New Brighton and Southport and made sure that everybody knew, especially about their first ride in a motor car. At Southport quite early in the century an enterprising young man was doing excellent business with his Daimler open saloon, taking half a dozen passengers a time for five-minute trips round the lake.

In general, slum life was far from being the jolly hive of communal activity that some romantics have claimed. They forget, perhaps, or never knew of the dirt that hung over all, of the rubbish that lay for months in the back alleys, of the 'entries' or ginnels with open middens where starving cats and dogs roamed or died and lay for weeks unmoved. They did not know those houses that stank so badly through an open doorway that one stepped off the pavement to pass them by. That people stayed scrupulously clean in such surroundings—and many did—only proves the tenacity of the human spirit.

On the light evenings after a day's work many men, even if they had the desire, possessed no means of occupying body or mind. Ignorance and poverty combined to breed, for the most part, tedium, a dumb accidie of the back streets to which only brawling brought relief. Summer evening leisure for men without the few coppers to go into a tavern meant long, empty hours lounging between kitchen chair and threshold. How familiar one grew in childhood with those silent figures leaning against door jambs, staring into vacancy waiting for bedtime.

Richard Hoggart's personal intimacy with the working class in its more 'respectable' reaches during the '20's and '30's of this century leads him into praising family unity and 'cosiness'.[2]

[2] *The Uses of Literacy.*

These qualities, however, do not, I think, appear either so evident or so laudable if one examines the working class at more levels and over a wider range of time. Certain nineteenth-century traits, of course, ran far into the twentieth and affected longest the ultra-conservative lower working class—among them, the gulf that stood between parents and children. From family to family there were naturally many variations in its importance, yet this division, I feel, made a profound impression on the minds and social attitudes of millions of manual workers. To ignore its influence is to distort any picture of working-class relationships in the first half of the twentieth century.

Round parents the household revolved, and little could be done without their approval. Especially was paternal consent needed. In compensation, perhaps, for the slights of the outside world, a labourer often played king at home.[3] Parents decreed on both one's work and leisure and set standards of conduct, taste and culture even if they didn't follow them. 'As long as you have your feet under my table,' a father would announce to one of his off-spring, 'it's not do as I do, it's do as I say!' There were, of course, many working-class homes where music and literature had long held honoured place, but at the lower levels reading of any kind was often considered a frivolous occupation. 'Put that book down!' a mother would command her child, even in his free time, 'and do something useful.' Teenagers, especially girls, were kept on a very tight rein. Father fixed the number of evenings on which they could go out and required to know precisely where and with whom they had spent their leisure. He set, too, the exact hour of their return; few dared break the rule. One neighbour's daughter, a girl of nineteen, was beaten for coming home ten minutes late after choir practice. Control could go on in some families for years after daughters had come of age. Such narrow prohibitions naturally led to much misery and frustration in the home, though there was a deal of conniving among the members of some families to help the young dodge the great man's strictures.

And how effective were his vetoes? The number of illegitimate

---

[3] It came as a shock to many a boy on errand to his father's workshop, to see the all-powerful at home go humbly scurrying off at some loud-mouthed chargehand's bidding. There existed, then, a child might discover, internal and external status.

births in the period 1900–10 was very small—in two separate years, the lowest since figures had been kept. This might be attributed to keen family overseeing; but even severer control in earlier decades had never been so successful in curbing illegitimacy. In the forty years before 1915 the national birth rate itself had fallen from 35·5 per thousand of the population to 24. It seems most likely that the general decline was due to an increasing knowledge among the working classes of the use of contraceptives and the bolder practice of abortion. Artificial checks on conception could be bought as early as the 1820's and rubber vaginal caps from 1881. Increasing literacy no doubt went some way to spreading a knowledge of their existence; yet in the ordinary working-class bed, while coitus interruptus remained permissible, any artificial interference with the will of God aroused nothing but abhorrence. Still, among the 'low', certain homely safeguards against conception had been known for generations, especially the small piece of oiled sponge[4] with tapes hopefully attached adopted by women. Common, too, was the home-made pessary, a compound of lard (later margarine) and flour. This, thoughtfully carried in the handbag and judiciously used, saved many a girl's honour. Bolder females had bolder methods, all designed for the same purpose. But by now the sheath, long bought discreetly by the middle classes, had become familiar to many manual workers. Even before 1914 several small societies were at work propagating methods of birth control, the most prominent perhaps being the 'Liberator League', with its manual *What women ought to know on the subject of sex*. From 1919 on Marie Stopes' pamphlet *A letter to working mothers*, price 6*d*, had a very wide sale. While such works would be read only by the more intelligent and liberal-minded in the working class, verbal instruction was undoubtedly passed on to those in the lower social layers. Here again the corner shop played its part. The fall in the bastardy rate seems to have been due more to newly acquired skills than to moral restraint or fear of father. By 1920 no youngster having gone from school into mine, mill or factory could remain ignorant for long of the existence of 'rubber'

[4] The method was said to have been introduced from France by Robert Owen of New Lanark in the early years of the nineteenth century. But many women scorn this theory; an artifice so obvious, they claim, must have been invented even before the wheel!

1 *A muffler—white, if possible, for the Lord's day*

2 *Some were too poor to buy at the old clothes shops*

stores and the uses of the goods they sold. By now 'surgical' was a dirty word.

Teenagers in the slums could find courtship extremely diffi-cult. Too early an interest in sex might be condemned by parents just feeling the benefit of a new wage-earning son or daughter. Most Edwardian elders in the lower working class, taking over still another prerogative unchanged from the previous century, looked upon it as a natural right that children, after leaving school, should work to compensate parents for all the 'kept' years of childhood. Early marriage robbed them, they felt, of their just rewards.

'Dancing rooms' being often taboo and visits to each other's crowded kitchens impossible, youthful couples walked the streets or stood in dark doorways, often to be duly marked and reported on. One moralist in our neighbourhood with half a dozen con-venient courting recesses round his warehouse, in order to fore-stall sin, kept them permanently daubed with sticky tar. But love apparently found a way. However promising national statistics, with us the hushed tones of matrons in the shop meant only too often that still another unhappy girl had shown herself 'no better than she ought to be'.

The Edwardian slum child, like his forebears, felt an attach-ment to family life that a later age may find hard to understand. Home, however poor, was the focus of all his love and interests, a sure fortress against a hostile world. Songs about its beauties were ever on people's lips. 'Home, sweet home', first heard in the 1870's, had become 'almost a second national anthem'. Few walls in lower-working-class houses lacked 'mottoes'—coloured strips of paper, about nine inches wide and eighteen inches in length, attesting to domestic joys: EAST, WEST, HOME'S BEST; BLESS OUR HOME; GOD IS MASTER OF THIS HOUSE (though Father made an able deputy); HOME IS THE NEST WHERE ALL IS BEST. To hear of a teen-ager leaving or being turned out of it struck dark fear in a child's mind. He could hardly imagine a fate more awful.

In some families one would come across a daughter who was 'devoted' to her mother. She usually had the parents' confidence and some authority and did much to ease the maternal burden that could at times be overwhelmingly heavy. But she did it at a price. From early days not expected to marry, the devoted daughter generally became drudge, unpaid servant and parent by

D

proxy to all the rest. When the mother died people said the shock would kill her; one half expected her to fall into a decline and pass away. Sometimes these family slaves dutifully accepted spinsterhood and kept pious memory warm, though occasionally, finding a mate in middle age, they burst free and lived to damn their years in bondage. If the husband died soon, however, they became for all their widow's weeds spinsters again in habit and outlook.

Men in the lower working class, aping their social betters, displayed virility by never performing any task in or about the home which was considered by tradition to be women's work. Some wives encouraged their partners in this and proudly boasted that they would never allow the 'man of the house' to do a 'hand's turn'. Derisive names like 'mop rag' and 'diddy man' were used for those who did help. Nevertheless, kindlier husbands, especially when their wives were near exhaustion at the end of a day or in the last stages of a pregnancy, would willingly do housework, cooking, washing the children or scrubbing a floor, provided doors remained locked and neighbours uninformed. Bolder spirits would even go out and shake rugs, bring in clothes and clothes lines, clean windows and swill flags, always at the risk of scoffing onlookers. One quiet little street in the village where several husbands dared to help their wives regularly became known in the pubs as 'Dolly Lane' or 'Bloody-good-husband Street'. A marital phenomenon observed with much puzzlement by some in this virile society was the woman who pushed open the vault door of a tavern and with cold eye and beckoning finger caused her husband (he could be a known 'fighting man', even) to put down his beer and follow her on the instant. 'It's a great big shame!' his pals might sing afterwards, 'and if she belonged to me, I'd let her know who's who!' Perhaps! But the knowing topers recognised well enough when they saw it a certain sexual relationship and could describe it, too, unequipped though they were with the Freudian terms common in a later decade.

The male weakling in certain households, often known even through manhood as 'Sonny', could be a subject of whispered concern among neighbours. He was usually 'delicate'. In pub and workshop there was plenty of talk, *sub rosa*, about the unspeakable. The working class, always fascinated by the great criminal trials, had been stirred to its depths by the prosecution of Oscar Wilde in 1895. As late as the first world war the ribald cry heard in factories, 'Watch out for oscarwile!' mystified raw young apprentices. The proletariat knew and marked what they considered to be the sure signs of homosexuality, though the term was unknown. Any evidence of dandyism in the young was severely frowned on. One 'mother-bound' youth among us, son of a widow and clerk in a city warehouse, strolled out on Sundays wearing of all things gloves, 'low quarters' and carrying an umbrella! The virile damned him at once—an incipient 'nancy' beyond all doubt, especially since he was known to be learning to play the violin. Among ignorant men any interest in music, books or the arts in general, learning or even courtesy and intelligence could make one suspect. This linking of homosexuality with culture played some part, I believe, in keeping the lower working class as near-illiterate as they were.

A typical victim of this sort of group hostility was D. H. Lawrence. Old working-class neighbours in his home village of Eastwood remembered him first, and with contempt, as one who in childhood 'played with the wenches', and later as a teenage effeminate who went with his walking cane to snoop on courting couples along the canal bank: the lonely voyeur. 'I've got something there!' said his worried father to miner friends. Had Lawrence's neighbours known or cared they would have smiled to think that such a youth in later life could have set himself up as an expert on sex virility in the working classes. 'Them as can, do,' they might well have said sourly; 'them as can't, scribble about it.' The lower-working-class woman, clamped firmly still in Victorian moral tradition, was in fact no subject at all for orgiastic pleasures, nor were men much freer. During serious sex talk in workshop and factory what one heard most was exasperated complaint about wives so prudish, 'virtuous' or uninterested in bed that copulation lost much of its attraction. I remember the savage dissatisfaction with his spouse of a young brass moulder. 'Last night', he said (during what was made plain had been the 'very lists of love'), 'she goes an' asks me not to forget to leave twopence for the gas!' The wife of a fettler in the same group was prone, it turned out, to reach her *crise d'extase* whilst eating an apple. A third, swathed in clothes, permitted her husband only the act *per se* and, on her mother's advice, allowed no 'dirty' manual contact whatever. 'It's about as exciting', he

said, 'as posting a letter!' This was a common inhibition. Only
the chargehand (apostate from a militant religious sect) spoke of
love life in a happier vein. He claimed that *his* partner, at the
peak of sexual congress (and on sectarian instruction) was wont
to cry, 'Rapture! Rapture! Praise the Lord!' Upon which he
returned the standard exclamation. But the noise, he said, disturbed the neighbours, who beat on the bedroom wall with a
boot. Another, a sad little man, complained that not only did his
wife take no interest in proceedings, but she also insisted on a
regular emolument of sixpence per session.[5] She was saving, he
said, for a holiday at Blackpool.

In a letter to Lady Ottoline Morrell in 1928 *à propos Lady
Chatterley's Lover* Lawrence writes:

I realise that one of the reasons why the common people keep—or
kept—the good *natural glow* of life, just warm life, longer than
educated people was because it was still possible for them to say ——
or —— without either a shudder or a sensation. If a man had been
able to say to you when you were young and in love: an' if tha ——
an' if tha —— I'm glad. I shouldna want a woman who couldna ——
nor —— —— —— surely it would have been liberation to you, and it
would have helped to keep your heart warm.[6]

This extract seems to me to typify Lawrence's false view of
working-class sexuality; earthy the Edwardian masses indeed
were, but only in certain strictly limited social situations. Men
had one language for the mine, mill or factory, another for home
and a third for social occasions.[7] Courtship was a time when one

---

[5] But married women generally, for all their lack of interest, felt bound in
duty to a fiction they thought existed, legally and morally, called 'conjugal
rights'. These, they believed, entitled a husband to the liberty of copulation
at almost any time, whatever his or his wife's state or condition. We knew
of a case where a married pair had not spoken a word to each other for
nine months; legal separation was on the way, yet he silently demanded,
'as a right', and she acquiesced in, coition three times a week. Wives who
complained to other women about the inconsiderate demands of their husbands usually got dusty answers. Such 'soft ha'p'orths' were thought to be
'odd'—natural old maids, perhaps, who had married in error, not knowing
what to expect. Really! One felt sorry for poor Joe! or poor Fred!

[6] D. H. Lawrence, *Selected Literary Criticism*. The words 'reluctantly suppressed' by the editor of *The Letters of D. H. Lawrence* were presumably
'shit' and 'piss'.

[7] It was an educative experience for every young apprentice introduced at
a trade union branch meeting to witness the courtesy and decorum of his

assumed the airs of a class superior to one's own; only a proletarian youth from the lowest grades would have used such words to his love *before* marriage, though familiarity, it is true, would afterwards have brought linguistic readjustments. This relaxation, however, did not in general spread to the use of sexual obscenity in the bedroom. Respectability sank deep through working-class womanhood; in the naming of sexual parts and actions a wife might have known all the terms on the tongue of the prostitute, but her husband, if he talked on the pillow at all, was permitted only euphemisms—private, infantile or dialectical. And that was how he wanted it, for the wife he so often called 'mother' was a 'good' woman and in her presence no sexually obscene words ever escaped his lips. In the proletarian bed Lady Ottoline would have stayed quite unliberated.

As for the young Lawrence,[8] timid as a child, mother-coddled, taken to school by a bodyguard of two older girls, scorned by young males, then drawn later into college and away from common life, it would seem that he had few opportunities, after childhood, of knowing the working-class man generally at first hand and a lack of male insight when it came to writing about him. His own father, as he admitted in later life, was a case in

---

elders. Stiff and sober in their best rig-out, they hardly seemed the same men he knew at work. Here, in union discourse, even an escaping 'damn' would be apologised for, and this, sometimes, by journeymen who in the workshop used every obscenity they could lay a tongue to. In the home, down to low social levels, a father (not often a mother) might 'damn', 'blast', even 'bloody' and 'bugger', but generally he would eschew excremental and sexual words there. If a drunk in the street began 'effin' 'n' blindin' ' (as the phrase went) in sobriety his social stock fell. One of our teenage friends, a foundry worker and a roughish type, turned down his new *amoureuse* after only one evening because in the cinema she had whispered, 'Excuse me, duck, I gotter rush for a piss!' This shocked him. 'You don't want that sort o' bleedin' talk from a bird!' he said. 'Then she's off down the aisle like an harrier!' This was not, he felt, romance as Pola Negri knew it. People always looked upon 'swearing' beyond the mild expletives as a serious matter; the working classes showed themselves as inhibited in language as they were in love. As for the petty bourgeoisie! 'Take this child home, boy!' the headmistress of the 'Mixed Infants' coldly ordered me once, pointing down at a sad soul, 'and inform his mother he's made an error in his trousers!' *Quelle delicatesse!* She was one of the people who taught us our manners.

[8] Lawrence says that he was 'delicate', a common word of the times for all the weak and ailing. His mother kept him from school until he was seven.

point. Lawrence, as did all the 'unvirile' throughout the working class of the time, drew upon himself the despisal and derision of his boyhood contemporaries. This might well have contributed to his later snobbery and intense dislike of the 'mob'. But it can, I think, be truly said that in Lawrence's Eastwood or anywhere else in early twentieth-century England the lower manual workers as a whole, philistine and sexually inhibited,[9] both feared the artist and despised his works.

[9] One remarkable feature of Edwardian times, difficult in the circumstances to understand, is the lenient attitude of many of the courts of law towards illegal sexual acts. In what would be considered nowadays, for example, a case of 'living on immoral earnings' serious enough to get an offender four years' imprisonment, a local court in 1908 gave the accused two months' hard labour. Three months for 'gross indecency' (women were often found guilty of this) and 'twenty-nine shillings, or one month' for prostitution were very common sentences.

Chapter 4

Governors, Pastors and Masters

The laws were made to keep fair play
William Blake

Before 1900 the 'undermass' went to gaol not only as a punishment but in order to receive punishment. In 1895 the Gladstone committee on crime decided that such an openly punitive system 'made for the deterioration of the prisoners, who on their eventual release into society were neither deterred nor reformed, but brutalised and embittered'. They concluded that 'prison treatment should be effectively designed to maintain, stimulate, or awaken the higher susceptibilities of prisoners and turn them out of prison better men, both physically and morally than when they had come in'.

Fair, well intentioned words; but what committees on penal reform have always tended to overlook is that while one may alter regimens and rules, it is far more difficult to change the minds of the custodians called upon to administer them. Nothing was done to educate the ignorant turnkey or the general public. Nineteenth-century attitudes on the treatment of prisoners lingered among prison staffs and the community far into the present century and caused untold suffering. They have by no means disappeared, even today. Yet the Gladstone committee certainly initiated change.

In 1902 no fewer than 170,000 people went to prison, 52,000 of these being 'females'. The commissioners noted with satisfaction that very few skilled workmen were to be found in our prisons. More than nine-tenths, in fact, of those incarcerated consisted of the labouring poor. The great majority had been committed for the most venial offences; a little over half, in default of payment of a fine.[1]

---

[1] For some reason there was a remarkable difference in the incidence of petty crime in Scotland compared with the other countries of the United Kingdom. In England and Wales the number of prisoners received in local gaols was 621 per 100,000 of the population; in Ireland, 744; but in Scotland the rate for the unco' bad stood at 1,489!

Of the 105 crimes listed to which the undermass was prone, the commonest were simple larceny, assault, drunkenness, begging and sleeping-out, neglecting to maintain family, prostitution and misbehaviour of paupers. The Prison Act of 1898 caused delinquents to be classified into three categories according to the nature of their offence and antecedents. The 'first division' now received all those who had been known previously as 'first class misdemeanants'. Its social intent was obvious: none of the very poor, whatever the offence, was ever sentenced to it. The 'second division' was 'intended to meet the case of persons guilty of offences not implying any great moral depravity, and to a large extent, the case of persons committed to prison in default of paying a fine imposed, where the antecedents were respectable'. The 'third division' took those in need of 'stern repression'. But whatever the Act intended, most justices, class-bound as ever, went on sentencing much as before. In 1902 more than 40,000 men and women who had failed to pay small fines for offences not warranting a prison sentence were sent to gaol *with hard labour*. The sybaritic second division, magistrates plainly felt, was no place for a poor offender, no matter how respectable his antecedents. There were women who had been imprisoned more than two hundred times!

The treadwheel as a form of hard labour had just been abolished, though it remained a little while longer in some gaols, notably at Derby, where the mill ground wheat for other prisons. Penal mechanical punishment had never been considered a consistent success: some smaller gaols had not possessed a wheel and at others medical officers had exempted many inmates because of their physical inability to tread a mill. The abolition caused changes in the employment of those prisoners doing hard labour. They now spent fourteen days of the first month in 'strict cellular separation', picking oakum 'without mechanical appliances'. This meant that the 'fiddle', a tool used to help untwist and comb old tarred rope, was forbidden. Without it, fingertips, after constant picking, would begin to bleed. In the second half of the month the prisoner made coal sacks, chopped wood and stones or performed any other 'heavy, disagreeable labour'. After twenty-eight days he continued with the same kind of tasks but did them in the company of others under the closest supervision and in strict silence. From the imposition of silence on prisoners in the nineteenth century a myth grew among the custodians that should this rule ever be relaxed inmates would at once exploit the new liberty to plan riot inside the walls and all kinds of villainy beyond. More stupid warders were convinced of this; they fought bitterly against the abolition of the 'no talking' rule until its final demise nearly half a century later. Certainly the earliest attempts by the commissioners to mitigate the severity of silence got little encouragement from prison governors. Prisoners, it was decided, who had done twelve months of their sentence would be permitted during one period of exercise, on one day a week, to walk and converse with another prisoner, provided that such a prisoner 'is of the same class and that, in the opinion of the governor, their association is not likely to be injurious. If the governor has reason to suspect that any prisoner is abusing this privilege he may withdraw the indulgence.' The governor at Birmingham seemed to voice the view of a number of his colleagues. 'Conversation at exercise', he said, 'is not much sought after; most prisoners prefer taking their exercise in the ordinary way [walking in a circle, six feet apart, in single file] and applications to converse are seldom made, and then usually by bad characters.' But in spite of every punishment men went on talking, somehow defeating each new prohibition, until finally inmates were (and are) penalised not for speech but for talking after being ordered to stop.

The prisoners' day ran like this:

5.30 a.m.	Men rise, wash and clean cells. Officers muster.
6.10	Labour in cell starts. Juvenile adults drill till 7 a.m.
7.10	Breakfast.
8.00	Chapel service.
8.15	Prayers commence.
8.30	Prayers cease.
8.45	Labour begins.
12.00 p.m.	Dinner
1.30	Labour begins.
5.35	Labour ends. Supper. Lock up.
6.05	Labour begins.
7.15	Labour ends.
8.00	Lock up.
8.20	Lights out.

Official belief held strongly that each day, in gaol, evil must be confronted by good. Prisoners, whether they liked it or not, got daily prayers, homilies in chapel and as many as three sermons a week. They underwent too a steady succession of lecturers who spoke at length on such subjects as 'Purity', 'The cardinal virtues', 'Industry', 'Formation of character', 'Moral obligations', 'Our world-wide empire', and 'Fresh air', all directed at 'uplifting the listener'. Sermons and lectures were 'much appreciated', and inmates invariably 'grateful'. With pleasure chaplains commented again and again on the 'heartiness' of chapel singing. 'We banged the tins and bawled the hymns,' wrote Oscar Wilde. This could have been due to fervour or perhaps to the chance to open one's mouth wide without being ordered to 'shurrup!' Again, all chaplains noted with great satisfaction that their congregation remained 'quiet and devoutedly attentive', which was not to be wondered at since discipline warders, on raised seats, backs to the altar, cast a cold eye on their charges throughout the proceedings: devotion was an alternative to 'bread and water'. Prison chaplains, rich in authority and power, wrestled hard with their flock, in the pulpit and out; one made 15,981 visits to cells in a year. Some plainly treated the lost sheep, across class barriers, with patronage and pomposity; others, wretched before so much human misery, were quite at a loss for solutions. But not the incumbent at Bodmin gaol! He claimed well-nigh total success. 'The behaviour of prisoners at all services', he reported, 'has been exemplary and there can be no possible doubt as to the excellent results which accrue from daily prayers and frequent exhortation. . . . The daily service and constant instruction help to train prisoners in habits of prayer and knowledge of the Scriptures and teach them how to carry into effect the desire for improvement.' 'A considerable number have professed repentance of their sins and a determination to amend their lives both spiritually and morally.' He asserted that no recipient of his ministrations had returned to prison, though it must be said that the percentage intake at Bodmin gaol in the following years varied little from that of any other prison. He admitted failure, however, with 'vagrants'. 'They appear', he said, 'to be wilful idlers and, according to their own confession, prefer to stay in prison to Union or casual ward.'

The chaplain at Northampton went in for services of a 'penitential character, in which one of the litanies of penitence is sung antiphonally by chaplain and prisoners'. But he too seemed to have got no co-operation, antiphonally or otherwise, from the vagrants inside. This 'idle pauper class' made him feel that it was 'a pity no severer punishment than confinement and bread and water diet can be administered'. And even this, he regretted, was sometimes evaded because some of the miscreants were too weak to receive it. Still, inmates everywhere were always 'respectful and seemly' and pastors ever on the look-out for any signs of self-improvement among them. The chaplain at Wormwood Scrubs, for instance, was quick to note a penchant among more educated prisoners for the novels of Lord Lytton and Thackeray. 'Also, by way of lighter literature, C. Dickens is by no means overlooked.'

The chaplain at Durham held a mission when 'many were brought to true repentance'. But he regretted, too, that so many came back to gaol. His colleague at Strangeways complained that those most eagerly applying to receive holy communion were often the worst characters in the prison. But he thought that a large proportion of the prisoners, especially first offenders, did try to live honest lives, 'as a result of the religious and moral influences brought to bear on them'. Yet the prison population continued to rise. It remained for the chaplain at Dartmoor to strike a melancholy note: 'With the desire to write temperately', he reported, 'and avoid being unduly pessimistic, the conviction is forced on me that a very large proportion of our prisoners are totally uninfluenced by moral considerations.'

One penal problem, however, was exercising authority more and more—the increasing number of vagrants who deliberately sought entrance into prison in preference to the workhouse. What had happened, the pundits were inquiring, to the famous principle of 'less eligibility'? Seventy years before, when workhouses were established, it had been emphasised in a Bill which Parliament welcomed with enthusiasm that conditions of living in the 'unions' must deliberately be made 'less eligible'—that is, more wretched—than those suffered by the lowest-paid worker outside. As conscious policy, any entrant to the workhouse had to be openly humiliated, and this was done with such thorough, cold-hearted effect that it cowed the undermass for the better part of a century. The workhouse system meant, said one of its inspirers,

having all relief through the workhouse, making the workhouse an uninviting place of wholesome restraint, preventing any of its inmates from going out, or receiving visitors without a written note to that effect from one of the overseers, disallowing beer and tobacco and finding them work according to their ability: thus making the parish fund the last resource of a pauper, and rendering the person who administers the relief the hardest taskmaster and the worst paymaster that the idle and the dissolute can apply to.

This enthusiast overlooked, of course, the unnumberable honest, hard-working men and women driven to destitution through lack of work; he forgot the old, the sick, the dependent children. Poverty, he felt, was a crime that should be sternly punished. For the rest of the nineteenth century and beyond, society left its 'idle paupers' in the hands of the overseers. But naturally it was understood that however bad a workhouse might be, prison would always be worse—the place of 'least eligibility'. Now, in the early 1900's, men were openly preferring gaol! The chaplain at Chelmsford gave at least one sound reason why they made this choice.

There are [he reported] large blocks of Jersey granite (most of them about ½ cwt) in many of the casual wards of this county. The quantity to be broken for a day's work is 14 cwt maximum; 10 cwt average. I have examined and personally worked upon the blocks, and am convinced that not more than half the quantity indicated can be broken without the most extreme exertion, excepting either by an expert, or a very strong man. I do not at all wonder that so many men who are in a somewhat low physical condition reject the task and elect prison. The diet of the casual ward is generally 8 oz of dry bread, morning, noon and night, 2 oz of cheese at noon and water the only drink.

The governor of Canterbury was perturbed by some of the prisoners sent to him for workhouse offences. One, he said,

aged 62 years, was ordered to break stones, but he was partially paralysed in his right hand and could not do the work.

H. S., No. 98, was sentenced to 14 days for refusing to work at breaking stones. He had recently undergone a serious surgical operation. The wound from this had not healed and required frequent dressing in prison.

W. H., Reg. No. 1263—sentenced to 14 days for refusing to do his task. This man was unfit for labour of any kind; he was epileptic and had recurrent fits the whole time he was in prison.

Attitudes of authority to the many thousands of men and boys tramping the country varied widely. The Discharged Prisoners'

Societies, who helped only the 'deserving' cases, expressed themselves in forceful terms on the 'idleness of these vagrants, who
are little better than mere animals and will not work'. It was
pointed out, however, that 'according to the last judicial statistics,
there were only 209 vagrants dealt with as incorrigible rogues
out of the many thousands who were perambulating the country
and filling workhouses and prisons'. The governor of one local
gaol where the number of vagrants had doubled since 1901 commented on the

severity of the tasks set by workhouse masters and states that the oakum
task prevailing in that district is an impossible one, even for an experienced picker. He states that many of the men convicted for refusing
to work appear to be genuine working men looking for employment
and he is of the opinion that if greater discrimination were shown by
the workhouse authorities in the treatment of the casual pauper class,
there would be far less committal to prison for begging and sleeping out
and crime generally.

But the prison commissioners were deeply disturbed by views
publicly expressed that the gaols had become havens from the
rigours of the workhouse. 'We are not prepared to admit', they
said, 'that the increase of the vagrant class sent to prison is due
to the fact that the conditions of prison life are unduly attractive.'

At several prisons where there has been a remarkable increase in the
number of offences against workhouse regulations, it is reported that
prisoners openly profess this preference for the prison on the grounds
of better treatment, greater kindness, better food and more humane
conditions. Any statement to this effect by a prisoner, especially if, as
often happens, it gains currency in the local press, is likely to lead to
misapprehension as to the principles and methods of prison discipline.

But they agreed that the problem required close examination.

On the preference of prison to workhouse [they announced later]
the evidence of governors in other parts of the country is to the same
effect, and the only opinion we can form, after careful consideration of
the matter, is that a remedy for this preference on the part of that class
of wastrels and ne'er-do-wells who hover on the borderland between
the two, is by the adoption by the workhouse authorities of a uniform
scale of dietary and task which should not be less favourable than the
standard adopted, after full inquiry, for persons convicted of crime.

But they found it necessary to add that on evidence received
from many parts of the country a large proportion of vagrants

committed to gaol were found by the medical officer to be unfit for any form of hard labour. What had happened, in fact, was plain to see. Though prisons still remained brutalising and inhumane dens, the Act of 1898 had mitigated some of their earlier evils; but the workhouse had stayed its old vile self. The undermass knew 'less eligibility' when they saw it!

In the first fourteen years of the century Board of Trade statistics continued to confirm the well-known fact that the number of those sent to prison during any one year varied in proportion to the number of unemployed. On average about 170,000 people were gaoled annually; but over 1908, a year of slump, the figure rose to 185,000, only to fall again to 139,000 in 1912, when economic conditions improved. Up to the outbreak of the first world war many thousands among the undermass went to prison, sometimes repeatedly, for the most trivial offences, thus forming a massive, clearly defined group within the working class. Over the five years ended 1908–09 an average of 177,500 people annually were 'summarily convicted' for minor offences and committed to gaol: a ratio of 514 per 100,000 of the population of the country. Not only men and women but children by the thousand were sent to prison.

'It is regretted', remarked the commissioners, 'that more than half those under 16 were committed in default of payment of a fine.' And the commonest crimes? Trespassing, playing games in the street, throwing stones and snowballs, sleeping out, and gambling. Sentences were short, usually three days to a month. The chaplain at Brecon prison had strong feelings about this.

A longer term of imprisonment [he thought], say three months, is better for a boy than one month. The sentence should be such as to allow the boy full advantage of the moral and intellectual training which prison affords. Special attention has been paid by me to the cases of juvenile offenders, visiting each in his cell daily and giving them a course in the Church catechism before release.

Go thou, and snowball no more!

The governor of Dorchester prison had similar views on longer sentences for boys. 'It takes some time', he said, 'before the novelty of the situation [going to prison] wears off and it is only when it is gone that the steady round of discipline and labour makes way for reflection, and the good offices of the chaplain, schoolmaster and drill instructor can be effectively brought into play.'

That the boys needed education *outside* prison could never have been in doubt. The chaplain at Durham reported that 'of 374 lads passing through my hands, 91 were unable to read, and in most of the other cases the school standard is disgracefully low'. The visiting chaplain to all the gaols noted that 'many of the juveniles sent to prison are illiterates. In one gaol 11 out of 27 boys did not even know their letters.' This was general, and he

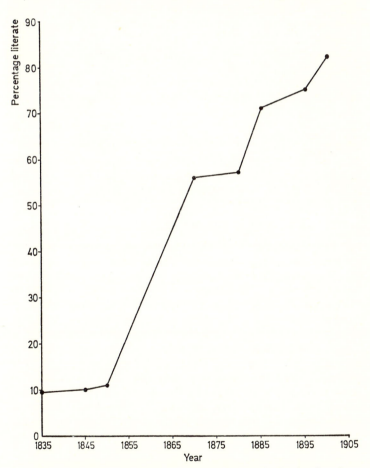

The percentage of literate inmates of prisons in England and Wales between 1835 and 1900

thought it 'difficult to account for in these days of enforced and free schooling'. He might have concluded, though, from the number of people then in gaol for offences against the Education Act, that strong resistance still existed among parents to the sending of children to school at all. Certainly many elders of the time, perhaps the majority, would have agreed wholeheartedly with the factory inspector who said, after the introduction of compulsory education: 'to keep young persons from work till they are 12 years of age will, I fear, create an objection to labour, which through life they may never be able to overcome'.

In a little over four years one young villain, clearly heading for a life of crime, had acquired forty-one convictions and been sent to prison on no fewer than thirty occasions; this in default of paying fines ranging from 1s to 40s. Among other crimes he was gaoled or fined seventeen times for playing pitch and toss, fourteen times for card-playing in the street, twice for playing football there, three times for stealing pigeons. For 'sleeping out' he was fortunately only cautioned. The sum total of his fines, in default of which he went to prison so often, came to less than £10. For 'refusing to move on' he was convicted twice and fined 2s 6d and 1s respectively. In each case (perhaps being flush after pitch and toss) he paid up and left the court a free boy.

'It is pitiful', said the governor of Pentonville in 1913,

to have to record that many lads continue to be sent to prison for what one must in all charity call trivial offences. There were no less than 226 cases here in the course of the past year. The facts point to a strong and serious defect in the administration of the law that there should be no other way of disposing of young offenders, who are neither vicious nor criminal, but just headstrong, stupid and foolish. Moreover, the length of sentence is ludicrously inadequate for any purpose other than to accustom the youth to an experience for which he should entertain a lifelong and wholesome dread. From a utilitarian point of view it seems little short of insanity to sit still and make no effort to check this pitiful waste of human life. It seems to me that the man who will invent some salutary method of treatment, not involving imprisonment for minor breaches of the law, will have earned well of his day and generation.[2]

---

[2] Lincoln prison was plagued by 'fishing apprentices', boys from ports along the east coast sent to gaol for absenting themselves from trawlers in contravention of the Merchant Shipping Act. 'All the cases seen by me', said the chaplain at Lincoln, 'express a great distaste for the life on board

3 *General dealer*

4 *The clothiers*

The prison commissioners themselves had no doubts at all on the iniquity. Commenting on the boy with forty-one convictions, they emphasised that 'for anyone who wanted to see punishment for youthful delinquency carried out according to humane and rational principles, the methods illustrating this one case cannot be the best. We venture to think they are the worst.'

And still they went on going to prison *en masse*. Those who escaped the law, young or old, still retained that 'wholesome dread' of gaol which, governors believed, was the prime purpose of their prison's existence. Like the workhouse, prison played a major role in keeping the poor profoundly deferential before any kind of authority.

The governor of Dorchester gaol, however, thought that

no anxiety need be felt that prison discipline is too severe for juvenile prisoners and should be relaxed; rather is it a matter of regret that they do not regard prison with the dread one would expect and desire to see. The majority come from habitations which it would be a libel to call home, ill-clad, ill-fed, frequently the victims of the violence of brutal and dissolute parents. What wonder that these children appreciate, as many say they do, the comforts of prison and the kindness of prison officers.

But in spite of all the amenities to be had in prison a few sensitive and civilised people of the time were fighting hard to abolish a system which sent so many thousands each year to enjoy them with so little reason.

The Criminal Justice Administration Act of 1914 had results which were both immediate and astonishing; in the first year after its introduction the prison population fell by 38 per cent. Offenders were now given time to pay, and sentences of less than five days were expressly forbidden. 'The Act of 1914', said the prison commissioners, 'may be regarded as the declaration of Parliament against the admitted evil of very short sentences which, while rendering persons familiar with the inside of prison walls, furnished no time for any improving influences.'

Here the commissioners were adding substance to a myth supported by many prison governors and chaplains then and for long afterwards. An extended sentence, they maintained, benefited

a fishing vessel and stated that they had been apprenticed without any option from the workhouse (their parents being dead).' After a boy had been convicted a certain number of times his indentures were cancelled.

the delinquent because he was subject longer to certain improving influences within the house of correction. In view of prison conditions of the time it seems incredible that this belief should have been asserted and repeated so often. A generation or so later, working myself for years in intimate daily contact with the inmates of a large local gaol, it was my experience that few men indeed, whether their stay was long or short, profited morally or in any other way from imprisonment. The 'improvers' were simply deceiving themselves. What kept men from returning to gaol was not Christian sermon and homily but (after 1914) an alteration of a law that had vilely oppressed the poor for generations, and an economic and social change which brought an easement of their poverty. In the year of the trade slump, 1908–09, 27,387 people—a record number—were prosecuted for begging and sleeping out. By 1917–18 the number had fallen to 1,478, and these, it was thought, were 'largely confined to the aged and mentally and physically weak'. There were vagrants who, to the last, avoided the workhouse at all costs.

Our own establishment, built in 1855 to hold 700 paupers,[3] stood, a massive pile, behind high walls, housing all those who had abandoned hope in this world, though frequent religious services offered brighter prospects for the next. Demands on inmates to follow the good life were rigorous; our local Church of England bishop, for instance, held the sternest views about the prevalence of bastardy among the poor. He felt great reluctance to having the illegitimate baptised at all. His *crise de conscience* came when a workhouse inmate—'a miserable girl', the guardians called her, 'who has been going downhill since she was sixteen'—presented the second fruits of her descent at the font of the Union church. The chaplain in charge, at his bishop's direction, refused to give the child a name. The mother seems to have been impertinent about it, saying that she didn't see why her baby shouldn't be christened in the church like everyone else's; but the guardians, skilled in the treatment of 'refractory paupers', soon put her in her place. Seldom a week passed without still another inmate turning 'refractory', which meant being disciplined by the board, being hauled off before a court or sent to gaol.

Our elected poor law guardians (six Roman Catholics, four

[3] Enlarged by 1900 to hold 2,000.

Protestants and two Independents) bore a heavy burden: for hours they debated over the problems of their charges, reported at astonishing length in the press. Typical was the case of an old lady brought before them for receiving letters from her daughter, 'a servant in a gentleman's house', containing money, 'sometimes to the amount of one shilling and sixpence'.

'She refuses', the clerk told the board, 'to let the workhouse master see these letters.'

Mr Brownrigg, of the board, said that 'if the master believed an inmate had money he should have a search made'.

Mr Simmons stated that 'if the master found an inmate with money he should turn out that inmate'.

The old woman, who is paralysed on one side, said she had been in the workhouse for two years.

Chairman. 'Can't you see that it is your duty to give up the money to the workhouse people for your maintenance here?'

Old woman. 'No, I can't see that.'

The guardians ordered a search to be made and said she could ask the workhouse master for a shilling from time to time.

Diet at the Union could always be relied upon as a subject for ribald comment among the Edwardian poor. In the local 'grubber' one broke usually half a ton of stones in return for a breakfast which consisted of six ounces of bread, margarine and one pint of skilly. For dinner one got six ounces of bread, tea and an ounce of cheese. Our guardians had special trouble with the travelling destitute (as many as two hundred a day), who queued at the workhouse, 'coughing and spitting', each evening, hours before opening time. Some sentimentalist suggested that in bitter winter weather they might perhaps be allowed inside early. This was scotched at once. 'These men', said an official, 'are breaking the law as it is. They should not be here at all. A vagrant has a legal duty to keep walking until the evening of each day.'

At Christmas time goodwill broke out, of course, even in the workhouse.[4] 'A dinner was served', the local press announced cheerfully, 'to seventy male tramps, ten female tramps and one

[4] Our elders told of a man with a large family struggling to keep his sick father with them. At last the old man insisted he should be taken to the workhouse. They set off, wife picking up his few belongings, and the father on his son's back. *En route* they stopped to rest a while on a stone seat. 'It was here', said the old man, 'I rested, too, carrying my

girl tramp aged nine.' Afterwards one among them rose and praised the quality of the beef, saying that in happier times he had dined at some of the best hotels where the meat had never been so tender. At these sentiments the mayor expressed his gratification.

---

father to the workhouse.' The son rose, took the burden on his back again and turned with his wife for home. 'We'll manage somehow,' he said.

Chapter 5

The Common Scene

I heard the sighs of men that have no skill
To speak of their distress, no, nor the will.
Wilfred Owen

Whatever it was that went to make the lower-working-class home 'cosy', parents had first, often sole, rights in it. They took, of course, the best bed and bedding and the two cushioned armchairs nearest the fire. In some families children were forbidden to sit on these at any time; during parental absence they had to remain vacated thrones of power. To many people the idea of sharing food and possessions equitably with their children would have seemed preposterous; yet adult life with all its little prerogatives was often no more than a stake in common poverty.

The homes of the very poor contained little or no bought furniture. They made do with boxes and slept in their clothes and in what other garments they could beg or filch. Of such people there were millions. Seebohm Rowntree's *Poverty: a study of town life* (1901), for example, showed that 'one in four of the inhabitants of York lacked the bare necessities of life'. Our village, like so many others that went to make the cities of thriving industrial Britain, was stamped with the same poverty, and this right to the outbreak and beyond of the first world war. In among the respectable rows of 'two up and two down' houses we had the same blocks of hovels sharing a single tap, earth closet and open midden: each house with a candle for light, an oil lamp or a bare gas jet. Coal the 'low class' and 'no class' rarely bought; they picked or stole it from spoil heap and wharf, or, in bad times, dragged the canals for droppings from barges. The more fortunate rolled home a hundredweight or so weekly in an iron-wheeled wagon from coal yards, dark, temple-like sheds where great cones of fuel rose along the gloom like a miniature volcanic range. Any customer wanting less than half a hundredweight was denied a vehicle and had to bear off his load in a sack over the shoulder. People like publicans who bought the stuff a ton at a time gave by this an impressive display of affluence. Few were so fortunate.

In 1906 the Board of Trade figures showed that half the women in industrial Britain earned under 10*s* for a week's work of seldom less than fifty-four hours. The Sweated Industries Exhibition organised by the *Daily News* in 1907 shocked at least the more sensitive visitors into realising the conditions in which so many of the poor were living. Women, they learned, working fourteen hours a day, made artificial violets and geraniums for 7*d* a gross, buttercups for 3*d* and roses for 1*s* 3*d* a gross. They put 384 hooks on cards for one penny and spent eighteen hours at it to earn 5*s* a week.[1] Matchbox makers got a similar sum. In sweated sewing shops machinists made pinafores and babies bonnets for 2*s* a dozen and ran up a gross of ties to earn 5*s*. Shirt manufacture brought them in less than a penny an hour. These were but a few examples in a massive chronicle of brutal exploitation. What it meant in terms of human suffering could be glimpsed, at times, only too terribly, in the columns of the local news-sheet. There was Emily Hughes, now.

One January day in 1913 Mrs Hughes, living in a street close by ours, found herself short of fuel. She went into the back yard and left her young daughter in the kitchen, where there was a small fire but no guard. When the mother returned her child was in flames. A neighbour ran in and wrapped a rug about her, but the little girl died the same day in hospital.

At the coroner's court the mother was questioned:

Coroner. 'You had a fireguard?'
Woman. 'I had no guard.'
Coroner. 'But one was seen on the same day as the accident before your fire.'
Woman. 'Someone came into my house and put it there while

---

[1] Of 304 women imprisoned in Strangeways between 4 August and 4 September 1914, forty-three were 'chars', thirty-two 'laundresses' (in court every washerwoman called herself a laundress), twenty-four 'servants' and thirty-seven 'hawkers'. At regular intervals the police made drives against 'illegal street traders'—those who tried to get a living by selling bootlaces and similar articles from door to door. Pedlars without licence, like the hawker with his hand-cart, they haunted the ways, a permanent part of the common scene.

I was at the hospital. I don't know who. It did not belong to me.'
Coroner. 'You know the police can prosecute you?'
Woman. 'Yes.'
Coroner. 'You know you can be sent to gaol?'
Woman. 'Yes.'
Coroner. 'It is very creditable of you to have spoken in this way.'
Woman. 'I could not afford a guard. I have had no fire for many days, but occasionally I managed to get a few cinders and make one to keep the children warm.'

A verdict of accidental death was returned and the woman put into touch with an officer from the NSPCC.

The local newspaper, in an earlier year, had reported too on a woman, unnamed, found lying by some workmen on bare boards in a property boarded off as derelict and insanitary. By her side lay a baby two days old. She was living on the food brought to her by neighbours, the poorest of the poor. 'Mother and child were removed to the workhouse', where she was visited later by a member of the Ladies' Health Society, who, 'not seeing the infant, inquired for it'.

The mother said, 'God has been good and taken it.'
'Is that the way you view it?' the lady asked.
'Yes,' she said. 'I have had nine, but thank the Lord I've buried six, and hard work I've had to find food for those left.'

The Ladies' Health Society worked bravely among us, especially in the early years of the century. Together with the 'Sanitary Society', they visited the 'lowest classes' and found

much that is saddening: but there are bright spots—clean homes, pretty little sitting-room kitchens, pictures on the wall, clean hearths, chests of highly polished mahogany drawers, a steady husband, a tidy wife and children.
The lime and whitewash brushes have done excellent service and have been in constant demand. They were lent out thirty-six times last year, thus sweetening and purifying the houses.

(Brushes were loaned by the corporation.) The Society also sold ten hundredweights of carbolic soap and distributed six hundredweights of carbolic powder. One woman who kept her windows dirty so that people couldn't mark her poverty was promised a blind if she would only clean them. Light was certainly needed by her neighbour: she was engaged in hemming handkerchiefs at sevenpence a gross (no cotton provided) and had to fetch and carry her materials to and from the warehouse.

The corporation lent out its whitewash brushes, distributed free, bags of lime and bottles of a preventive medicine popularly known as 'diarrhoea mixture', and urged hygiene on all the populace. And no wonder. In summer house-flies and bluebottles swarmed, every kitchen alive: sticky, foul-smelling paper traps dangled about, dark with their writhing bodies. And the bed bugs! With the warm days they appeared in battalions, first in the hovels, then in the better-class houses, where people waged campaigns against their sweet-odoured, sickening presence. They lime-washed bedrooms ('bug binding' was the delicate term for this) and drenched them with 'Klenzit Kleener' disinfectant.[2] The blue flames of blowlamps licked spring mattress, floorboard, cracked walls and ceilings; but still they came, creeping along joists and through party walls until even the valiant cleanly housewife gave up in despair and prayed for cold weather. Through summer days one saw the 'fever' van carrying off some child, who only too often would be seen no more. In school, inspection showed whole classes of children infested with head vermin; many had body lice. The worst would sit isolated from the rest in a small sanitary cordon of humiliation. They would later be kept at home, their heads shaven, reeking of some rubbed-in disinfectant. Their status did not suffer from this treatment: they had already reached rock-bottom.

One saw a quarter of a class sixty 'strong' come to school barefoot. Many had rickets, bow legs or suffered from open sores. It is true that from the early years of the century the health of the people as a whole was improving steadily. Infant mortality, for instance, in the first decade decreased by 40 per cent and there was a considerable decline in the number of deaths from children's diseases generally. Nevertheless, in great slum pockets the late nineteenth-century social and economic pattern still persisted and it is doubtful whether the health of their inhabitants was much better than it had been twenty years before.

In 1899, of 12,000 men from the city who volunteered for

[2] A local firm—'Bed Cleaners & Purifiers'—promised short-term immunity at 3s a bed, but this was considered exorbitant.

service in the South African war, 8,000 were rejected outright and only 1,200 accepted as completely fit, though army pass standards had been lowered to those of 1815.[3] The figures did not take into account the 'large number' who applied and who looked so obviously unfit that doctors 'did not even bother to examine them'. Fifteen years later, at the start of the first world war, men poured again in thousands from the ginnels eager to serve and again they were turned down in vast numbers, the authorities being shocked at their wretched physical standard. The new century, it seemed, had done little as yet to improve Britain's slum manhood.

Our medical officer's report to the education committee in 1905 noted outbreaks among children of 'small-pox, typhus fever, enteric fever, scarlet fever and diphtheria', only a few of the diseases mentioned. 'A large proportion of the pupils', the report added, 'show signs of rickets.' There had been considerable distress during the winter, but the children had 'much appreciated the free breakfasts provided'. Some went hungry every day. In our own school the more ravenous were known as 'bread horses'. At playtime the bread horse would stagger across the yard with another boy on his back in return for a scrap to eat from the rider's lunch. At the local mission hall, where scores of men went for a night's rest, those with twopence were asked to go to a doss house, so that the entirely destitute could have a mission bed. Yet no one in public seemed unduly depressed by it all.

Our village, like the rest, had its quota of feeble-minded, dummies (deaf mutes), hydrocephalics, grotesque cripples, and its elderly women, broken like horses, who could be hired to drag a hundredweight of coke in a wagon a mile or more for threepence. One knew others, the unnamable, mere living bags of rags who existed mostly on local charity and who stood draped in a creeping subservience that only years of beggary could confer. These were they who came shuffling into the shop late Saturday night pleading for the day's scraps of cheese and bacon to make Sunday's only meal the economic lowest of the low. They and their like are all gone now from our 'dull' Welfare State. In the England of 1912, according to official statistics, a mere ninety

[3] In 1902 the minimum height for entry into the army was reduced from 5 ft 3 in. to 5 ft, the smallest soldiers later forming the 'Bantam' regiments.

people died through 'starvation or privation due to destitution'.
Judging by the number of those in our own world of the time
who did 'not strive, officiously to keep alive', the figure seems
a little conservative. There was, for instance, Albert J. Ainsworth,
who according to a report in the local news, typical of many not
unlike it, was found

leaning against a wall in Brook Street. He told Constable Hare that he
was ill and destitute. The kindly policeman took him to the infirmary,
where he was treated by a doctor and removed to the workhouse. He
had slept the previous night, he told the Resident Medical Officer, on
a bundle of paper. He remained in a comatose condition until 11 p.m.
on Friday, when he died. His body was much diseased. The man had
a brother residing in the district, but personally had nowhere to lay
his head.

And through those years (so beloved now by the elderly middle
classes), and for long after, my mother kept shop among it all,
noting what passed with a mixture of shrewdness and sardonic
compassion. 'In the hardest times', she said, 'it was often for me
to decide who ate and who didn't.' If bankruptcy, always close
in a slum corner shop, was to be avoided, one had to assess with
careful judgment the honesty, class standing and financial
resources of all tick customers. Not one but scores of families
could lie in a poverty that left them with hardly any food at all.
They appealed for credit. Then a shopkeeper's generosity and
humanity fought with his fears for self-preservation—to trust, or
not to trust?

After closing time at 11 p.m. shop windows were covered
with wooden shutters bolted together from within, this to dis-
courage dangerous thoughts among those who stared in hungrily
during the day. A wife (never a husband) would apply humbly
for tick on behalf of her family. Then, in our shop, my mother
would make an anxious appraisal, economic and social—how
many mouths had the woman to feed? Was the husband ailing?
Tuberculosis in the house, perhaps. If TB took one it always
claimed others; the breadwinner next time, maybe. Did the male
partner drink heavily? Was he a bad time keeper at work? Did
they patronise the pawnshop? If so, how far were they committed? Were their relations known good payers? And last, had
they already 'blued' some other shop in the district, and for how

much? After assessment credit would be granted and a credit limit fixed, at not more perhaps than five shillings' worth of foodstuffs in any one week, with all 'fancy' provisions such as biscuits and boiled ham proscribed. Or the supplicant might be turned down as 'too risky', after which she would trudge the round of other shops in the neighbourhood while the family waited hungry at home. With some poor folk, to be 'taken on at a tick shop' indicated a solid foot at last in the door of establishment. A tick book, honoured each week, became an emblem of integrity and a bulwark against hard times. The family had arrived.

In the struggle for solvency corner-shop economics demanded a wily system of trading. My mother kept grocery travellers from two different wholesalers on what she gleefully called the 'hop'. Each arrived hopefully on different days and, monthly, a pair of rival patent medicine men called too. By getting goods from all these, then settling with one until the others grew restive, she stretched her credit to the uttermost, a necessity in a shop with so many doubtful 'trust' customers. One of her subterfuges infuriated me. Immediately our grocery traveller had left the shop with his order she would despatch me to the warehouse two miles across the town, whence I would return with 24 lbs of packet tea, or with half a roll of bacon lolling over a weary shoulder, and all my play-time gone. Since goods ordered from a traveller one day were delivered by cart the next, I was convinced that she devised these trips merely to keep me occupied. She did not stoop to explain her economic stratagems to small boys. Only much later did I discover that any items ordered after the traveller's visit did not appear on the current week's invoice. The trick brought still another few days' vital credit. And how we needed them!

But in the blazing summer of 1911, she recalled, bankruptcy finally stared us in the face. Half our customers, either strike-bound or out of work, had failed to clear their tick books. My mother in turn, already owing on earlier accounts, was unable to meet a current bill with our major supplier. Nastily Mr May, the traveller, gave her an ultimatum from the boss himself— pay the outstanding debt amounting to £5 2s 0d in full or no further groceries would be sent, which meant shutting the shop door for good—and this only a few days after the old man had once again lost his job. My mother offered Mr May all she possessed—thirty shillings. Haughtily he refused, snapped his order book closed, turned on his heel with a curt 'good day' and fell in a fit on the shop floor, where he rolled and foamed for some little time, then lay still, with a small stick of firewood in his mouth inserted 'to stop him biting himself'. He recovered, she said, with remarkable speed, and without a word, handing off all help, staggered away in a daze, only to return that evening, pale, toothless and shaken. 'My dentures!—where are they?' Abjectly he begged my mother not to mention his seizure; knowledge of it at the 'office', he said, and him carrying all that money, would mean instant dismissal. Mr Belson, the boss (as my mother knew), was a hard man. She, in turn, went on at length about scorning to get anyone sacked: nobody better than her, she told him, knew how bad times were for *everyone*. Meanwhile my sister searched the shop floor for his teeth—without success. But Mr May's mind was now on business: happily, since the afternoon he had seen a way of mother's paying her debt by instalments—while he himself would 'cover' for her. By now my sister had discovered the false teeth where Mr May had cast them—behind a box of herb beers. Our greatest economic crisis was over!

Among the more thrifty of our credit customers were those who did a little cash shopping at the Co-operative stores (an organisation detested and railed at by shopkeepers and publicans alike). With Co-operative dividend at 3s in the £, quarter day brought them a small bonanza which they often used to clear off arrears on their tick book at the shop. This practice enraged my father, who, in his cups, swore he was being 'used'.

Throughout the years money always seemed to be 'tight', especially with the elderly among us, who suffered most, and with good reason: from 1896 to 1912 the purchasing power of the pound fell steadily from 20s to 16s 3d. Economists estimated that between 1902 and 1909 the cost of living rose by 4 per cent, and between 1909 and 1913 by nearly 9 per cent. Ever since the German Reichstag in 1889 had passed the model 'law of insurance against old age and infirmity' there had been much talk, but no action, in England about making similar provisions for the aged. At last, in 1908, the Liberal government allocated £1,200,000 for the establishment of a non-contributory old age pension scheme and an Act was passed to become law on 1 January 1909. Pensions, however, would be withheld from those 'who had failed to work habitually according to their ability and need, and those who had failed to save money regularly'. Here was a means test with a vengeance. Paupers were not entitled to any pension.

There was to be no doling out of largesse under the scheme. Pensions were graduated from 1s to 5s a week, provided the recipients had already an income of less than £31 a year. The combined weekly allowance for a married couple was fixed at 7s 6d. Nevertheless, even these small doles meant life itself for many among the elderly poor. Old folk, my mother said, spending their allowance at the shop, 'would bless the name of Lloyd George as if he were a saint from heaven'.[4] The government met with much opposition to the introduction of a pension scheme at all from both the middle and working classes. Free gifts of money, many urged, would dishearten the thrifty who saved for their old age, and encourage the idle. Lord Rosebery, the great Liberal peer, had even graver misgivings: the provision of old age pensions, he thought, 'might deal a blow at the Empire which could be almost mortal'. Meanwhile our elderly paupers still went to the workhouse—a word that rang like a knell among us—or died, to be borne away in a black, glassless hearse to a common grave. There lay the final indignity. For old folk well known in the district, now dead and under-insured, people would have the usual whip-round to prevent the deceased being 'put away on the parish'. My mother would often give a sheet to make a shroud. Two women went from house to house to collect enough for a wreath. For the very poor who lost a child at its birth or soon after, Mother found a box so they could take their young to the burial without expense.

A recurrent event in the district was the death of some baby suffocated by its mother in bed. In 1901 national figures showed that no fewer than 1,550 infants had died in this way. A baby overlain could give rise to much searching gossip. Did it happen in the small hours of Sunday morning after the mother had been out drinking? Was the child illegitimate? Had it been insured,

---

[4] After the passing of the National Health Insurance Act of 1911 people receiving sickness benefit used to say they were on the 'Lloyd George', a compliment to the tremendous part he had played in introducing that measure.

and for how much? Had it been ailing, or was another baby on the way? And, in a few cases, the final whispered question—was this the stifling of a living sin within the family itself? Most folk, though, talked kindly of it all—poor little soul! A tragic accident. Too many, most likely, sleeping in mother's bed. But now and then the coroner's exonerating verdict was greeted by some among the matriarchs with a sniff of doubt.

In bereavement, fortunately, all but the poorest could fall back on that bulwark of the times, the funeral friendly society. Our own, founded 1 April 1815 in a public house with the licensee as treasurer, reached a membership a century later of more than sixty thousand. Artisan families, however, had a second stake in one of the great friendly societies; in our district, the Oddfellows. These latter organisations, requiring weekly premiums well beyond the pockets of the indigent, insured workers mainly against sickness and accident. But our local club's purpose stood plain and unequivocal—to provide members, on payment of one penny a person a week, with enough money to bury their dead.

Death benefits were not fixed, but varied in proportion to the annual mortality rate of the membership. The two competing clubs in our neighbourhood offered little in the way of inducement to join. The older, perhaps as a remembrancer of its birth in a pub, added a bottle of whisky to the usual £15 death benefit, whilst its rival settled for about £14 but always included 'a good, oak coffin: priced 25 shillings'. Members of long standing who lapsed through poverty were usually kept on the books. A club official paid out death benefit to the deceased's nearest and dearest. This, at times, set problems of 'kinship' whose solution would have lain far beyond the skills of the mere social anthropologist. No policies were issued: a committee conducted all business 'on trust'. A brother might have his name on the weekly premium card whilst a sister had done all the paying. Our friendly society office saw many a bitter family struggle over spoils, he, or (often she being 'next of kin' who succeeded in grabbing the cash as it was pushed across the counter. Occasionally the official had to pay out entirely on 'good faith' but, well versed in the ways of the community, when facts were clear he seldom made an error. One elderly woman, for instance, came into his office and claimed death benefit on a widow (no relation) who had lived next door to her.

'I settle only with next of kin,' he said.

'You settle with me!' she told him. 'Lizzie had no one left, and I've no one left and all the street can prove it. We promised each other that her as went first would be put away nicely by the other. I put her away nicely last Tuesday. Here's the bills! Now pay up!'

Breaking all the insurance laws in sight, he paid up.

The club collector called at week end: to knock anywhere after Monday was a waste of time. Somewhat better educated than his members, he was usually welcomed in homes as a friend and acted often as a walking citizen's advice bureau. One in our village, however, combined his activity with money lending, at a penny in the shilling per week interest, which made him unpopular among the more respectable. This man had one driving ambition, often voiced: to amass a thousand pounds in the bank 'before decease'. This he achieved with a few pounds to spare after a lifetime of grind and self-sacrifice that would have warmed the heart of Samuel Smiles. Then he dropped dead. Merrily his half-brother went through the lot in fifteen months, a 'death benefit' that both delighted and scandalised the village for half a generation after.

According to its annual report, the year 1903 was a prosperous one for our burial club: only 720 claims for benefit had been made, and of these 330 were on behalf of minors under five years of age, where the highest payment could not exceed £5 3s 0d per child. Thirty-two infants under one year (benefits were low here) had died of 'convulsions', and eighty-four of the 390 adults from tuberculosis. Mrs Cleary, however, club member in the house next door to us, had a poor year. On 5 January her Jessica, aged three, succumbed to diphtheria; death benefit (reduced through arrears)—£1 0s 0d. On 19 May Charles, her husband, died of pneumonia; benefit—£4 3s 0d. Then at the end of August she lost James, aged five months, with enteritis. The club[5]

[5] Our burial club was run by a committee of five trustees chosen by ballot and almost invariably elected year after year. In its latter days, however, the power appears to have stayed in the hands of a professional treasurer manager. When finally in the '30's, after some chicanery among agents, the society had to be compulsorily amalgamated with a large insurance organisation, an investigator, seeking out trustees, found a couple of the five, 'senile to the point of indifference to any commercial affair', and the other three elders 'illiterate'. The society's assets stood at more than £165,000.

paid her £3 10s 0d to bury him with. Death often swept through a house in this fashion; it behoved a woman to keep straight with the burial books—if she could! To have a body put away on the parish was to bear a lifetime's stigma.

So our neighbours, and many like them, in this 'thrice happy first decade' fought on grimly, certainly not to rise, but to stave off that dreaded descent into the social and economic depths. Under the common bustle crouched fear. In children—fear of parents, teachers, the Church, the police, and authority of any sort; in adults—fear of petty chargehands, foremen, managers and employers of labour. Men harboured a dread of sickness, debt, loss of status; above all, of losing a job, which could bring all other evils fast in train.[6] Most people in the undermass worked not, as is fondly asserted now, because they possessed an antique integrity which compelled 'a fair day's work for a fair day's pay' (whatever that means); they toiled on through mortal fear of getting the sack. Fear was the *leitmotif* of their lives, dulled only now and then by the Dutch courage gained from drunkenness.

A craftsman thrown out of work sought another job at his 'trades club' or in a certain public house. If these failed him he began the weary round from firm to firm or from town to town, a journeyman in reality, asking for work. Building labourers I have seen as a child follow a wagon laden with bricks from the kilns, hoping to find a job where the load was tipped. For the same reason, too, they would send a wife or child trailing behind a lime cart. On some building sites a foreman might find fifty labourers pleading for a mere half-dozen jobs. It was not unknown for him to place six spades against a wall at one hundred yards' distance. A wild, humiliating race followed; work went to those who succeeded in grabbing a spade.

In many firms and industries the battle for social justice still remained unjoined. There it was perilous for employees even to mention trade unionism. At the local dyeworks, in a meeting between masters and workers, one man had the temerity to say that since the employers had 'combinations' he saw no reason why workers should not have them too. The manager sacked him on the instant, in spite of his thirty years' service, together with another who had called 'Hear! Hear!', and refused to pay

---

[6] They had reason for fear: as late as the 1890's a quarter of all people over sixty-five years of age were paupers and half died in the workhouse.

5 *Women of the time* 1

6 *Women of the time* II

them anything in lieu of a week's notice. One man fought his case in the courts, where magistrates after some heart-searching decided that he was entitled to his full wage of 28s for a 59-hour week. Yet 'combinations', in fact, in pre-war Britain were by no means the powerful, sinister force that employers and the general public seemed to believe.

By 1911 the trade unions in Britain possessed 3·1 million members, yet for all their numbers the movement as a whole lacked both status and influence. The great majority of workers remained unorganised. Until the Liberal government in 1911 sought the aid of trade unions (much flattered by the invitation) to help administer the National Insurance Act, governments looked upon unions as a nuisance to be tolerated, and the leaders of craft societies, often achingly respectable men, as no more than small, misguided persons of liberal leanings. Even in 1903 a Conservative government could set up a Royal Commission on Trade Disputes and Combinations and not appoint one single trade unionist to serve on it. Union weakness lay in its parochialism and disunity. Of the 669 organisations in existence fewer than a score had a membership of over 20,000: many small industrial unions formed and faded like will o' the wisps. Only the Amalgamated Society of Engineers and one or two other smaller craft societies were really organised on a national basis and had the power to implement country-wide agreements; the others, at best no more than regional, but usually district, bodies, fought, often in bitter rivalry against one another, to wring what concessions they could from local employers. Owners and managers of many industries would on no account deal with a trade union representative. His mere appearance on the premises could be a signal for a call to the police. Railway and shipping companies were especially obdurate. In some firms well into the 1900's proved membership of a 'society' could lead to a tradesman's dismissal and victimisation, a form of malevolence to which my father was more than once subject. And for the industrial unions, their membership drawn mostly from the undermass, and their leaders, worthless 'agitators' spouting of 'direct action' and 'general strikes', the English bourgeoisie felt nothing but contempt. But the time came when they had to listen.

Despite the increasing population, trade union membership during the first six years of the century had remained static at about two millions. Certainly from 1901 the unions had been demoralised and their activities shackled by the Taff Vale judgment, which had made it legal for a union to be sued for the losses caused by a strike of its members. Nevertheless, general apathy stemmed not from despair at the unions in chains nor the failure of such political action as there was; it sprang from mass ignorance: the millions did not know and did not want to know. At that time one had to work hard indeed to convince the unskilled labourer of the need for trade unions at all. An individualist, he was simply not interested in easing the common lot, but concerned entirely with improving his own, and that not too vigorously. From what little he understood, the aims of trade unionism seemed quite impracticable and those of socialism utterly unreal. In the end not persuasion, but dire want, changed his views.

In 1905 the Conservative government's reaction to serious unemployment was to pass the 'Unemployed Workmen Act'. This empowered but did not oblige local authorities to establish 'distress committees' to find work for their unemployed or to provide them with relief. Many councils did nothing and the Act proved blatantly inadequate. 'Right to work' committees sprang up in many parts of the country. Then in 1908 and 1909 came those years of real slump which at last drove many in the undermass to recognise their parlous condition. Yet there was little to be accomplished then by industrial action: in the depths of depression strikes could be broken by the employers' calling in workless men desperate for any kind of job. From the start of the century until 1909 the average number of days lost annually through strikes and lock-outs was only 3½ million, although the Taff Vale judgment had been reversed in 1906. With the revival of trade, however, in 1910 a great wave of industrial unrest broke over the land. The three years which followed saw a sudden inflow of more than 1½ million recruits into the trade unions, most going into the industrial combinations of semi-skilled and unskilled workers. In 1910 the number of days lost through strikes and lock-outs rose to 12½ million. Indeed, in the two years which followed there was not a single coalfield, port or railway company in the country that did not experience labour trouble: in 1912 days lost in strikes and lock-outs soared to more than 38 million!

Some historians have discerned in all this turmoil a proletariat ripe at last for revolution. In thinking so, I believe they have seriously misunderstood the mind and temper of the working men of the time. Whatever their quarrel with *local* employers, the ultra-patriotic mass[7] remained intensely loyal to the nation and the system as a whole. One week a striking docker might hurl stones at the police and the next, assured of his daily bread, applaud the marching Territorials or cheer a passing prince to the skies. Oratory during strike time about 'direct action', 'general strikes' and the 'one big union' might sound fine, but in the day-to-day struggle to live it meant nothing at all.

Nevertheless, the syndicalist ideas of men like Tom Mann, aimed at uniting workers, industry by industry, into great unions, had some success and lasting results with the semi-skilled and unskilled, especially among railway and transport workers.

By 1909, 1,168 unions existed, many of them ill-run. The syndicalists believed that no more than fourteen were necessary. Some went on dreaming of that 'one great combination' which would, in due time, take over the capitalist State itself. But members of the craft societies in general met such ideas with ridicule or hostility. Industrial unionism, they realised, would strike at the very heart of the working-class caste system. Artisans who had served seven years to acquire place and skills, citizens who considered themselves culturally and socially superior beings, would have none of it. They had no intention at all of being incorporated into one big union with floor sweepers, tea brewers and common fetchers and carriers, and perhaps even having to strike on their behalf. The older the craftsman the more furious his indignation. 'Some of 'em', said my father, more prophetic than he knew, 'will be askin' us to learn 'em the trade next!' Here then was the common suspicion, that industrial unionism would weaken the craftsman's bargaining power and finally undermine his social position. Many employers sympathised: better the trade union devil they knew than syndicalism!

Yet over the country as a whole, except for tiresome strikes and labour disputes, all in the glorious June of 1911 seemed well.

[7] In this they stood at one with some of their leaders: in war-time Blatchford, Tillett, Clynes, Thomas, Thorne, Havelock Wilson—all showed themselves as jingoistic as any rabid Tory.

Government and people were busy making preparations for the crowning of King George V. At home, though, we put out no flags. My mother did not say why. That summer her husband, with two other mechanics, had gone to Greenock to work on 'submarines', jobs found by the labour 'bureau'. The manager of our recently opened exchange boasted about it in the local press—'A fine example of how the new system operates,' he said, 'finding skilled men work in a town two hundred miles away. And this isn't charity, mind!' But Father was forgetting to send his wages home as often as he drew them. Several customers at the shop with husbands on strike or unemployed couldn't pay for what they had had to eat. Times for us were bad indeed. 'I don't know', my mother said, 'which way to turn. They'll have us in the workhouse!'

A traveller called with twopenny packets of paper bunting and union jacks on little sticks. 'There's fifty per cent on this stuff,' he said. 'You'll make a mint!'

'We didn't stock it for King Edward,' she told him, 'and I won't for this one.'

'We should buy what'll sell,' advised my sister. 'That's what I think.'

'When I want your opinion,' my mother said, 'I'll ask for it.'

But on the great day Zinc Street looked gay enough without any help from us. As for our 'royal borough', 'Utterly transformed!' the local weekly announced. 'A glorious blaze of colour! Everywhere there are outward and visible signs of people's rejoicing and demonstrations of loyalty to the throne. From countless thousands of little shops and dwellings, flags and banners and devices of wondrous kinds express the people's gladness.' 'The whole nation from the highest to the meanest in the land are as one in showing devotion to our new sovereign.' Some of the meanest, however, had other things on their mind besides monarchy.

Throughout June strikes had been spreading that finally involved 65,000 seamen, firemen and dockers. Thirty-six other trade disputes began. Indeed, coronation month, with nearly a million and a quarter working days lost through strikes, turned out to be the worst in Britain's industrial history. Men, it seemed, were demanding bread besides circuses.

Then, with us, in the heat of the finest summer for a century, came the explosion. The local seamen struck first, to be followed almost at once by the dockers, carters and miners, who came out both in sympathy and with bitter grievances of their own. By mid-week the city ground almost to a standstill. 'Forty thousand people idle!' cried the press. 'Many workshops and factories close down altogether. No coal! No supplies! Eighty-four ships unmanned in the docks! Food is being cut off!'

Strike breakers, shielded by the police, attempted to move coal and food. Pickets determined to stop them. In a dozen places fierce fighting broke out that lasted all day. Five hundred police from other towns poured in at once. 'Never before', sobbed the local newspapers, 'has this community witnessed such scenes!'

Beyond the end of our narrow lane we saw huge crowds go milling past in the stifling heat, then, a few minutes later, the rout! Men rushed yelling and cursing into the alley-ways. A score ran towards us, their clogs clattering over the setts, pursued by mounted police. A child, standing terrified by the door, I saw an officer lean forward on his horse and hit a neighbour with his truncheon above the eyes, heard the blow like the thump of wood on a swede turnip. The man ran crouching, hands to his face, into a wall and collapsed. Then my mother grabbed me, screamed after the charging police, fled into the shop and slammed the door. For half a lifetime afterwards the same man stayed amongst us, but did little work after. Something about him seemed absent. 'They knocked him silly,' old people said, 'in the dockers' strike.'

In one day more than a hundred strikers were treated at hospitals for injuries. 'Police charges', explained the newspapers, 'were necessarily vigorous, but officers generally showed a fine restraint under trying circumstances.' That same night the mayor, in a panic, appealed to the government for help. On the Home Secretary's—Winston Churchill's—instructions, the War Office promptly despatched 'C' squadron of the Scots Greys, four hundred men of the 2nd Battalion, South Staffordshire Regiment, two squadrons of the 16th Lancers and three hundred officers of the Metropolitan Police (fifty mounted)—a veritable army, all under the direction of General Macready. 'The troops,' reported the national press, 'fresh from duty in India and Egypt, are standing up well to our tropical heat.' On Friday afternoon of that week they met the enemy face to face. A local newspaper, not noted for its tenderness to the lower orders, described the scene:

A remarkable procession was witnessed yesterday when a demonstration was held by the wives of the dockers. About two thousand women, many of them carrying babies in their arms, took part. The procession in its every aspect bore the impress of poverty, but the women in their tattered shawls and gowns strove cheerily to keep its pathetic side in the background and chatted together in lively fashion and joked with the spectators. Nineteen out of twenty had no head covering and many bore the marks of their long struggle to keep homes going on small wages.

The procession, headed by a brass band that played 'Hearts of Oak' and 'Tom Bowling', carried banners bearing inscriptions—'No Alms, But A Living Wage', 'Our Poverty Is Your Danger! Stand By Us!' 'Live And Let Live!' 'Give Us Each Day Our Daily Bread', 'Our Right To Live!'

The object of the demonstration, said one of the leaders, was to show the rich people that dockers had wives and children they were proud of and who required looking after. Some of the women found the heat and the long march too much for them, but as they fell out their places were taken by others.

At the end of the march appeals were made to the women to stand by the men in their efforts to get an increase in wages proportionate to the rise in the price of food. These words were received with cheers and cries of, 'We will! We will!' Another speaker said that women and strikers knew how to control themselves without the need for military and insolent authority.

Milk was then served to over a hundred children and babies. It was evident that many of the women were exhausted. Afterwards many made their way back as best they could to the dockers' headquarters, where a hundred gallons of soup had been made with meat given by sympathetic butchers.

Some few strikers, reported the newspapers later, gave the soldiers a nod and a smile, 'but their womenfolk would have none of them'.

As the strike continued, suffering grew acute. The miners, protesting without official backing, received no strike pay. Most of the dockers and carters, members of no union, had little hope of any financial support. 'Actual want and privation is now evident,' said one newspaper. 'Many a home is darkened by despair, but the situation is quietly borne and there is now no threatening manifestation of any kind.' Backed by the overwhelming show of force, the dock gates stood wide open for any strike breaker wishing to enter. Not one man now of the four thousand returned.

A pitiless sun went down each day. Seamen, dockers, carters, miners stood in sullen little knots at a hundred slum street corners and talked and waited. A local priest spoke to the press of conditions:

> These men are not hooligans. I live among them and know their poverty. Seamen here have rarely been bringing home more than two to three pounds for a whole month's trip. Work three or four days a week is all most dockers get here. [They drew 4s 6d for a ten-hour day.] With these men and their families there is want within twenty-four hours of stopping work. Home conditions are terrible. I often have to visit dying people in a room where a family of seven or eight lives. I have seen many instances of approaching starvation. One day I watched a man take off his coat and vest outside a pawnshop and, after a visit inside, give the money to a waiting child. Another man with his wife near confinement raised cash on the last thing the pawnshop would take—his boots. Recently I had a girl of sixteen, housekeeper to her father and five other children, appeal to me for help. All the children went hungry to school. She didn't mind hunger herself but she couldn't stand their crying. Strikers are not hooligans, but decent men. Poor people are helping. Only today one woman sent me 6½d in stamps and a weaver left me two shillings. A collection among the local shopkeepers has brought in five hundred loaves and other necessaries.

At home in our own shop my mother was racked with indecision—she stood heart and soul with the strikers—but how much more food could she let go to those who, we knew, had no money to pay for it at week end? One wholesaler had finally stopped supplies; another threatened. 'A few more days of this,' she said, 'and we'll have to close!'

Then miraculously it was all over and the dockers had won! 'Askwith!'—the name ran down the streets—'a man from London, sent by the government! He settled it! He told the bosses!' People gabbled it out again and again, overjoyed at the news. The dockers had gained three major demands—'a wage increase from 4s 6d to 5s 0d for a nine-hour day; full recognition of the union; men engaged on any day but not required, to receive 1s 6d "disappointment money".'

Carters' wages were fixed at 25*s* 0*d* a week for drivers of one horse and 27*s* 0*d* for drivers of two, plus 6*d* an hour for all work done before 7 a.m. The day's work had to stop at 6.30 p.m. (Carters had suffered a notoriously long week, putting in as many as seventy hours.) Very soon, however, many employers repudiated the agreement.

Seamen received a rise of 10*s*, increasing the union rate to £4 15*s* 0*d* a month; but some railway workers who had struck against their own vile conditions got nothing except a promise that the employers would not prosecute them for leaving their service without permission.

The dockers' success gave heart to unorganised groups of workers who before had never dared to strike. Notorious for a generation with us had been conditions at the local flax mill. Some employees there were among the very poorest of our customers at the shop. Even in those times one had to be hard put to it indeed to take a job in flax and labour for 'starvation wages'. After a week of 55½ hours' heavy work a woman drew 9*s*, with a bonus of 1*s* 6*d* provided she had lost no time. Girl helpers of eighteen years of age got 5*s* 0*d*. Men received 15*s* 6*d* for a 55½-hour week, or 17*s* 3*d* for one of 64½ hours. Spurred on by 'agitators' from outside, members of a cotton union, the whole mill struck work: six hundred women demanding an increase of 2*s* a week and the men a minimum wage of £1. Helped by sympathisers all over the town, they held out against employers adamant in their refusal to concede any increase whatsoever. 'We consider', they said, 'the women's demands unreasonable.' But failing to get workers from elsewhere, and after a deal of hard bargaining, they caved in and finally agreed to pay 'females an extra shilling and men one pound for a 55-hour week'.

Next, labourers at the local cabinet factory walked out. Having worked 59½ hours for 12*s* they now boldly asked for 20*s* and a reduction in the working week. Outraged, the employer sued some of the strikers for breach of contract and lost his case. Blacklegs came in from as far away as Newcastle and Grimsby. Union organisers gained the newcomers' sympathy, got them out of the shop and promptly paid their fares back home. In the end, and with the greatest reluctance, the firm conceded its workers' demands—a signal victory.

Soon the local railwaymen struck again, and in greater force[8] this time, demanding that all wages be increased to £1 for a 54-hour week. But once again they had to go back with little to see for their militancy, beyond a 'commission' to study 'grievances'. On resumption of work the directors of the Lancashire & Yorkshire Railway Company sent a circular full of unctuous praise to all those who had 'stuck loyally to their work in the most trying circumstances'. 'We have pleasure to inform you', they concluded, 'that it has been decided to grant double pay for all the time those men worked through the varying period of the strike.' Later the men did gain some advantages and the companies, through government pressure, eventually recognised their unions.

Unrest continued through the winter and many realised that the turbulence no longer stemmed from traditional trade union disputes. 'These upheavals', cried one of our street corner speakers, uttering a common thought, 'are spontaneous uprisings on the part of large sections of the working class against poverty and want. They are, to a great extent, vast, unorganised outbursts against a system in which the poor get poorer and the employers wealthier.' And the economics of the time bore him out. 'Between 1899 and 1913', wrote Cole and Postgate,[9] 'real wages actually declined by about ten per cent . . .' Over the same period 'Gross assessments to income tax under schedule D (profits and interest) rose by 55 per cent'. The profit makers in coal and cotton, the rentiers and investors in foreign markets did particularly well.

Several times during our troubles 'syndicalists' (a strange word to the simple) had appeared among us and spoken impassioned words about the might of the worker and what could yet be done to organise a brand new society based on union power. In the town hall, a thousand or more had massed to hear Tom Mann himself on the subject: but our chief constable, who had but recently received some silver plate, suitably inscribed, for his part

[8] The chief constable, remembering services rendered by outside police on the previous occasion, rushed out telegrams to twenty other authorities in the region asking for help. Every single one refused: they had, they said, similar troubles of their own, or were expecting them. The chief constable then swore in fifty-two 'specials'. No conflict of any kind occurred. Members of the auxiliary force were paid 5*s* a day and on disbandment were allowed to keep their truncheons and armlets as souvenirs.

[9] *The Common People, 1746–1938.*

in restoring civic order, had him arrested for disaffection. The trial, something of a *cause célèbre*, ended in Mann's being sentenced to six months in the second division. This was soon reduced. In fact he served only six weeks, and told the press on release that he had been 'treated well'. Authority saw little menace in syndicalism; but it was wily enough not to make martyrs. Still, in the North and Midlands it took the precaution of underwriting police loyalty by introducing a better scale of pay and conditions. In the new regime of 1912 constables received 27s 0d–36s 0d a week, sergeants 38s 0d–43s 0d, with pensions amounting to two-thirds of pay.

Altogether, among the lower working class the actions of the police during these troublous times had left them no better loved than they had been before. In 1908 the Chief Constable of Manchester, in his annual report, thought that modern police duty bore 'little resemblance to that of thirty or forty years earlier. Then the policeman dealt largely with the criminal: now he is rendering a public service to all classes.' That he was rendering some sort of service to the poorest of the day there can be not much doubt: during 1908 more than 180,000 of them went to gaol, mostly for miserable little offences; the highest number in the decade.

At that time, says T. A. Critchley,[10] noting a 'spirit of change' in the police generally, 'the policeman as a social worker was a new phenomenon, introducing a concept of policing in which the policeman's wife also had a part'.

Again in 1908, a leading article in *The Times* pointed out that:

The policeman in London is not merely a guardian of the peace, he is an integral part of its social life. In many a back street and slum he not merely stands for law and order, he is the true handyman of our streets, the best friend of a mass of people who have no other counsellor or protector.

In spite, however, of the happy seeming state of affairs down Hoxton or Whitechapel way, nobody in our Northern slum, to my recollection, ever spoke in fond regard, then or afterwards, of the policeman as 'social worker' and 'handyman of the streets'. Like their children, delinquent or not, the poor in general looked

[10] *A History of the Police in England and Wales.*

upon him with fear and dislike. When one arrived on a 'social' visit they watched his passing with suspicion and his disappearance with relief. Here was no counsellor or friend. Except for common narks, one spoke to a 'rozzer' when one had to and told him the minimum. In view of the low cultural and educational levels of the policeman of the time and his recruitment from the ultra-conformist section of the working class, it is hard to see how he and his wife could have even begun to act as effective social workers. The 'public' (meaning the middle and upper classes), we know well enough, held their 'bobby' in patronising 'affection and esteem', which he repaid with due respectfulness; but these sentiments were never shared by the undermass, nor in fact by the working class generally.

After the days of uproar we fell again into the common round. One thousand disaffected might cheer the syndicalists and many more strike work, but city and borough together held close on a million people, for the most part solid in allegiance to society as it was, and these had no time at all for 'foreign' ideas or discontented labourers. The bulk of the unskilled workers, conformist, chauvinistic, went on accepting their lot unchanged. And beneath them the underdog, according to his lights, worked when he could, begged or pilfered, fighting his own battle for existence and sensing only too well how narrow now lay the border between want and destitution. Soon in music hall and street they would be singing a new ditty—'There's a good time coming'— and, strangely enough, for many of those in direct need the words ran true: old poverty would have an end. But that time was not yet.

Chapter 6

Food, Drink and Physic

Pinched and poor are we, while they, the knaves, are rich and fat!
Song

Man seems to have adulterated food ever since he began to sell it. In industrial England of the nineteenth century its sophistication became both widespread and highly profitable. By 1900 government action had stamped out most of the blatantly dishonest practices, but even in that year public health analysis proved that 13 per cent of coffee and 9·9 per cent of milk were adulterated, and this in spite of vigilance and innumerable prosecutions. In one working-class district alone one in every five samples of beer examined was found to have been watered. A favourite trick of some publicans, well enough known to our imbibers, was to dilute their ale, then add salt[1] to 'flavour it up' and stimulate thirst. My father, who loved liquor as he loved life, considered this to be a crime that called for the ultimate penalty.

The minds of the very poor of the time were constantly preoccupied with food—where was it to come from tomorrow, or even today? How best could a pittance be spent? Board of Trade figures for 1904 give the bald facts.

The majority in our area came within the first group listed, with a weekly income of less than 25*s*, but a good twenty per cent of the whole lived at a much lower standard; their income each week reached 18*s* or less. As the century grew older we know that the poor grew poorer; real wages fell and rumblings of discontent increased. By 1912 the workhouses of England held 280,000 paupers: an all-time record. Some of our neighbours went there, honourable men and women, after a lifetime's work; old Mr Molson, a one-time waiter; Mrs Gray, char for the 'Live and Let Live', and her husband, degraded beyond measure. At least in the 'Union' they would get food, such as it was.

---

[1] They sell the salt now with potato crisps.

Average weekly cost and quantity of certain articles of food consumed by urban workmen's families

Limits of weekly income	*Under 25s*		*25s and under 30s*	
Number of returns	261		289	
Average weekly family income	21*s*	4½*d*	26*s*	11¾*d*
Average number of children living at home	3·1		3·1	
	s	*d*	*s*	*d*
Bread and flour	1	0½	3	3¾
Meat (bought by weight)	1	8	3	4¾
Other meat (including fish)		7½		8¾
Bacon		8¾		9
Eggs		5¾		8½
Fresh milk		8		11¾
Cheese		4¾		5½
Butter	1	2	1	7
Potatoes		8¾		9¾
Vegetables and fruit		4¾		7
Currants and raisins		1½		1¾
Rice, tapioca, oatmeal		4½		5
Tea		9¼		11¼
Coffee and cocoa		2		3¼
Sugar		8		10
Jam, marmalade, treacle, syrup		4¼		5¼
Pickles and condiments		2		2¼
Other items	1	0½	1	3¾
	14*s*	4¾*d*[2]	17*s*	10¼*d*

[2] Farthings in the shop were common currency. They bought, among other things, one of those slim candles which served at night to make darkness visible in the bedrooms and sculleries about us (often only the living-room of a house would have gaslight), and down the ways when day had gone what a dim, flickering world it was! For some reason my mother always segregated the farthings from other cash; they ranged in a series of martello towers rising and diminishing along a shelf by the shop window. All the rest of her takings (up to 30*s* on good days) she dropped into a double-pouched calico 'till' taped about her waist, tipping it on the table each night for counting. Out of the larger pocket slid a mass of pence and halfpence and from the other, a mere slit, a patter of silver; poverty did

The Board of Trade list of provisions gives little idea in human terms of how people eked out their earnings. Many varieties of 'fancy' food common in middle-class grocery stores were quite unknown in the slum. What 'luxuries' people bought at a corner shop often figured only in the father's diet, and his alone. 'Relishes' consisted of brawn, corned beef, boiled mutton, cheese, bacon (as little as two ounces of all these), eggs, saveloys, tripe, pigs' trotters, sausage, cow heels, herrings, bloaters and kippers or 'digbies' and finnan haddock. Most could be bought from the corner shop. These were the protein foods vital to sustain a man arriving home at night, worked often to near-exhaustion. When funds were low a pennyworth of 'parings', bits from a tripe shop (sold by the handful in newspaper), staved off hunger in many a family. Another meal in such times, long known and appreciated, was 'brewis'. It consisted merely of a 'shive' of bread and salted dripping broken up and covered with boiling water.

Boiled ham on the bone we highly esteemed and ate it so often after funerals (provided the 'late lamented' had been 'well backed' with the insurance) that to be 'buried with 'am' became a comic's cliché. Many children yearned for the taste of it. One urchin of our day was sent to the shop to get two ounces of the delectable stuff for his father's Saturday tea. Returning, the Devil tempted. He tore off the tiniest morsel. 'It tasted', he said ruefully fifty years after, 'like the food of the gods! I took a little more and, terrified, found I was hooked! Two ounces went down to a piece about the size of a postage stamp. I swallowed that too and fled!'

The very poor never fell into debt; nobody allowed them any credit.[3] Paying on the nail, they bought in minimal quantities,

---

business through the copper coin. Those customers finding a half sovereign in their wages on Saturday would often come in at once to get it 'changed down' for fear of losing it. Any money at all passed over by one of our 'regulars', a big, slow-moving woman, my mother washed immediately. Once I watched her and opened my mouth. 'Ask no questions!' she ordered, 'and mention it to no one!' Only years later did I learn that this customer, a bookmaker's mistress, had been suffering in the later stages of syphilis.

[3] In the early days of his career as 'mixed' grocer Father took down a card hanging on the wall by the boot and stay laces. 'Please Do Not Ask For Credit', it begged, 'As Refusal Might Offend.' He turned the notice over and, using a stick of Berry's Blacking, daubed on it for the benefit of simpler natives a translation in basic English—'NO TICK'!

sending their children usually for half a loaf, a ha'p'orth of tea, sugar, milk or a scrap of mustard pickled cauliflower[4] in the bottom of a jar. Generally, two ounces of meat or cheese was the smallest quantity one could buy; to sell less, shopkeepers said, was to lose what tiny profit they got through 'waste in cutting'. Yet poor folk would try again and again, begging for smaller amounts—'Just a penn'orth o' cheese—to fry with this two ounces o' bacon.' My father would not deign to attend to any of these 'shipping orders', as he called them; an elder sister took indigent pence. 'It's all cash,' she said briskly. Nor would Lipton, or 'Sir Thomas', as my mother named him, have truck with any who tried to buy a single boot-lace or asked him to divorce a pair of kippers.[5] Such things, he seemed to believe, came to man in natural pairs, binary as bosoms.

Customers always preferred my mother to cut their meat because she could slice it so finely that 'two ounces looked like half a pound', and it 'spread plenty on the plate'. When Mother sold a quarter of anything it weighed exactly one fourth of a pound: the old man's 'quarter' varied from three and a half to five ounces, according to the customer's face, reputation and antecedents. Whenever I or any member of the family saw a heavy, cold-eyed man in the neighbourhood we sped home on the instant—'Weights 'n' Measures!' The one nearest rushed to the scales and slid off a piece of fat bacon attached under the pan. But once the ogre arrived without warning! Both parents knew their peril. While the old man engaged him in converse, Mother, in the kitchen, grabbed me by the arm. 'Get in there!' she ordered. 'Crawl on your stomach and knock it off!' That ten-

[4] Some families who dealt with us had male members (all unskilled workers) who had soldiered in the outposts of empire during the late nineteenth century and after. Their experience seemed to have gained them little beyond a contempt for lesser breeds, a love of family discipline and a passion for hot pickles.

[5] Later Father banned kippers, swearing that their 'pong', as he called it, amalgamated with the odour from tarry firelighters under the counter to give a certain *je ne sais quoi* to the milk. At times, too, Mother thought she detected in it the distinct flavour of 'Lively Polly', a pervasive washing powder we stocked. 'This isn't milk,' I heard her say once, dabbing her lips in distaste, 'it's more of a disinfectant!' Still, the liquid, highly esteemed in the neighbourhood for its 'creamy taste', went on selling in large quantities. And each day the family did their best, scrubbing and scalding every milk bowl and measure in the endless war against investing dirt.

foot journey was among the longest of my life. At last I lay under the scale pan, reached clumsily, hooked with my finger at the meat and missed. The scales trembled. I stretched again, hooked, and it fell, to bounce once before the cat, whipping round, snatched it and fled. Yet this 'equaliser', though strictly against the law, of course, did no more than balance our decrepit scales; Mother was painfully honest.

'That little lot's not right, yer know!' the inspector would say, feeling again the scales and testing with weight and finger. 'Not by a long chalk! You're yer own worst enemy!'

'We don't mind givin' a bit of "over",' Father would smirk hypocritically.

'That's not it,' the inspector told him. 'Give what's the weight, see! No more an' no less. Then you won't be in no trouble. Now let's have them scales down at our place today!'

Here I would groan silently. This meant that the heavy iron balance, weights and pans would be pushed into a sack and I would have to hump them a mile or more, for adjustment in a dark little room under some railway arches, then carry them all back. And only a few months later, there he would be again!— 'That little lot's not right! . . .'

Cockles and mussels bought from buckets or off push-carts were a common delicacy; but in the early years of the century only the 'low' in the working class ate chips from the shops. Good artisan families avoided bringing them, or indeed any other cooked food, home: a mother would have been insulted. Fried fish without chips one could already buy from cook shops. One could eat at these shops or take out a fourpenny hot dinner in a basin. Many working women among our three thousand or so inhabitants took advantage of the basin meal; engaged as they were all day in the weaving, spinning and dyeing trades, they had little time to cook,[6] or indeed to learn how to, since their mothers before

---

[6] In the forty years before 1914 a new eating habit developed in the industrial areas of Britain, especially in those towns which used female labour. After 1871 and compulsory military service in a united Germany, thousands of Bavarians emigrated, mostly to North America, but some arrived in Britain. Among them came a steady stream of young pork butchers, humble followers in the wake of the German cotton merchants and woollen men long established in Manchester and Bradford. The newcomers saw at once that the kind and variety of pork products they could make for sale far exceeded anything on show in the conservative English shops. Establishing

7 *Water for the wheel: a knife and scissors grinder*

8 *Hawkers at rest*

them had often been similarly occupied in the mills. This contributed, I think, to the low culinary standards which existed in the Lancashire cotton towns before the first world war. Most cooking was done, of course, on the open fire, though single gas rings had come rapidly into general use. The frying pan, because of the ease and speed with which it produced cooked food, was the most esteemed utensil despite the medical profession's pronunciamento that fried foods were ruining the health of the working classes. One local doctor whenever he called upon our humbler neighbours with stomach troubles would demand the family frying pan, then go outside and smash it to pieces against a wall; a gesture which compelled the housewife to borrow one from next door until she could afford to buy another. She made no protest at the act: a doctor was a demi-god.

Among us there was still a great deal of prejudice against corned beef and boiled mutton in tins (not shared by the very poor), though condensed milk and tinned salmon were readily accepted; but a dietary revolution was on the way. Until the mid-nineteenth century and the coming of railway transport the working classes ate very little fresh fish, though the salt variety and pickled herrings were popular enough. The introduction of deep sea trawlers in later decades and the use of ice as a preservative brought vast quantities of cheap Icelandic cod into the country. Towards the end of the century new cotton seed oils, often vile smelling when heated, came on to the market; neighbourhoods were polluted by still another odour and a further 'offensive trade' was added to the official list. Well before 1914 'chip' shops had mushroomed all over working-class areas and fish and chips became an integral part of proletarian diet. Many of the élite, however, still rejected this new-fangled food, but not so the poorest; they would buy, and gladly, even a farthingsworth of 'scratchings'—scraps of cooked potato and the broken bits of batter which had fallen from frying fish.

---

themselves first in Hull and other east coast ports, they slaved, prospered, married—usually other German pork butchers' daughters—and set up their sons in the same business. By the outbreak of the first world war it is doubtful if there was a single Northern town, large or small, that did not have its German pork butchers. Each one, versed in Continental culinary skills, introduced a range of new tastes in cooked meats to the British working class, and incidentally established the image of the 'typical German' for the next several generations.

G

Dining precedence in the homes of the poor had its roots in household economics: a mother needed to exercise strict control over who got which foods and in what quantity. Father ate his fill first, to 'keep his strength up', though naturally the cost of protein limited his intake of meats. He dined in single state or perhaps with his wife. Wage-earning youth might take the next sitting, while the younger end watched, anxious that any titbit should not have disappeared before their turn came. Sometimes all the children ate together: a basic ration of, say, two slices (and no more) of bread and margarine being doled out. There was, however, a tremendous resistance to eating 'Maggie Ann' (margarine[7]): it stood as the very symbol of a poverty-stricken diet. Whenever they could, even the poorest would try to buy butter. This reluctance to substitute margarine for butter has persisted in Britain, though not in other European countries, far into the twentieth century. In the apportioning of food, small girls often came off very badly indeed: mothers felt that they didn't need much—'not the same as lads'. In the streets, therefore, none looked more pathetically 'clemmed' than the little schoolgirl. Through ingrained habit this stinting could continue even after she had started work. If women generally possessed a stronger will to live than men some certainly needed it!

Sunday dinner, taken between mid-day and 2 p.m. (there was no such meal as 'lunch'), all the family partook of together. This was the only adequate meal many children got; a time for stuffing in as much food as possible against the meagre days to follow. But whatever a child ate, filling or not, he had to announce at the end of it, 'Thank God for a good meal. Please may I leave the table?' In the poorest households, through a lack of both knowledge and utensils, little cooking of any kind went on, except for the grilling on a fork[8] before the kitchen fire of bits of bacon and fish. Many never cooked vegetables, not even potatoes. Irish families, however, were ridiculed for their Sunday habit of boiling cabbage, pork ribs and 'murphies' all in one iron pan, then letting the mess serve for every meal far into the following week.

[7] From 1909 to 1913 the annual consumption of butter per head in the United Kingdom stood at 16 lbs, that of margarine 6 lbs.
[8] There were two types—one the common long-handled kind, the other which slid over a broad top bar and allowed meat, hung on two hooks beneath, to grill, parallel to the glowing coals

But even this, our local xenophobes sneered, was for the 'Micks' a cultural step forward—'Before coming to England they didn't know food *had* to be cooked.'[9]

When bad times came out tick customers at the shop were, of course, forced to adjust their diet; it began to fall off in quality, quantity and variety. Some made the change-down with great reluctance. Often a housewife would go on buying the cake or biscuits her family had grown used to in prosperity at the expense of plainer, more nourishing but less palatable fare. Then, forced by degrees to give them up, she went in for small quantities of jam and finally the cheapest sweet of all—black treacle. In the end sheer hunger, or my father's flat refusal to sell 'fancy relishes to them as can hardly buy bread and scran [margarine]', put a term to indulgence. And here again he crossed swords with my mother: 'If', she told him, 'a woman can still pay at week end for what she's getting, let *her* choose the family's food, not you!'

When destitution stood at a house door a father still claimed the lion's share of what sweetstuff came in, usually condensed skimmed milk. This was not necessarily due to greed or selfishness: a man simply had to store energy against a sudden call to do some casual job, short in duration perhaps but physically exhausting: here, then, another example of how economic necessity shaped small dietary rites. Tea the woman of the house brewed in her husband's pint pot: the teapot being a luxury article unbought by the lowest social order; so too was the cup. Parents and perhaps wage-earning children supped from pint pots, the rest from half-pound stone jam jars. A treat for the smallest child consisted of a 'round' of bread lightly sprinkled with sugar—the 'sugar butty'. But such was the craving for sweetness[10] among the most deprived, some children I have

[9] Irish families long established in the neighbourhood and figuring, if only modestly, on our social register, disliked the influx of raw compatriots whose poverty and ignorance of local *mores* might again raise doubts about their own standing. In the shop they would, at times, apologise for or try to condone the habits of those who were 'just off the bog' or had 'come over with the cattle'.

[10] The very poor seldom went weekly shopping; they bought, not even for the day, but for the meal. This meant that some children spent nearly all their leisure running errands, always in the expectation of some tiny reward. A halfpenny brought them rushing to the shop for 'gobstoppers', 'Everlasting Strips' (licorice), 'Kali Suckers' (sherbet) and, above all, 'Lucky

known would take leaves from the bottom of their father's pot and spread them over bread to make the 'sweet tea-leaf sandwich'.

Meals one frequently helped out with sauce and vinegar sold in penny bottles: in bad times sauce on bread became the meal itself. Pickles of all kinds, milk and jams we dispensed unhampered by hygiene from open vessels, purchases being taken away in cups and jars. The manual worker neither then nor later dined regularly on tinned salmon (a middle-class myth); it was far too expensive. When, by judicious buying at a 'Greedy corner' auction late Saturday night, a housewife could get a Cheshire rabbit, 5 lbs potatoes, 2½ lbs carrots and turnips and 1 lb onions all for a shilling, few would spend 9½d on a small tin of salmon. For less than a shilling one could have bought, too, a couple of pounds of New Zealand lamb or 9 lbs of flour. Many tinned fruits to be had very cheaply in the '30's were unheard-of luxuries then, though we did stock pineapple chunks and one or two other tinned delicacies for customers paying cash. We sold, besides, great quantities of condensed skimmed milk at two tins for 3½d. This contained plenty of sugar and no fat at all and doubtless contributed to the fact that around 1904 one in six babies in the district died within the twelvemonth.

Many workers either had their mid-day meal brought from home by one of the children (a chore that could take up most of a boy's own meal time) or took a packed lunch. They ate this, in the smaller workshops at least, sitting by machine or bench with a tea can on the floor; no canteen, not even a table being provided. There was much domestic friction about sandwich content, some men demanding fillings which the family budget could not sustain. One mechanic, I remember, after a violent quarrel with his wife found next day that lunch consisted of the rent book between two slices of bread. Not all women called their husbands 'master'!

Bags'! These gave a trinket, a few cachous and the hope of discovering that 'golden sovereign' which, we firmly believed, the 'government' compelled confectioners to put into one in every ten thousand packets. A 'boy in London', our myth went, had once found two in a single week! A hush would fall on the little knot of children as a packet from our shop was broached. But one there stood around careless; if any seeker had struck gold after my fingers had felt over Lovell's Monster Lucky Bags he would have been a fortunate boy indeed!

Our local carters working the city warehouses seldom took food with them. Public houses, avid for trade, put on some kind of a free snack with their 1½d 'carters' pints'. Certain pubs went further and supplied potato pie, cheese and pickles, a pint of beer and a piece of thick twist tobacco—all for 4½d. A carter had to prove his *bona fides*, though, by bearing a whip in hand or round his neck.

Milk was either bought from corner shop 'dairies' or from vendors' churns in the street, the latter product usually becoming so dirty in the four winds that even our boldest itinerants poured the last grey inch away. Before 1900 formaldehyde, often in large doses, had been used by dairymen to prevent milk souring. They either did not know or did not care that this preservative could cause intestinal troubles. When the practice was banned by law in 1901 the trade objected strongly. Milk sold to the public, dealers claimed, would now deteriorate in quality. In fact the precise opposite happened. But the industry in its lower reaches had still to pass through years of substantial and often enforced change before it put fresh milk in a sweet condition regularly on the tables of the poor. Eggs, mostly Irish, selling as low as sixteen for a shilling, came uncleaned in crates packed with straw. Nearly always some were broken and bad. We had a steady trade in cracked eggs, on the basis of *caveat emptor*. Luckily a few of our rougher customers did not at all mind their age and condition: an egg was an egg was an egg.

Just as topers believed there was no 'bad' beer—only good beer and beer—so the poor considered there was no 'bad' food. They had, of course, few worries about food deteriorating after purchase; it was dispatched too quickly for that. Not so a small shopkeeper. With the first warm weather he needed to be constantly on the alert for meats and cheese going 'off'. In the absence of a refrigerator or even an ice box, bacon and raw ham (easily the most popular of the meats) arriving none too fresh from the wholesaler could be alive with maggots in a few hours. Washing with charcoal water would stave off putrefaction for a time, but in the end only the cutting away of affected parts, with a considerable dent in profits, gave rather more permanent relief. Many shopkeepers washed and then sold these trimmings, but my mother would have none of it. 'If they're rotten for us,' she said, 'they're rotten for them.' She felt strongly, and repeated her belief often, that much disease among our poorest neighbours was caused by their eating decayed food bought cheaply late at night off barrow and stall, where greengrocers ran a line in what they euphemistically called 'faded fruit'. Butchers too used market stalls to get rid of meat they had been unable to sell in their shops earlier on Saturday. A few sold surplus beef salted, though this product rapidly declined in popularity throughout the century, except in country districts, where a butcher, having no market stall, found 'pickling' the only way to dispose of his left-overs at a profit. This was even preferred by many to the fresh chilled variety, which met generations of solid resistance. Not until the days of mass unemployment between the wars did the working class as a whole accept chilled meats. Before 1914 no respectable artisan's wife would have been seen in a butcher's shop which dealt exclusively in imported 'frozen' beef and mutton.

The butcher, who had what was commonly considered a 'good' shop, employed one or two adult assistants and a boy and took up to £30 a week. An 'apprentice' to a working-class butcher before 1914 received from 4s to 5s a week, and for this, in spite of Board of Trade inspectors, could work on Saturdays from 6 a.m. until nearly midnight; then, at some shops, if stocks remained unsold, he would go in again on Sunday morning from 8 a.m. until mid-day. At seventeen years of age he got 8s a week and at twenty £1. Standard rate for an experienced man ran from 25s to 30s a week, with usually a free joint to take home at week end.

A butcher bought meat on the hoof from farm and cattle market and killed his own or had them despatched at a neighbouring slaughterhouse. Since motor trucks had hardly come into use, a common sight of the times was a troop of cows or sheep passing through the streets, leaving their droppings to mingle with the ever-present horse manure. In a field or yard near their premises some butchers would keep a 'pet' tup lamb that came at a call and led in all the newcomers meekly to the slaughter, then skipped back with its reward. But one day (such is the vileness of man) it gaily headed the little flock to return no more.

The highway close to our corner shop ran, a main artery, from one of the great Northern cattle markets to the city abattoirs. Along here every Tuesday, running to their doom, came masses of cattle and sheep bought by the wholesale merchants. And nearly every week, or so it seemed, at least one harried beast (it was always a 'mad bull') would take off from the herd and escape into the by-ways, followed by dogs and cursing drovers. Women screamed, children fled, doors crashed to. Soon, beaten to numbness, it would be driven back into the tide of flesh. Sometimes a prolonged chase would end with a beast collapsed in utter exhaustion against a wall, whence, its legs tied, its eyes great pools of fear, it would be dragged by net in a horse drawn wagon. Sixty years afterwards these poor fugitives rush through my dreams still.

The drovers, with their Welsh collie dogs, registered very low indeed on our social register. Many travelled from outlying districts with the cattle trains, slept in doss-houses by the market and lived off beer and free pub snacks. We knew them as our chief hazard on Tuesdays, when the boldest amongst us went with ginger beer bottles, climbed the pens and stripped milk from the restless cows—a job that, in the circumstances, required no little expertise. A drover often hired out his services to cattle dealers. Wages were low but he could earn a little extra by staying on night duty at the abattoir when pens had been packed to excess with sheep. If he saw an animal dying through suffocation he roused a slaughterman, who killed it at once. Next morning a visiting inspector could then pass the carcass as fit for human consumption.

Slaughtermen earned much better money than drovers but rated little higher socially. They usually worked on the job in small teams, each man with his special task. For killing and dressing a sheep the group received 1*s* and 2*s* 6*d* for a beast. Renowned as a class for their drinking and independence of spirit, the one or two we knew in the neighbourhood were pleasant enough men, seemingly unaffected by a lifetime of daily killing.

As in everything else, 'meat' shops had rating. They ranged from the high-class 'purveyor' of home-killed beef to the 'slink' butcher who sold meat of the lowest quality, including 'slink'— the flesh of prematurely born calves—and braxy, the flesh of sheep that had died of disease or accident. Not for him sirloin and legs of lamb at 1*s* 6*d* a pound: his was the place for breast of mutton at a penny, sheeps' heads for threepence and lumps of frozen beef for a few coppers. He daubed prices on his window, too—a practice every decent butcher scorned. On the whole, it was a poor household indeed that did not try to get some kind of meat to make a Sunday dinner.

Many families had queer inhibitions about the very process of eating. No meal would be put on the table unless everyone not belonging to the family had left or been asked to leave. Sometimes the front door would be locked before dinner or tea began and all those seeking entrance ignored until every sign of food had been cleared away. These practices may have originated in efforts at hiding from the world how little there was to eat. A family often boasted when it had had a good, or unusual, meal: class points, of course, could be picked up by those known to keep a 'good table'. But even when a household had food in plenty men and women (men especially) often seemed embarrassed to be observed eating it.[11]

Many food 'illiterates' existed—those who would eat only the few meagre dishes, ill-cooked and worse served, known to wife or mother. Being faddy about food gave them one of the very few areas of free choice that they possessed. For years among the working classes both bananas and tomatoes were looked upon with great suspicion. Our elderly doctor sent up the sale of the first fruit locally by assuring us that every banana eaten gave one an 'extra ounce of blood', though he would not deny, as many neighbours were fond of pointing out, that 'tomatoes could be responsible for cancer'. The food illiterate, when odd occasion took him to dine away from home—often on fare more varied and far better than his usual diet—would sit through a meal in confusion, eating little or nothing. Though he was the extreme, one would have been hard put to it to find any working-class household free from ignorant prejudices of all kinds about food and cooking.

Some families' custom forbade the young to speak to one another at meal times, talk when father was present, or address, until spoken to, any visiting adult. At table children were often obliged to stand even when chairs were available. This was supposed to be good for the moral fibre. Kindly fathers would save

[11] I have known elderly men in gaol who refused the privilege of 'dining in association' and who always took their food alone. In confidence they confessed a fear of not having the 'proper manners' for eating with others.

a bit of their 'relish'—the tail of a finnan haddock, the top of a
boiled egg—and give it to each child in turn, and there would
be much fun and jollity over it. My father, who had an Olympian
contempt for all young children,[12] never indulged us in this
fashion. Whenever possible we avoided him: his drunken roaring
had too often frightened us, but, drunk or sober, he never laid
a finger on any child. During meal times, Mother serving in the
shop, we used to sit in quiet patience whilst he, appearing from
time to time from behind the pages of the *Daily News and
Leader*, took a portion of stew or tomatoes and chops from his
plate and bobbed back again. At once my eldest sister, a girl with
nerves of piano wire, would rise silently, step forward and, taking
a piece of dry bread from her pinafore, rub it vigorously in his
gravy, sometimes popping in her mouth the very titbit he had
left for his next foray. I used to watch, trembling at what might
happen. Yet he never caught her. Once or twice he half laid down
his paper, staring puzzled at his plate, at the cat, then at Jenny;
but she sat grave as a nun beyond the fireplace. None of us,
though, ever wanted for food. 'We don't keep a shop,' my mother
would announce, bringing in still another two large loaves, 'the
shop keeps us!' We were lucky and knew it.

'At least one third of the children in the working classes', it
was said in 1904, 'go hungry at some time.' The scene at our
factory gate with workers leaving would have attested to its
truth. There every evening stood some of England's young
starvelings, each asking hopefully, ' 'Ave yer anythink left from
yer dinner, mister?'

Ever since the passing of the Compulsory Education Act
private charities in the cities had struggled to provide breakfast,
in winter at least, for a few of the many thousands of children
who came to school hungry. By 1900 attempts were being made
to have such meals subsidised from the rates. But *The Times*
would have none of it:

There is a section of the School Board for London [announced an
editorial in 1901] which aims at the saddling upon the ratepayers of
the responsibility for the feeding of the children sent to school without
their proper meals; a policy which we have contended from the first,

---

[12] A handsome man himself, I used to catch him on occasion, though,
staring down vaguely at me, a thin, ugly child, in some puzzlement,
suspended perhaps between hope and fear on my origins.

will inevitably tempt a large class of parents to starve, or half-starve their boys and girls in order to escape a burden to which they are legally subject and one which they are well able to bear.

But if money from the rates had to be used at all to feed hungry children, the dissuasive scheme devised by our local authority would have met with the editor's full approval. All children arriving at school in winter with empty stomachs were divided into three 'categories': (*a*) those 'where temporary illness, loss of employment, or other unavoidable causes have, for the time, incapacitated the parents from making necessary provision for the child', (*b*) those whose parents were 'permanently impoverished', and (*c*) those whose parents, 'though capable of making this provision, have neglected to do so'. (These last, in fact, were found to be very few indeed, as *The Times* could easily have discovered.)

Of parents in classes (*b*) and (*c*) preliminary investigation was made by school attendance officers, men of little education and known authoritarianism, and the 'applications were entered on a form prepared for the purpose and forwarded to the Guardians'. 'In only a small proportion of cases was relief granted,' said an official report, 'the applications being withdrawn in many cases by the parents when they were informed that the granting of relief would involve disfranchisement, and in other cases being rejected.'

This, in short, meant that the child most in need of a breakfast had least chance of getting one. It was pointed out, however, that if a pupil from categories (*b*) and (*c*) did have the good fortune to be accepted, 'no distinction was made'—he got coffee, bread and margarine just like those children whose parents were starving only temporarily. Of the annual sum subscribed to pay for these meals, four-fifths came from private sources (including an appreciable amount from better-off schoolchildren) and only one fifth, about £50, from the rates. Yet this gave the guardians powers, which they used, either to deny breakfast to the very poorest children, or allow it to a few on condition that the parents became disfranchised.

That the Roman Catholic part of the community was much poorer than the rest may be plainly seen from the statistics given for free meals. During the winter of 1905–06, 3,388 free breakfasts went to the hungry in Protestant schools with an aggregate of 3,500 pupils, whilst among an equal number of Roman Catholic scholars in the same area 8,368 breakfasts were served.

After 1906 the Education (Provision of Meals) Act was adopted by the council, but it was still thought that 'as far as possible the expense of feeding the schoolchildren should be defrayed out of a voluntary fund'. By 1911, however, the cost was being met almost entirely from the imposition of a rate of $\frac{1}{4}d$ in the £.

What Lord Harcourt called the economic cleavage of England could perhaps best be seen in the mere quantities of food eaten by the rich and poor. In 1902 one survey of domestic budgets showed that upper-class families consumed about three times as much meat per annum as working-class households, four times as much milk and three times as much butter; all of which may go some way to account for the fact that children of twelve years of age who went to private schools were, on average, five inches taller than those who attended State schools.

Of soft drinks in vogue at the time, herb beer and 'pop', sold in stone bottles,[13] had the largest sale, followed by lemonade, ginger beer and the more expensive squashes, but compared with today the range was very limited. Soda water in small bottles for hang-overs and in syphons for the seriously ill sold steadily. But no 'real' man would touch any of the stuff. This was drink for 'women and kids'.

'Beer!' my father would bawl whenever some elder dared to chide his tippling. 'Beer is my food!' To maintain his strength he seldom drank less than four quarts a day. Many men, like him, had come to believe the common nineteenth-century myth that 'bees' wine' as they called it was vitally necessary for their health. To the great mass of manual workers the local public house spelled paradise. Many small employers of labour still paid out their weekly wages there. In the main fetid dens, they held an attraction with which nothing in present-day society can quite compare. After the squalor from which so many men came there dwelt within a tavern all one could crave for—warmth, bright lights, music, song, comradeship, the smiling condescension of a landlady, large and bosomy, for ever sexually unattainable, true, but one could dream, and her husband (the favoured called

---

[13] Once in our district a drowned mouse decanted itself from a stone bottle of dandelion and burdock. Sales of drinks in opaque containers slumped for some time afterwards. We had our standards.

him by his first name), a man of the world dispensing wit and wisdom—and Tory politics too, of course: publicans were Tories almost to a man, and the party's self-appointed agents. But above all, men went for the ale that brought a slow, fuddled joy. Beer was indeed the shortest way out of the city. Then, driven at nearly midnight into the street, their temple shuttered and barred, the company lingered on, maudlin, in little groups, loath to face a grim reality again.

Our village loyally supported its fifteen public houses and a single hotel, the only one permitted by law to sell wines and spirits. As if by natural order each establishment had its status rating over and above the social gradations to be found within a house itself. Lowest on our scale came the 'Boatman', haunt of bargees, loose women and thieves, and at the pinnacle—the 'Duke of Clarence', frequented by shopkeepers, foremen (in the 'Best Room') and artisans in the Vault. Tenanting the 'Duke' was a little dark widow of such refinement that not more than half a dozen of her customers were considered worthy of verbal salute. Others received her nod and the lower breeds a cold stare. Seldom seen, she delegated authority to two solemn barmen who allowed no singing, drunkenness or bad language. So select was our hotel its respectability hung in a beery aura over all the immediate neighbourhood. The poorest frequenters felt in no way affronted by their hostess's contempt. Publicans, after all, were powerful figures in every slum. They spoke of her, in fact, with the profoundest respect—'a proper lady if ever there was one!'

A great deal of beer bought in jugs from the 'Outdoor Department' was drunk at home. This happened in families where a wife, perhaps, had put her foot down and demanded some share in the good things of life, or where the husband, having 'filled his slate' at all the taverns around, felt no compulsion to 'pay old debts with new money'. Lower-class women, bold enough to enter a pub but too 'overfaced' to sit, beshawled, in one of the rooms, stood crushed together drinking in the 'Outdoor', the barmaid, not the landlord (he was too important), serving them. Beer and stout were the staple liquors for all, gin being little drunk except as a micturitive. Men who did not frequent public houses or drink at home were usually sneered at by other males, but not by women, as 'tight-fisted', 'hen-pecked', 'miserable' or 'not proper men at all'. He who took the pledge, however, was looked upon with a solicitude similar to that bestowed on some-one gone 'low' or melancholy. The boozers sighed and hoped that even yet kind nature would restore him to normality.

One hoary folk tale in Northern towns is that concerning the man who returned home helplessly drunk, only to be tied up by his wife and beaten into unconsciousness and future sobriety. This may well have taken place, but not, surely, with the frequency that legend has it. A more authentic cure for intemperance I know of was the horse blistering liniment applied regularly by an irate wife to her husband's bare soles as he lay in 'swinish sleep'. His was the only case known of a man who gave up drink because it made his feet sore.

Every week the Salvation Army planted itself monotonously across our street end, in moral intimidation. To push through its ranks, a jug of ale in each hand, while some fervent convert howled against the evils of drink needed a bold face, but no one ever seemed to shirk the duty. Father, though, did not force any of his children to walk this hazard; he went to the beer-house himself, returning with a quart vessel through the ring of singing Salvationists, their leader, a large, ginger man, staring hard and bawling across, 'He wrote my name down for a carriage and crown, A wonderful Lord is He!' But the old man passed on insouciant; his chances, he knew, of a diadem and free transport hereafter were slim.

Drunkenness was, of course, the major social problem.[14] In the year 1908–09, 62,882 people were sent to gaol for it. Before 1914 my father spent weeks of every year idle, sacked because of his trade union activities or through over-drinking. For a long time he worked for an old-fashioned firm where everyone, management included, drank daily to excess. Many a Monday

---

[14] In 1908 England and Wales still had a hundred thousand public houses, despite many closures. The government introduced a Bill to abolish about a third of those still in existence, a proposal which shocked the less temperate. Great protest meetings took place up and down the land. Working with singleness of purpose, the House of Lords, the Conservative party and the brewers of England fought as one to foil the scheme. At Stockton on Tees a 'crowded service for publicans' even called upon the Almighty to assist. Against such opposition a government could do little. The Bill failed, brewery shares rose again and the picture drawn of a nation full of starving barmaids faded. Like her sisters the country over, our Lizzie Matson at the 'Duke' went on working her ninety hours a week for a wage of 10s, 'less breakages'.

when Father didn't appear on the job the foreman, a notorious 'ale can' himself, arrived at the house in mid-morning and from beyond the shop counter (Mother would not allow him in the kitchen) he would set up loud cajoleries aimed to persuade his henchman, still stupefied on the sofa, back into work. 'We're stuck, Bob, lad!' he would call. 'Can't get on with that job! Mister Barton' (the owner), 'Bill Barton's sent me 'isself!'

The old man would raise his head, moan and fall back into torpor. But sometimes by long persuasion the foreman succeeded. Father staggered to his feet, pushed his head into a bowl of water while an elder sister rushed a few sandwiches together, and they would be gone. Then he would return at close on midnight, dirty and hollow-eyed, having worked himself to the point of collapse. There were occasions, though, when he and the foreman left home full of high purpose and got no farther than the nearest pub, from which they both rolled out again hours later, aggressively drunk.

Before 1914 in many workshops ale was sent out for and consumed on the job. Though the annual beer consumption had steadily declined from the astonishing 1876 figure of thirty-four gallons per head for every man, woman and child in the country, excessive drinking was rife and the inebriate staggering home an everyday sight that aroused no comment. Drunkenness was by far the commonest cause of dispute and misery in working-class homes. On account of it one saw many a decent family drift down through poverty into total want.

Some craftsmen whose inebriety the boss tolerated because of their long service or special skills were notorious for habitual absence on the first working day of the week, celebrating, as they called it, 'St Monday'. Most men, though, either through a sense of responsibility or fear of their wives, drank heavily only on Saturday nights. With us this led the following morning to a run on stomach settlers from the shop: we sold Seidlitz powders galore. The man unfit for work on Monday because of week-end drinking, though, was marked and points were deducted from his social stock. The family would suffer a fall in prestige too. This could be another home on the slippery slope.

In spite of abounding poverty it would be wrong to assume that the district lay slumped in despair. Much banter and good-natured teasing was to be heard. People laughed easily, whistled, sang, and on high days jigged in the street—that great recreation room. A barrel organ called Tuesdays and Saturdays: children danced solo in a kind of private ecstasy. Only top persons and a few avowed Christians renowned for their clean doorsteps and 'amen' faces kept aloof from it all.

Knocks, bruises, ailments one accepted stoically enough. Death, after all, called often. Children made a common habit of visiting a house where someone had just passed away to ask reverently to view the body, a request that was never refused. One friend of my youth boasted of having seen thirty-seven corpses over a wide area. This was the heyday of quack medicines, a time when millions of the new literates were reading newspaper advertisements without the knowledge to gauge their worth. Innumerable nostrums, some harmless, some vicious, found ready sale among the ignorant. One had to be seriously ill before a household would saddle itself with the expense of calling a doctor,[15] in our case an elderly Irishman famous for kindness and wheezing whisky fumes. At week ends people purged themselves with great doses of black draught, senna pods, cascara sagrada, and their young with Gregory powder, licorice powder and California syrup of figs. For all these on Friday they came to the shop in constant procession. Through the advice of doctors and wide advertisement the working class had an awful fear of constipation, a condition brought on by the kind of food they ate.

The sick too found relief in medicaments from the corner shop, supplied by manufacturing 'chemists'. Few of these had any qualifications. One of the traders who sold to us had entered the profession via the mineral water business. His early attempts at a cough medicine (6*d* per two-ounce bottle), though attractive in colour, had run thin as ginger beer and fallen a drug on the market. But he learned quickly. With such mixtures content and colouring meant little; high viscosity was all. His next concoction slid down the gullet like warm pitch. Bronchitics swore by it and sales soared.

[15] In our district more people were sued in the county court for non-payment of doctors' bills than for any other reason. This somewhat dents the myth of the golden-hearted medico 'forgetting' the debts of his poorer patients. But in that world of private enterprise many slum doctors were hard up enough until the Health Insurance Act of 1911 (against which the BMA fought tooth and nail) put them off their bicycles and into motor cars.

Pills sold at a penny a box, any doubts as to their potency
being quieted by the venerable image of their maker smiling
from the lid. He had cause for amusement. Nearly all the pills
appeared to possess a dual purpose: they 'attacked' at one and
the same time the ills of two intestines—'Head and Stomach',
'Blood and Stomach', 'Back and Kidney', 'Back and Bladder',
and indeed almost any pair of organs that could in decency be
named. Whatever their aim, however, for ease of manufacture
all pills contained the same ingredients—soap and a little aperient;
but they differed in colour, the 'blood and stomach' variety being
red, say, and the 'back and bladder' a pea green. Some colour
sense was required, it seemed, in marketing. A pink blood and
digestive pill might go down famously in Leeds, only to be
rejected entirely by Liverpudlians, whose stomachs would settle
for nothing but a pellet in a warm brown shade.

With us a week seldom passed without somebody's baby
having 'convulsions'. 'Mother's Friend', known in the district
as 'Knock-out Drops', was always in demand for the fretful,
especially on mid-Saturday evenings. 'It relieves your child from
pains,' said the advertisement, 'and the little cherub awakes
bright as a button.' This 'Soothing Mixture' (laced with tincture
of opium) would guarantee to keep baby in a coma until late
Sunday morning. Meanwhile mother spent two happy hours in
the Snug of the 'Boilermaker's', undisturbed yet not unmarked.
Tincture of opium figured too as the kick in a pricey cough cure
we sold. A good dose would grip for a short while even the
consumptive's spasms, to bring flickers of renewed hope that
soon died.

'Therapion' had a good run. This 'New French Remedy' was
unique in that it claimed not only to induce venery but also to
heal any unfortunate consequences of it. 'Therapion', we read,
'stimulates the vitality of weak men, yet contains besides all
the desiderata for curing gleet, discharges, piles, blotches and
premature decay.' 'French and Belgian doctors' swore by it.
Floratino, too, was 'highly recommended'. At 2s 6d a bottle it
'imparted a peculiarly pearly whiteness to the teeth [before the
enamel flaked] and a delightful fragrance to the breath'. With
his best suit out of pawn, a dose of Therapion and a mouth
washed with Floratino, a young man could feel all set for
Saturday night. 'St Clair's Specific for Ladies' had more serious

9 *'The shortest way out of Manchester'*

10 *A barrel organ called* **Tuesdays and Saturdays**

aims; this 'prevented', among other ailments, 'Cancer, Tumurs [*sic*] and varicose veins'.

The boldest purveyor, who took a quarter-page spread in the local newspaper, appeared to be a 'Mr W. H. Veno'. A charismatic figure, he was shown standing before a screen in a great beam of light. 'His marvellous diagnostic power', the advertisement assured us, 'borders on the superhuman. He sees a sick person at a glance, reads his disease without asking a question and with the utmost accuracy.' He could do this 'blindfold', too, and had withal a 'rare gift' which enabled him to 'cure the sick and diseased in a manner that reads like miracles'. 'Priests and ministers of every denomination' were numbered among his patients. They all took, we were informed, 'People's Strengthener and Health Giver'—Sea-Weed Tonic at 1*s* 1½*d* and 2*s* 9*d* a bottle. Doctors used it too, because 'they recognised in Sea-Weed Tonic the most successful medicine that science has yet produced for liver, kidney and blood diseases'.

The imposition of the first tax on patent medicines put their manufacturers in a dilemma. A clause in the Act appeared to imply that proprietary medicines could still be sold free of tax provided their purported curative powers were not advertised. From then on, until the Act was revised, some firms merely announced the title of their product: others paid the tax and hired professional advertising men. The pushers of one pill, in keeping with a claim to have 'the largest sale of any patent medicine in the world', made boasts of almost megalomaniac proportions. Their pellet 'Cured Biliousness, Nervous Disorders, Wind and Pain in the Stomach, Sick Headaches, Giddiness, Fulness and Swellings After Meals, Dizziness and Drowsiness, Cold Chills, Flushes of Heat, Loss of Appetite, Shortness of Breath, Costiveness, Scurvy and Blotches of the Skin, Disturbed Sleep, Frightful Dreams and All Nervous and Trembling Sensations, Etc.' 'This is no fiction,' the ad-man went on. 'These are FACTS testified continually by members of all classes of society. No Female should be without them. They will restore Females of all ages to sound health.'

And the females took his advice: we sold them at the shop in screws of paper, three for a halfpenny, in endless succession. A simple aperient had taken on magic potency.

Tucked away in corners of the local newspaper one saw other

H

medical announcements. These offered assurances to 'Ladies', 'Women' and 'Females' of their ability to remove 'obstructions' of all kinds, 'no matter how obstinate or long-standing'. The advertisers usually had foreign names and obscure London addresses. But most of our women in need of such treatment relied on prayer, massive doses of pennyroyal syrup, and the right application of hot, very soapy water. There were even those who in desperation took abortifacients[16] sold by vets for use with domestic animals. Yet birth control continued to be looked upon as a sin against the Holy Ghost.

Fine tooth combs (sold in great quantities), powders of all sorts, and even small bottles of various liquids were displayed in shops, fastened by elastic onto show cards about a foot square. Swinging freely from shelves, the 'slow movers' gathered layer after layer of dust. When manufacturers were forced finally into packing goods in boxes, sales fell off at once and took a considerable time to recover.

Following age-old tradition, whenever occasion allowed, poor folk stuffed and swilled themselves, then took a strong purge to quell the after-effects. So they combated the twin subconscious fears of starvation and illness. Stomach trouble was by far the commonest ailment of the time. Not until 1917, when the demands of war compelled it, did authority make an effort to educate the nation generally in simple food values. Then the poor began to learn that some beer could be bad beer and not all was grist that came to the molars.

[16] The 'old queens' favoured concoctions of aloes and the vigorous use of turpentine. The controlled fall downstairs also had its advocates. But if all else failed someone always knew a woman who knew a woman who . . . The skilled abortionist, though, valued herself by no means cheaply. Our local practitioner, my mother told us long afterwards, was never crude enough to mention fees for kindly services rendered. 'Any little trinket will do, dear,' she used to say—'in gold'! This meant: rock-bottom price—half a sovereign!

Chapter 7

Alma Mater

And all the lore its scholars need,
Pure eyes and Christian hearts.
John Keble

Little sound statistical evidence seems to have been published on the number of adult illiterates[1] in Great Britain before the first world war, but there appears to be general agreement that elementary education, after the Acts of 1870 and 1880, had swept basic ignorance away. Our modern historian writes that by 1900 illiteracy had been virtually wiped out.[2] And another: 'In the last decade of our period [1890–1900] illiteracy had been razed from the map.'[3] Yet as late as 1887 inspectors in north-east England alone reported that there were still 'many thousands of children over five who have never seen inside a schoolroom'. Were conditions any better in other parts of the industrial North? A glance at the cultural standards reached by prisoners in British gaols around 1900 makes confident assertion about the abolition of illiteracy suspect indeed.

The degree of education enjoyed by the poor in the early Victorian era may be gauged from official prison statistics:[3] 'Of

[1] Nineteenth-century parish registers are often used as evidence to show the rapidly increasing literacy levels of the people. 'In 1838' (to cite one frequently quoted example) '58.4 per cent of the population of England and Wales could sign the marriage register; in 1893 the percentage was 94.6.' In a period, however, when reading and writing skills had become highly valued generally, the ability just to sign one's name, *and no more*, was much prized. Parish register figures, therefore, when offered as proof of literacy should be viewed with caution. In my own experience, based on years of teaching many hundreds of adult non-readers, I have found that nearly all beginners had already learnt to write their names, but many were otherwise quite illiterate.

[2] P. Gregg, *A Social and Economic History of Britain*.

[3] Stephen Neal, *Special Report on the State of Juvenile Education and Delinquency in the Borough of Salford*. Neal quotes figures from George R. Porter's *Progress of the Nation* (three volumes in one, London, 1836–43).

252,544 offenders (1836–45) 229,300, or more than 90 per cent, were illiterate. Only 1,085 persons had enjoyed the advantage of instruction beyond the elementary degree, and only 22,159 had mastered, without advancing beyond, the arts of reading and writing.'

But by 1870, *before* the introduction of the Elementary Education Act, the illiteracy rate of those going to prison had fallen to 33·8 per cent: an astonishing decline of more than 56 per cent. It may perhaps be that the twenty years of great economic prosperity after 1850 brought as one of its many material benefits a startling advance in voluntary education. In view of the Education Acts of 1870 and 1880, later figures seem more remarkable still. By 1900 the prison illiteracy rate had dropped by only 0·2 per cent and the number of those who 'read imperfectly' remained about the same. Now, over the country as a whole, schooling was made compulsory, more accommodation found for pupils and sterner action taken against parents who deliberately evaded the Act in order to send their children out to work. Nevertheless by the turn of the century the prison illiteracy rate stood at 19·2 per cent—a drop of only 14·6 per cent in more than thirty years of compulsory education, compared with a fall of over 56 per cent during the previous thirty years of the 'voluntary' era.

So much for the illiterates. But in viewing cultural standards of the time through the masses of poor delinquents, what can be made of the great numbers of prisoners officially classed as 'imperfect readers'? 9,799 inmates examined at local gaols in the early 1900's gave these results:

Totally illiterate	1,845
Successful at standard I[4] (seven-year-old level)	2,591
Successful at standard II (eight-year-old level)	3,137
Successful at standard III (nine-year-old level)	2,226
	9,799

[4] Prison education gradings were based on those set in the elementary schools, where, to pass from the first standard, a child had to read aloud a 'short paragraph from a book not confined to words of one syllable'. In standard II he read a 'short paragraph with expression'. Finally, in the sixth standard he was expected to read 'with fluency and expression'. Writing grades were fixed too. To be promoted from standard I the pupil needed to 'copy in manuscript character a line of print on a slate'. In the sixth and final class they required him to write a 'short theme or letter; the com-

More than nine-tenths of the men, women and children going to prison at that time were not a special class of professional criminals but ordinary members of the community, no different in cultural and educational standards from those among the lowest social orders who managed to escape the attentions of the law. In spite, then, of what some historians believe, it seems plain that about twenty per cent of the poor working class were illiterate and about as many nearly so. In 1900 children generally left school at twelve (in our district 70 per cent before that age), almost all of them going into jobs that made no call on 'book learning'. Most, of course, kept up some reading skill in leisure, but the need to write occurred seldom and there were those who lost that ability, and even some who lapsed into illiteracy. Whatever improvements were made in the English educational system during the forty years after 1870—and they were revolutionary in scope—it is true to say, I think, that the cultural levels reached in that time by the unskilled worker and his family left them still at an abysmally low level, and the world I knew, typical of so many similar that proliferated in industrial Britain at that time, gave proof of it.[5]

In the years before 1914 my mother, a woman of intelligence and self-education, had opportunity at first hand of judging the literacy levels of our neighbourhood. All her tick customers (and these comprised at some time or other most families in the district) were given a small notebook in which they wrote, against an account kept in the shop, their daily purchases. The illiterates showed themselves at once: she had to write in their books too. My mother acted besides as village scribe, communicating on behalf of the unlettered with magistrates, county courts, boards of guardians, charitable societies, hospitals, sanatoria, or soldiers

---

position, spelling and grammar to be considered'. Proficiency in arithmetic ranged from a 'knowledge of simple addition and subtraction and the tables up to 6 × 12', in grade one, to the 'use of decimals, vulgar fractions and proportion' in the final class.

[5] Of the many thousands going to prison in the early 1900's the chaplain inspector in charge of education wrote: 'The chaplains and schoolmasters generally assert that the education which many of the prisoners have received in their early days is so limited and indifferent that when they are examined on reception at the prison they are found to be almost illiterate. The little which they acquired has been forgotten, no effort has been made to retain it and the schoolmaster has to teach them from the beginning.'

serving away from home. Very often she was called upon to read aloud and advise on letters and forms received in reply. Through all this and daily contact one could gain a pretty accurate idea of local literacy standards. At a conservative estimate she thought that about one in six of our adult neighbours were either illiterate or nearly so. And what kind of education had Church and State provided for their poor?

Among many other advances the great Education Act of 1902 allowed local rates to be used to support voluntary schools and for the first time gave education committees the power to nominate one third of their school managers, who as a group now had authority over religious teaching. Nevertheless, the local incumbent, previously in complete control of such instruction, still wielded great personal power among the six managers in Church schools. Often enough teachers were appointed there not through ability but because they had proved themselves devoted and active members of the Church and could be relied upon to further its interests among pupils.

The Church of England school[6] which served our area (built in 1839) housed about 450 scholars and had a staff of eight, for the most part highly unqualified.[7] When I was twelve one lady assistant, teaching English, gave me a tap on the skull, scornfully crossed out the word 'masticated' from my composition and substituted 'massicated'. 'Chewing food to a mass,' she said, 'not a mast!' The sycophants about us sniggered. Back home with a dictionary I found myself gleefully right, though of course dared not mention it; but my respect for her scholarship plummeted. From our mentors we expected and got 'omniscience'. Soon afterwards, as it happened, she took another dive, socially this time, and with us all, by leaving to become the wife of a 'Sweeney Todd'. Teachers, we knew, might not be perfect ladies, but they didn't marry penny-a-shave barbers![8] Barbers generally had little 'class'.

Still hardly accepted as members of a profession, teachers in

---

[6] One November night a few years before the turn of the century Paul Verlaine had lectured in a room close to the school. One can only wonder now what the audience made of him and he of a district as grim as any around the Rue Mouffetard.

[7] In 1902 55 per cent of all teachers had not attended a training college of any kind.

[8] Although an efficient safety razor had been invented well before 1900, most males rejected it as effeminate and stayed loyal to the old 'cut-throat'.

Church and State schools fought respectfully for social recognition. Sons and daughters very often from top working-class families, they felt the need to conform as closely as possible to what they knew of middle-class standards.[9] Disseminators among the poor of bourgeois morals, culture and learning, they remained economically tied to the lower orders, living in genteel poverty with an income little higher than that of the skilled manual worker. In 1905, after increases in that year, our headmaster received £120 per annum and his assistants £110. As the century grew older both the economic and the social gap between teachers and the skilled manual workers widened: teaching became a 'profession' and its members establishment figures in the lower middle class.

Under appalling conditions in our school the staff worked earnestly but with no great hope. The building itself stood face on to one of the largest marshalling yards in the North. All day long the roar of a work-a-day world invaded the school hall, where each instructor, shouting in competition, taught up to sixty children massed together. From the log book it is clear that rarely did a week pass with all teachers present. 'Miss F.' or 'Mr D. absent today—ulcerated throat' appears throughout with monotonous regularity.

Fortunately for the size of the classes, anything up to a quarter of the pupils would stay away too, perhaps in sympathy. One of our dominies, a frail young Scot, had, we thought, the disgusting habit of coughing into his handkerchief, then staring into it. We could not as yet spot the active consumptive looking anxiously for signs of haemorrhage.

His Majesty's inspectors seemed permanently dissatisfied with us. These gentlemen we learned to recognise: they came in pairs like comedians, addressing us with some unction. Teachers feared them as they feared the Lord; scholars knew and enjoyed their

---

Before 1914, however, lower-working-class men did not generally shave themselves, but patronised a barber twice a week, which occasioned a large demand for lather lads. These boys were often grossly exploited, working till all hours for a weekly five shillings. Our local barber, a wit and a drunkard with a palsied hand, generously gave regular customers two, 'cut-price', shaves for three-halfpence, but squalid premises and the danger of catching 'devil in the beard', a skin disease, kept his connection small.

[9] Six of my cousins, all children of aunts married into the 'middle' classes, became schoolteachers. We had plenty of occasions for observing their values.

terror. Many the looks of gratitude we, the bright boys, got for responding smartly to these god-like questioners.

One inspector early in the century had complained that 'Classrooms are insufficient [four for 450 pupils] and one is without desks. Yet writing is taught in it, thus inducing awkward attitudes and careless work.' Error, though, was easily emendable; scholars wrote on slates and made erasures with saliva and cuff. In a school nearby, however, this method was frowned on. There the pupil wishing to 'rub out' had to raise a hand and a monitor swung to him a damp sponge fastened to the end of a rod. Another inspector deplored the fact that all our 'offices' were without doors, 'even those under the classroom'. Doorless privies, our school managers believed, eliminated 'certain practices' among the pupils. They were mistaken. One HMI urged an innovation—'a cloakroom with taps and bowls'. Months later the 'washing appliances' were installed—cold water taps and bowls—'two for the girls' end; two for the boys''. The uproar from the street another inspector found 'intolerable'. 'Wooden blocks laid down', he thought, instead of the 'cobbles' (setts), 'would be a great boon.' The blessing remained unconferred fifty years even later, when the school fell down.[10] Time and again others condemned the wretched lighting (open gas jets) and the stench of classrooms. They seem, however, to have overlooked the 'pit'. Under a shed where we gathered when it rained, our small play yard contained a hole six feet square and six feet deep, with a loose lid, into which all the school's refuse was shot, to be removed at intervals. Meanwhile we salvaged what we could. One pupil spent so much time there, looking for 'treasure', that he was known among his contemporaries even thirty years after as 'Dusty Dan'.

At first the inspectors, conscious of the conditions under which teachers worked, refrained from attacking the staff. 'The children are well behaved', wrote one, 'and under industrious if not very intelligent instruction.' 'Scholars are orderly', wrote another, 'and attentive to their work, which is practised under careful conditions.' 'Pupils work willingly,' added a third, 'under teaching of creditable regularity and endeavour.' But whatever it was we practised under careful conditions and with creditable regularity,

[10] Alarming structural defects suddenly appeared and pupils had to be removed at a few hours' notice.

inspectors later in the decade grew sharply restive about it. 'Some of the teachers here', complained one, 'work in fixed and narrow grooves, hence there is in several classes a marked want of power to reason and a lack of independent effort.' He might have noted, though, that when one is jammed holding a slate with fifty others in a fetid classroom, power to reason and independence of effort do not perhaps come easily.

'The staff here must be strengthened at once,' demanded still another inspector, 'both in numbers and qualifications.' But the qualified and competent whom necessity had forced into such a school left again at the first chance. Many other criticisms followed and at last came a thundering from the Board of Education itself about the 'inadequacy of staff and the want of intelligent teaching'. But nothing changed. With sad repetition the headmaster went on recording in his little book—'Examined standards II and III today—poor, very poor. Standard V—no better.' Yet all was not gloom: in spheres beyond the secular he knew consolation. 'The religious tone of this school', diocesan examiners had assured him in writing, 'is admirable.'

Our school, lowest scholastically and socially of the three attached to its parish church, was ruled by the rector, a large man of infinite condescension. Once a week he called upon us, booming; the Head at sight of him seemed to shrink into a stoop of deference. They went into conference at the end of the hall. To judge from the log books, while both seemed happily agreed on the school's religious 'excellence' there were other points to which the Head had nervously to call attention—'the overcrowded classrooms', 'the great numbers of children with bad eyesight', the numbers of those taking free meals—'64 at the Ragged School today'. Then the regular apology for the great drop in attendance after a visit from 'Nurse'—'Sent out many "verminous" notices'. Children often stayed away for this and to earn a copper or two whenever possible to add to the family income, but the most frequent excuse for absence was 'visits to hospitals and dispensaries, or minding babies while mother goes'.

Rector and Head together considered many grave matters. They both agreed, for instance, that 'no child be allowed to remain at school who is not in time for morning prayer';[11] a

---

[11] Despite cheap clocks and watches many homes had no means at all of telling time. Professional knockers-up tapping each morning with long canes

rule that must have done much to aid local illiteracy. They bemoaned the frequent absence, through illness, of staff and its rapid turnover. They worried about absenteeism and truancy. Then there were the prize-givings to arrange, when the rector would address all the school and the few parents present, urging them to be 'ambitious; the children to get on spiritually and materially, the parents for their children's welfare, in the best sense of the word'. Then they would sing together, 'The fox and the crow', 'Three kings of Orient', and 'Lest we forget'. 'Afterwards each child was presented with a bun and dismissed.'

One bitterly cold autumn day we had no heat in school. As one of the more presentable boys in the class, I was dispatched by our headmaster with a letter to authority requesting that fires be lighted before the allotted date. Away I trotted in mid-morning across town to ring at the Rectory, a double-fronted villa deep in a garden. The maid let me in, took my note away and returned, beckoning across carpets—'The Breakfast Room!' Awed, I followed a second servant bearing a tray into the aroma of coffee and cooked meats. The rector, wearing a red dressing gown, slouched side-on to a table, a newspaper spread, in an apartment warm, and dark with mahogany. He was holding my letter in his hand and looked at me over his glasses. Then he crumpled it and tossed it a yard across a thicket of fire-irons into blazing coals. 'Very well!' he grunted. 'Just for the cold snap, tell him!'

I left overwhelmed. Such grandeur!

At intervals lessons were suspended while the rector gave us homilies aimed to 'exercise influence on the scholars' conduct'. To the same end we received other clerical visitors, including the Reverend Septimus Barker, who impressed upon us the 'necessity of missionary work in India.'[12] Temperance lecturers called regularly, though not perhaps with the enthusiastic encouragement of the minister himself—a known good liver. 'I do not agree with teetotalism,' he had been heard to say, and to this his complexion bore witness. In due time our incumbent became a canon of the cathedral. He may have been a worthy man: the poor are often prejudiced.

---

on bedroom windows roused the early workers. A minor nuisance of the day was the number of children in the streets anxiously asking the hour.

[12] At that time some sixty thousand missionaries were at work in Asia and Africa, two-thirds of them Roman Catholics.

Discipline in schools inevitably reflected the class pattern of society beyond the walls. Teachers were only too well aware from the physique, clothing and cleanliness of their charges just how far each one stood from the social datum line. In spite of their compassion for the neglected and deprived (not always in evidence), some teachers publicly scolded the condition of their dirty and ill-dressed pupils, too often forgetting the poverty from which they came. It was difficult for a child to keep himself clean in a house where soap came low on the list of necessaries. Children of the quality they might reprimand but seldom punished; the rest were caned (it seldom amounted to much) with fair indiscrimination.

Parents saw their children's teacher passing through the streets with a proper awe—a tribute which doubtless gave pleasure to the recipient and all his working-class relations. The school staff patronising their flock were condescended to in turn by the rector, visiting clergy and His Majesty's inspectors. Our headmaster, ever conscious of his standing, spoke politely to the mothers of his pupils whenever they called, timid and deferential, at the school. He cared about them and their children, 'but', complained the women in the shop, 'he speaks to you like you was half-witted!' In this the headmaster merely followed common practice. Many in the working class talking to their betters used their normal speech but aspirated most words beginning with a vowel in an effort to 'talk proper'. This habit *Punch* found extremely funny. As a whole, the middle and upper classes, self-confident to arrogance, kept two modes of address for use among the poor: the first was a kindly, *de haut en bas* form in which each word, of usually one syllable, was clearly enunciated; the second had a loud, self-assured, hectoring note. Both seemed devised to ensure that though the hearer might be stupid he would know enough in general to defer at once to breeding and superiority. Hospital staff, doctors, judges, magistrates, officials and the clergy were experts at this kind of social intimidation; the trade unionist in his apron facing a well-dressed employer knew it only too well. It was a tactic, conscious or not, that confused and 'overfaced' the simple and drove intelligent men and women in the working class to fury. Some middle-class women, impudent magistrates, prison governors, military and small public school types still exploit it.

The inspector who had placed our school on the humblest social

level lacked a certain subtlety in class perception. All of us indeed
were low, but some, we knew from talk at home, were lower
than others, far lower. Confidently any member of a class, if
called upon, could have pointed a finger at the bottom dog,
provided of course he was in attendance—an infrequent event.
Our 'Huck Finn' was a wizened Irish lad who could despise no
one. The illegitimate son of a prostitute, socially and economically
Ignatius hit rock-bottom. He wore the cast-off clothes of an adult
that brought him much ridicule, and had taken to truancy and
sleeping out by brick kilns. After weeks of absence from school
he was once escorted back, dirty and evil-smelling: an exemplary
case indeed. The teacher put him on display before the class, drew
about him a chalk circle and proceeded to dust him with a cane.
Clouds rose from what appeared to be no more than a shrinking
mass of clothes. When justice was done the heap crouched there
for another half hour while lessons continued, then as the master
turned his back a face rose from the rags, gave a grimace to
authority and, to us, a perky smile. This 'warning' to us all had
plainly not developed those 'habits of submission and respect
for superiors that education', as one MP had once put out, 'would
give the working classes'. Our mentors prophesied confidently
that Ignatius would go to the bad, and in due time he did.[13]
Truants haunted our headmaster's life. Every morning he despatched a dozen or more reliable pupils to scour the streets and
knock on doors seeking backsliders. They rarely returned before
ten o'clock, so that each of us lost five hours a week of what
teaching there was.

In its day our school, gaunt and black by the marshalling yards,
could have been among the worst in England, though several about
us seemed little better, yet for all its poverty it still gripped the
young mind through the variety and intensity of experience to be
gained there. Within it we received the first intelligence about the
planet beyond the railway lines, where, we understood, there were
'five oceans and five continents', most of which seemed to belong
to us. We picked up besides a lot of inconsequential facts on India,
parts of Africa, and that tired cliché, known even in Alexander the
Great's time, about the 'empire on which the sun never sets'—

[13] I taught him in a prison class forty-two years afterwards and we chatted
happy as two old Wykehamists, about our Alma Mater. In all, for petty
offences, he had done nearly thirty years in gaol.

all ruled over by Edward the Peace-maker (pacemaker, my father called him) and later by George the Fifth—'Our Sailor King'. History lessons ran, all kings and queens, right to the awesome Victoria. Her we knew only too well: she sat plump and un-smiling in oleograph on innumerable slum kitchen walls, the slab-faced William Gladstone coming a very bad second. It was at school too that one felt the first strange stirrings of puberty. As eight-year-olds, I remember, we fell into the care of a gay, flossy-haired young woman who filled out a sateen blouse and smelled delightfully of scented soap. With her we grew forests from carrot tops in saucers of water on the classroom window ledge and one hyacinth in a puce glass vase. She brought twigs from home, too—'off the tree in my garden' (this made a pro-found impression) and we put them in water and saw the miracle of the bursting bud. 'Miss' seemed to spend a deal of her time behind the blackboard with a bandy young man who taught standard iv, and, once, after inspectors had called, she cried openly in class, dabbing her nose with a scrap of handkerchief. Our hearts bled. Maybe with fifty children huddled in that little room she did not teach well; but she did it with 'good grace'. On her behalf one or two of us would have martyred ourselves and over the deserts of the weekends we yearned for Monday mornings.

On 9 May 1910 the headmaster gathered all his 450 children into morning ceremony and, deeply moved, announced that 'our beloved King and Emperor, Edward the Seventh, ruler of our great empire, has passed away, and all the world lies in mourn-ing'. On instruction we said a prayer for his widow. Soon after-wards the Head gave notice that the Great King Edward Memorial Fund had been established. Monitors distributed pamphlets and envelopes for contributions to every class. He urged us all, staff and pupils alike, to make a sterling effort. We should vie with each other, he said, class against class, boy against girl, to show our loyalty and send in a sum that would be worthy of the school. We vied. When the fund closed one month later our contribution totalled 6s 4½d.

Close to the entry in the school log book on the passing of King Edward the headmaster noted 'with sorrow' the death of a scholar—'Thomas Judge (aged 10) from pneumonia. The third in four months.' A fourth followed a few days later. Causes of death were listed as 'enteric fever', 'double pneumonia' and 'heart failure'. We heard and felt a passing sorrow too, but in the swarm of young life four small boys were soon forgotten. We had our eyes fixed on the coronation, in celebration of which each one of us was promised and duly received 'a medal, a bun, an orange, a banana and a small box of chocolates'. King George V had no more loyal subjects in his empire.

Teachers, fed on Seeley's imperialistic work *The Expansion of England*, and often great readers of Kipling, spelled out patriotism among us with a fervour that with some edged on the religious. Empire day of course had special significance. We drew union jacks, hung classrooms with flags of the dominions and gazed with pride as they pointed out those massed areas of red on the world map. 'This, and this, and this', they said, 'belong to us!' When next King George with his queen came on a state visit we were ready, together with 30,000 other children, to ask in song, and then (in case he didn't know) tell him precisely the 'Meaning of Empire Day'.

'The children were first presented with a bun', says the log book, 'and a piece of chocolate kindly provided by Alderman F. and after forming fours on the croft proceeded to a stand erected on the road. Each boy wore a rosette of red, white and blue ribbon and each girl wore a blue sash over a white dress.' (Those without white dresses were allowed to stand at the rear.) In happy unison we sang, 'Here's a health unto His Majesty', 'Three cheers for the red white and blue', and

> What is the meaning of Empire Day?
> Why do the cannons roar?
> Why does the cry, 'God save the King!'
> Echo from shore to shore?
> Why does the flag of Britannia float,
> Proudly o'er fort and bay?
> Why do our kinsmen gladly hail,
> Our glorious Empire Day?
>   *Réponse*
> On our nation's scroll of glory,
> With its deeds of daring told,
> There is written a story,
> Of the heroes bold,
> In the days of old,
> So to keep the deeds before us,

Every year we homage pay,
To our banner proud,
That has never bowed,
And that's the meaning of Empire Day!

'The children gave their Majesties a great reception,' wrote the headmaster, 'and after they had passed we returned to school. The national anthem was sung and the pupils dismissed. A brilliant afternoon,' he ended contentedly. And so it was, that fourteenth day of July in the fourteenth year of the century. All was still right with the world.

And how, indeed, did the nation's poor profit from the possession of empire? Compulsory State education had been introduced with overt propagation of the imperialistic idea: especially was this so after 1880. Schools—and none more than those belonging to the Church of England—set out with vigour to instil in their charges a stronger sense of national identity and a deeper pride in expanding empire, an exercise stimulated by a whole series of events that demonstrated Great Britain's might and glory, from the Ashanti wars of 1873, through Victoria's dazzling jubilee to the crowning of George V. Yet 'the actual increase in British trade', writes C. J. Lowe,[14] 'derived from the vast territories annexed after 1880 was negligible: by 1901 it only amounted to $2\frac{1}{2}$ per cent of the total, 75 per cent of which was still with foreign countries.' What the undermass got materially from empire, old or new, is hard to see, unless it was the banana—or rather, the plantain—which, exported from the colonies, began to appear increasingly in slum greengrocers' shops during the later years of the nineteenth century. Once instructed, however, the indigent remained staunchly patriotic. 'They didn't know', it was said, 'whether trade was good for the Empire, or the Empire was good for trade, but they knew the Empire was theirs and they were going to support it.'

In this, we in our school would have fully concurred. With a deep consciousness of global possession, a grasp of the decalogue[15]

[14] *The Reluctant Imperialists.*

[15] Daily exposure for nine years to Christian teaching left me with an active distaste for the Lord. He was, they had for ever told us, a 'man of sorrows and acquainted with grief', who, in his passage through our vale of tears, had never been known to smile. Now this, I felt, was overdoing it; things were not as bad as all that! On Ascension Day our whole school trailed along the 'cart road' to church, jerked into rhythm now and then by two

and a modicum of knowledge we left in droves at the very first hour the law would allow and sought any job at all in factory, mill and shop. But, strangely, I myself wanted to go on learning, and with a passion that puzzled me; an essay prize or two, won in competition against the town's schools, had perhaps pricked ambition. 'Isn't there some examination you could take?' asked my mother. I inquired of the headmaster. There were, he said vaguely, 'technical college bursaries', but he didn't put pupils in: one needed things like algebra and geometry to pass—quite difficult stuff. Some homework, then, I suggested. He shook his head; he didn't give homework. Still, my name could go up. I could sit, of course. The old man raised no objections, merely instructing me to 'get through!' I sat an incomprehensible paper and failed. When the results were announced weeks after, without having a possible hope of success, I felt sick with disappointment.

One dinner time I saw Father, half-drunk and frowning, fingering a slip of paper. 'I see yer passed!' he shouted down the kitchen.

'Yes,' I said boldly, 'I came top!'

He rose, threatening, from his chair. 'Get out!' he roared. 'Get out and find work!'

I went out and found work. The girl at the Juvenile Labour Bureau was very pleasant about it. She gave me a green card. 'Fill it in,' she said, 'and put what you would like to be at the bottom.'

I completed the form and wrote on the last line 'Journalist'. They did not require any journalists. A boy was needed, though, to sweep up, brew tea and abrade union nuts in a brass shop. I took that.

---

buglers and a drummer from the Boys' Brigade. The place took us in like a tomb. And yearly the canon cried of Death and Dissolution and the Glory yet to come, on and on, interminably; one felt oneself growing old. Then it was all over and we burst into the spring sunshine, wild with relief. For many among us the Son of God had long become the epitome of misery and boredom. Soon, in the workshop, with other apprentices, I fell across the Opposition in the shape of a chargehand over the brass foundry who, in between slopping about with kegs of molten metal, found time to dismantle Christianity for us. A jocular type, he called Christ 'Jesus Josephson', gave us stale copies of the *Freethinker* and quoted entertainingly from a booklet entitled *One Hundred and One Obscenities in the Bible*. All this duly turned us into violent atheists, much concerned with the problem of Cain's wife, the size and content of the Ark and the mystery surrounding Adam's navel.

11 *Theatre by the market*

12 *Boys haggling at the hen market*

Chapter 8

Culture

The men of culture are the true
apostles of equality

Matthew Arnold

Before 1914 most working men put in not less than a 54-hour
week, starting at six in the morning, with a break of half an hour
and one hour for breakfast and dinner. The day's work usually
finished at 5.30 p.m. People generally lived closer to their work
than they do now but most were too tired at the end of it to
take part in leisure activities outside the home except at week
ends, when factories closed on Saturday at mid-day or one o'clock.
The many looked for amusement, the few for education. And all
suddenly found at hand a new mobility.

The introduction of all-electric tramcars in British provincial
cities during the first years of the century profoundly influenced
the lives of the common people. As early as 1903 horse-drawn
trams vanished from the streets of Manchester. Having spent no
less than £1½ million the city now had 140 miles of line and
400 tramcars of four different kinds. Salford was equally prompt
in electrification, and city and borough possessed together a tram-
way network that remained for a decade the envy of the country.
For the first time in history the undermass enjoyed the benefits
of cheap urban travel. Municipal electric trams would now take
passengers three-quarters of a mile for ½d and more than two
miles for 1d, and even three miles for the same sum on a work-
man's ticket. Soon the tramcar, of far more practical importance to
the poor than railways, occupied a place in conversation much like
that of the motor car today. In summer, loads of children were to
be seen rattling along the rails *en route* for fields and parks, and
innumerable families experienced the pleasure of day trips to
attractions in far corners of the city, delights which previously
time and expense had made impossible: now journeys were about

half as dear and more than twice as fast as those made on the
old horse trams. More important still, rapid transport sparked
off a building boom in the outer suburbs which continued until
1909, when Lloyd George's famous budget introduced the taxa-
tion of land values. Some among the lower middle class moved
into new homes on the outskirts, allowing richer artisan families
to shift from dowdier streets in the inner suburbs into the houses
they had left empty. The electric tramcar enabled more working-
class people than ever before to find and keep a job beyond their
immediate neighbourhood, to visit relatives and friends, to go to
parks, libraries, theatres, concerts, cinemas, museums, schools
and technical colleges. Except for war itself, this revolutionary
new form of transport contributed more than anything else to
breaking down that ingrained parochialism which had beset
millions in the industrial slums of pre-1914 England.

Fear of Germany's great technological advance in the later years
of the nineteenth century had caused a demand for wider voca-
tional training in Britain. Our own technical institute had opened
its doors in 1896 and had been dubbed 'Royal' by Edward VII.
The sons of under-managers, foremen and top-class mechanics
were soon flocking there. We in the village looked upon it with
awe, but nobody would have had the courage to enter. We had
a relative, a young millwright of real ability, who did venture
there, then walked round and round the building and came
home. He had decided, he said, that it wasn't 'for people like
me'.

For the tired and unambitious there were other allurements.
In our midst stood the usual 'Blood Tub', a low-grade theatre
whose presence impinged on life social and cultural over a wide
area. With actors, as with bookmakers, feeling remained ambiva-
lent. Star performers, of course, were wholeheartedly admired
save by the narrowly religious few, but ordinary theatricals who
made up the weekly touring companies and who lodged, keeping
themselves, in the larger houses close to the theatre, both impressed
and shocked us. We watched the small-part actors with cheroots
swaggering through the stage door in lush coats, astrakhan
collared, and were amazed to discover through the matriarchs
(who knew everything) that many of them owned but a single
shirt apiece or one pair of socks. Though when 'the ghost walked'
—pay night—and they popped in at the shop to buy generously

of boiled ham, mustard pickles and pineapple chunks, they seemed well-heeled enough. Undoubtedly some kept up a bold face on most meagre incomes: a pair of sisters we knew, competent artists, as late as 1913 kept going in some style on the combined pay of 35*s* a week, out of which they had to find 8*s* 6*d* for a place to sleep. We saw actresses powdered and mincing, befurred and large-bosomed, cheeks bright with rouge ('Red John' the matrons called it), and we knew they had shared a pair of kippers for lunch. And all were immoral! Of that the respectable had no doubt. Yet they brought glamour, new ideas, titillating catchwords, beauty, fantasy and a sense of style to our wretched reality, and we loved them for it. Occasionally a girl in her early teens, to the envy of all others, would leave us to 'go on the stage', i.e. join a touring dance troupe. On fleeting visits home afterwards, 'dolled up to the eyes', she would often pass down the street and ignore everyone. But neighbours had the satisfaction of thinking the worst.

Nowhere, of course, stood class division more marked than in a full house at the theatre, with shopkeepers and publicans in the orchestra stalls and dress circle, artisans and regular workers in the pit stalls, and the low class and no class on the 'top shelf' or balcony. There in the gods hung a permanent smell of smoke from 'thick twist', oranges and unwashed humanity. Gazing happily down on their betters the mob sat once a week and took culture in the shape of 'East Lynne', 'The Silver King', 'Pride of the Prairie', 'A Girl's Crossroads', 'The Female Swindler', 'A Sister's Sacrifice' and the first rag-time shows. The drama critic of our weekly press invariably ladled handsome praise over all plays and performers, though when, in 'A Woman of Pleasure', the heroine was abducted in the first act, and again (by balloon) in the second, chased through the third across Africa by natives and wild beasts, then, in the finale, snatched at the last moment from a burning ship—all this to the rattle of the South African war—he felt that the title was 'somewhat misleading'.

In later years, after cinema had begun to outstrip live entertainment as an attraction, our theatre, like many others, tried 'go as you please' competitions on Friday evenings when local amateurs, good to outrageous, trod the boards. Two turns, at least, after debut could not have pursued their art much further, and the first, a nerve-fraying soprano, brought down what, for a moment, looked like a genuine protest from heaven. In the middle of her rendering of 'The Holy City' a bolt of flame burst from the upper dark and fell like a judgment to consume itself over vacant seats in the stalls. It turned out, however, that some careless smoker had ignited a lady's cotton shawl and she had cast it forth blazing from the gods. The altercation which followed, aloft, added much to our evening.

The other artist, who called himself Houdini II, performed to slow piano music. He invited members of the audience to tie him with ropes, guaranteeing to be free 'in a trice'. Two dockers then trussed him up so effectively that a few minutes later the stage manager and his aide had to carry him off like a parcel, bent double and almost asphyxiated, the audience having watched his frenetic struggles in dead silence. Later he appeared at the tail end of the prize winners and received a five shillings consolation award for 'effort'.

Many patrons of the cheapest seats in the theatre, lacking the benefits of literacy, revelled in song and the spoken word much as Shakespeare's 'groundlings' had done three hundred years before. Often two friends would go together; one to learn by heart the air of the latest hit, the other to concentrate on getting hold of the lyric. Songs first heard in the theatre were taken up in pubs then rendered with dreary iteration by street buskers for the next several years. Professional 'cadgers' came among us in hard times, as many as ten a week. Some made no attempt to earn reward but begged openly from door to door; others strutted in a stylised walk down the middle of the 'cart road' quavering loud enough for householders to hear. Local members of the fraternity, though, never had the bad taste to perform in their own district. Some after singing broke into oratory, when reasons for their destitution came crying along the wind. This form of appeal, however, was generally frowned on. 'I didn't know where to put myself!' said one woman in the shop, 'when that —— today started shoutin' the odds!' There was common agreement that a man should not 'cry poverty'. One doubts if beggary ever profited much by it.

Melodies so often and so long repeated served to fix words and tunes in the minds of all. At that time singing solo or in small groups as one strolled along the pavement was a daily and welcome feature of working-class life. Broadsheets of popular songs[1] and their parodies were hawked until well into the '20's and found ready customers. At festival times when street jigging occurred tipsy women would form up across the flagstones and to barrel organ or concertina music execute till they collapsed a kind of hey, remnant perhaps of some long-forgotten folk dance. There was a great hurrying for beer in washstand jugs and much shrieking sodality.

A deal has been written about the old music hall and its cultural importance to the working class. Certainly popular song did not concern itself then, as it does today, almost entirely with the yearnings and deprivations of sexual love; composers linked their lyrics to reality. Until the flood of American rag-time songs most topical hits merely satirised passing fads, fashions and novelties or reflected the tragedies, patriotism and politics of the time. But the bulk of these were of a wretched quality, with airs painfully banal and lyrics of an inanity that even the sub-literate rejected. Only a handful, in fact, of music hall songs gained anything more than an ephemeral vogue. Among the lower working class these were thumped out on pub pianos and bawled in chorus with a devastating regularity. Folk songs were entirely unknown. Certain pub soloists became esteemed locally for the rendering of this or that ditty, sentimental, or, as the night grew uproarious, obscene even, like the famous 'Clancy's wedding'. These solos were given over and over again with apparently little demand from listeners for a change in repertoire. With music, as with the printed word, the working masses seemed easily satisfied. From time to time the morris men, miners from local pits, brought a sudden breathless gaiety to the streets, but I never saw them again after 1921. Though the Salvation Army[2] came often, they

---

[1] Until the copyright law was strengthened in 1910 scores of people a year, usually poor Jewish peddlers, were convicted for selling pirated music in working-class districts of the city.

[2] Like many socialists of the time my mother was bitterly opposed to the Salvation Army, with its acceptance of society and indifference to the economic causes of poverty. 'So long as you're saved,' she said, 'they don't give a damn why you're starving.'

'Oh! how I see the emptiness and vanity of everything,' wrote Catherine Booth, in 1881, 'compared with the salvation of the soul. What does it matter if a man dies in the workhouse? If he dies on a doorstep covered with wounds, like Lazarus—what does it matter if his soul is saved?'—*War Cry*, 7 July 1881.

soon departed, gleanings spiritual or material being few; but one stood grateful for the burst of glory and hated the silence as it flowed back.

With music and song the discerning learned early to discriminate between 'low' pub soloists, full-blooded stage professionals and the genteel efforts heard at chapel and church concerts. Many of the élite who were already making 'electric tramcar' journeys to the city to hear Gilbert and Sullivan felt contemptuous of 'common' beer-house performers, whom they condemned for using many of the very gimmicks so favoured by today's pop singers.

In pre-1914 Britain, until the introduction of cinema, there was little organised entertainment for deprived children except that provided by the Band of Hope. Founded in Leeds in 1847, this combine of juvenile abstinence societies had a membership, by the end of the century, of more than three millions, all children under sixteen years of age. For most boys and girls in industrial slums an evening at the Band of Hope beckoned as the cultural highlight of the week. Held in a chapel hall (I never knew of one on Church of England or Roman Catholic premises), ours pulled in up to two hundred young 'abstainers' per session; among them I recall one, 'Pudding' Whitaker, who, though sworn like the rest of us never to 'touch, taste nor handle', confessed, at twelve, to loving the 'smell' of it. He defected early!

Our meetings opened sluggishly with the singing of temperance hymns, a bearded man bellowing half a line in front of us from the platform. Then followed a tedious lecture about some worthy in the Movement and a talk with lantern slides on the evils of drink. As the evening wore on, though, our programme usually turned skittish. Sometimes we enjoyed dire performers out of the audience; at others, galumphing young men, teetotallers every one, worked frantically to keep us amused, capering on the stage in song and uproarious sketch, all aiming to prove that one could be both happy and sober. Soon under the influence our own pleasure frothed over and ran reckless among the benches. Suppressions eased: boys scuffled and cat-called; girls shrieked in private laughter; song books clove the air. Chaos crept near. But a stern call to the closing hymn, in which each and all remembered pledges made, returned the meeting to its high purpose. We left happy at 8.45 with little blue cards and the promise renewed of a field day or Christmas treat. Wonderful value, we juniors thought, for a penny a month. But older *habitués* tended to sniff at it as very much *déjà vu*; especially one notorious sketch—'The Lodgers', which Pudding claimed to have seen performed no fewer than 'ten soddin' times!' He, like millions of others in the Bands of Hope, fans of another decade, stood waiting for the 'picture houses' to open.

Well before 1914 the piano and gramophone, two status symbols of the highest significance, had already penetrated deep into top working-class homes. The gramophone, however, was one of the few objects valued which had not previously established itself among the bourgeoisie. Upper- and middle-class people tended to look down on the instrument and thought it 'all right for servants'. Children of the better-off workers now paid trips to the suburbs, where cards in bow windows announced piano lessons at a shilling an hour. Mr W. A. N., for instance, gave instruction there, advertising himself as 'Pianist, accompanist and experienced vamper. Terms moderate'. Nor were other art forms quite neglected. Miss H. in the same district provided facilities for 'painting, decorative art and Chrystoleum painting at 10s 6d for 10 lessons. Payable in advance'. Nearer home the voice of Caruso sobbed across Sunday morning streets and people leaned in doorways, both enjoying a free concert and paying homage to possession. On almost any fine evening, too, there were other al fresco enjoyments to be had.

In the first quarter of the present century children's singing games in the streets reached their hey-day. This form of self-entertainment provided a ritual that gave young Edwardians pleasure unalloyed. Home duties done, children came together at some accepted place in the street, by a lamp or along a blank wall, and quite spontaneously a performance would begin, while parents, sitting on doorsteps, watched indulgently. Certain unwritten rules existed. The choice and order of the games were usually decided upon by the eldest girl present, infants being excluded, whilst all boys above about the age of eight and all girls who had left school for work excluded themselves.

It seems unlikely that many of these games were learnt first in school and then passed on to succeeding generations, since the participants chose 'lovers' openly, gave wedding rings and went to 'church' in a way no Victorian schoolma'am would have approved of. In one of the most popular, children formed a large circle and, holding hands, moved round singing:

> Up the streets and down the streets,
> The windows made of glass,
> Oh, isn't Annie Taylor,
> A nice young lass,
> She can dance, she can sing, she can show a wedding ring,
> Oh for shame, oh for shame, turn your back behind you!

Then the girl named would face the outside of the ring, still holding hands, while the others continued to face inside. The singing and circling began again to the second verse:

> Annie made a pudding, she made it very sweet,
> She daren't stick a fork in for her life's sake,
> Hurray! Hurray! don't be afraid,
> For next Sunday morning it's your wedding day,
> Oh, it's your wedding day, oh, it's your wedding day,
> For next Sunday morning it's your wedding day.

Another child was chosen and the chorus started again. This went on until everyone was facing outwards, after which the singers snaked into a single line and hopped the length of the street, chanting:

> Hop, hop, hop, to the butcher's shop, for I can stay no longer,
> For if I do my mother will say, 'You've been playing with the boys over yonder.'

'There came three dukes a-riding', 'There stands a lady on the mountain', 'A big ship sailed' and many other simple songs with movement lightened the dull evening, the young voices ringing clear and sweet, bearing on unaware a folk tradition that was soon to die from the streets. Then, as the lamp-lighter made his way one would hear weirder cries, so typical of the slum scene —those eldritch screeches, like jungle calls at evening, that mothers used to bring their young to bed. Each child knew its own shriek and turned obediently for home: the play was done.

Night sounds from the narrow streets were mostly of human agency. One lay, the gas flame a blue bud, waiting for sleep. A breeze far off slapped window frames and a wooden roar ran in crescendo until it hit one's own panes, then rolled grumbling beyond. From one or other of the rival railways an express would sear the dark, leaving our iron bedstead trembling. Nearer, engines idled, coughing, then chuffed into action—pock! pock! crash! Endless shunting punctuated the night. Cows standing hours in trucks along the line lowed for release. The night-soil carts passed rumbling over the setts. Half a street away a drunk went by singing himself home, sometimes most melodiously, and one sighed as the last notes faded. Below they raked fires for morning, sound rustling up the party wall. One drifted into sleep. But that lowing again. Sad cattle was it, or the moan along the canal of some ship on its way to the ocean? Father passed in his stockinged feet: the light flicks out. Sleep now. Soon a knocker-up scourging some early window would announce the morning.

The groups of young men and youths who gathered at the end of most slum streets on fine evenings earned the condemnation of all respectable citizens. They were damned every summer by city magistrates and unceasingly harried by the police. In the late nineteenth century the Northern scuttler and his 'moll' had achieved a notoriety as widespread as that of any gangs in modern times. He too had his own style of dress—the union shirt, bell-bottomed trousers, the heavy leather belt, pricked out in fancy designs with the large steel buckle and the thick, iron-shod clogs. His girl friend commonly wore clogs and shawl and a skirt with vertical stripes. That fraternity of some thirty to forty teenagers who lived in the street where our Church of England school stood achieved such a fearsome reputation for gang battle that they were remembered by name in *The Times* seventy years after. By my youth most of these were married and worthy householders in the district. In many industrial cities of the late Victorian era and after, such groups became a minor menace. Deprived of all decent ways of spending their little leisure, they sought escape from tedium in bloody battles with belt and clog —street against street. The spectacle of two mobs rushing with wild howls into combat added still another horror to the ways of slumdom. Scuttlers appeared in droves before the courts, often to receive savage sentences. In the new century this mass brutality diminished somewhat, but street battles on a smaller scale continued to recur spasmodically in our district and in others similar until the early days of the first world war.

This form of violence, vicious and purposeless, seemed to have its root in a subconscious wish to establish 'territory'. Not only children but adults too felt that the street where they dwelt was in some way their personal property. Householders would even order youngsters who lived in the street away from their doors with a—'Get down to the other end where you live!' Boys and youths walking alone in the evening would at times have to avoid those thoroughfares where territorial aggressiveness was strong, through fear of molestation or assault. All the warring gangs were known by a street name and fought, usually, by appointment—Next Friday, 8 p.m.: Hope Street *v.* Adelphi!

The street group, however, far from being the entirely degraded element deplored by social writers of the time, had certain values of which bourgeois society knew nothing. For those young workers too immature, inhibited or indifferent to join what few boys' clubs there were, the group constituted an open-air society, a communal gathering which had great importance socially, culturally and economically. By tradition, membership stood hedged round with restrictions, all unformulated: indeed, participants were hardly conscious of a bond. Generally, all boys after a few weeks at work were eligible, though upper-class parents frowned on their sons' entering except perhaps to join in football games. Schoolboys, girls, women and married men kept their distance, the last, of course, having their own rendezvous socially much superior in the tavern. For certain older men rules of the 'youth club' were relaxed. The victims of cuckolddom or other public ridicule, the notoriously henpecked, the moronic, those who had completely lost caste through chronic illness or feckless poverty, the dwarfish, the cripples—all were *personae gratae* within the fold, and indeed, because of age and experience, enjoyed some esteem there, though their social stock stood low in adult circles. As a provider of light entertainment the village 'idiot' found himself ever welcome (ours, 'Daft Alfie', went berserk at times, which added to the 'fun') but any child brash enough to approach the club in session was ordered or chased out of earshot.

During each nightly meeting the young worker, once fully integrated, listened, questioned, argued and received unawares an informal education. Here work-a-day life beyond his personal ken came up for scrutiny. Jobs in factory, pit, mill, dock and wharf were mulled over and their skills explained. From first-hand experience, often bitter, youths compared wages, hours, conditions, considered labour prospects, were advised on whom to ask for when seeking a job and what to say. All this was bread and butter talk vital at times to the listener, talk that had an economic scope and variety to be heard nowhere else.

Before 1914 apprenticeships of any kind were not generally open to the children of the labouring poor. One had to be 'spoke for' and usually tradesmen spoke only for the sons of tradesmen. Well before they left school most boys from the undermass had been working part-time in shops or as street traders of some sort. At that time railways held a glamour for the young that has long since faded. Round all the city termini 'station boys' gathered in great numbers daily both to watch all the bustle and excitement and earn coppers by doing odd jobs. Gamblers with what they got, like all street boys of the time, they were constantly being hauled off before the magistrates. At one Birmingham station in 1912, out of 174 lads in regular attendance no fewer than 167 had been convicted of at least one offence. In our city, like the rest, errand boys, telegraph boys, van boys swarmed like summer flies. Outstanding among them were the nippers, carters' helps. The nipper looked after the horse and sat guard over goods at the tail end of a vehicle. Always he was to be seen about the ubiquitous railway lorry. Nippers hoped some day to become carters, but supply far exceeded demand: at eighteen most lorry and van boys found themselves thrown again on to the labour market.

Part-timers in shops lucky enough to be taken on fully after leaving school often enough put in a 74-hour week which allowed them, late Saturday evening, to bring home five or six shillings to grateful parents. Many skilled workers used boys, not as apprentices, to assist them. There were the printers' devils, the feeders, the piecers and those in boot factories who placed the tacks ready for the soling machines. There were our local lads in the glass works on twelve-hour night shifts taking bottles to the blowers. And of course we had the youngsters who spent their first teenage years almost wholly engaged in fetching beer for thirsty bricklayers on building sites. Most of these lads travelled each day to those outer city suburbs to which in the first decade of the century new transport had brought the building boom.

These young pot carriers experienced the pleasure, much sought after then, of a regular daily ride on a tramcar.

In more modern, Americanised factories mass producers had quickly seen the advantages to be gained from the use of juvenile labour. Some shops ran almost entirely on young teenage workers; one notorious sewing machine factory managed to turn out its wares with only four or five skilled adult workers to every hundred adolescents, all of whom were sacked before they reached twenty. There were innumerable other jobs besides in foundry, ironworks and shipyard, all of which led youth nowhere except to dismissal on approaching manhood and a place among the mass of unskilled labourers fighting for jobs of any sort in the industrial maelstrom.

But youth then, like the young of all times, bore its burdens lightly. After serious discussion, our club at the corner would go on to gayer things. Perhaps, a girl passes on the other side, or a 'pro' flounces by: conversation veers to sex. Long familiar with some basic facts, the newly inducted aches to learn more. Well aware that the known sex ignorance of any lad within the group makes him, until the next innocent arrives, the butt of all, he treads very carefully indeed. At all costs he must snigger at the right innuendo and when the next obscene 'Pat 'n' Mick' story is told guffaw with the rest. Smirk and nudge he must if Aristotle or Oscar Wilde is mentioned, though who or what they are he has no idea at all. Every music hall ditty has spawned a parody,[3] often smutty, and this he sings confidently in chorus. Most of all

---

[3] In grown-up company, though, one had to be wary about street parody. I recall a gay party at home in war-time when my elder sisters sat around the piano with soldier friends. Naïvely hoping to entertain, I burst into a variant of 'Men of Harlech' which detailed, I learned later, in terms idiomatic but unmistakable to adults, just what it was that the British forces loved best of all. It stopped the party dead. One corporal in the corner sat jack-knifed in dumb mirth; the others smiled about at one another, glassily. At once my mother found an errand and on my return dispatched me privately to bed with a curt 'Never dare sing that song again!' Copied gesture could also be dangerous. That 1940 'victory' sign which brought forth a roar of delighted derision to the astonished Churchill's ears when he first made it to troops on parade was well understood in our day, since it was then accompanied by verbal instruction. But there were other hand signs and finger interlockings, too, some mere youthful fun, others of sexual significance. A boy had to learn the hard way what modes of speech and gesture, common in the street, were strictly forbidden at home.

he must look knowing when the vulnerability of certain girls is mentioned or vague aberrations are hinted at. Altogether, to gain face the newcomer must register a sophistication he is far from feeling. But one learns fast. Now he hears value judgments on people and practices which differ substantially from those he had grown to accept at home and, making mental readjustments, he deepens his own social awareness.

Discussion moves to matters literary. Newspapers are brought out, racing form read aloud and analysed—a boon, this, to the several illiterates within the group. Non-readers profit too from hearing headline news of the day announced and interpreted. Now periodicals and paperbacks change hands and have their contents appraised.

Even before the first world war many youngsters in the working class had developed an addiction for Frank Richards's school stories. The standards of conduct observed by Harry Wharton and his friends at Greyfriars set social norms to which schoolboys and some young teenagers strove spasmodically to conform. Fights—ideally, at least—took place according to Greyfriars rules: no striking an opponent when he was down, no kicking, in fact no weapon but the manly fist. Through the Old School we learned to admire guts, integrity, tradition; we derided the glutton, the American and the French. We looked with contempt upon the sneak and the thief. Greyfriars gave us one moral code, life another, and a fine muddle we made of it all. I knew boys so avid for current numbers of the *Magnet* and *Gem* that they would trek on a weekday to the city railway station to catch the bulk arrival from London and buy first copies from the bookstall. One lad among us adopted a permanent jerky gait, this in his attempt to imitate Bob Cherry's 'springy, athletic stride'. Self-consciously we incorporated weird slang into our own oath-sprinkled banter—'Yarooh!' 'My sainted aunt!' 'Leggo!' and a dozen others. The Famous Five stood for us as young knights, *sans peur et sans reproche.* Any idea that Harry Wharton could possibly have been guilty of 'certain practices' would have filled us with shame. He, like the rest, remained completely asexual, unsullied by those earthy cares of adolescence that troubled us. And that was how we wanted it.

With nothing in our own school that called for love or allegiance, Greyfriars became for some of us our true Alma

Mater, to whom we felt bound by a dreamlike loyalty. The 'mouldering pile', one came to believe, had real existence: of that boys assured one another. We placed it vaguely in the southern counties—somewhere between Winchester and Harrow. It came as a curious shock to one who revered the Old School when it dawned upon him that he himself was a typical sample of the 'low cads' so despised by all at Greyfriars. Class consciousness had broken through at last. Over the years these simple tales conditioned the thought of a whole generation of boys. The public school ethos, distorted into myth and sold among us weekly in penny numbers, for good or ill, set ideals and standards. This our own tutors, religious and secular, had signally failed to do. In the final estimate it may well be found that Frank Richards during the first quarter of the twentieth century had more influence on the mind and outlook of young working-class England than any other single person, not excluding Baden-Powell.[4]

Older teenagers went on reading the *Magnet*, the *Gem*, the *Boys' Friend*, 'Nelson Lee—the schoolmaster detective' and 'Sexton Blake' in the *Union Jack*, but other periodicals more adult in content could be brought to the street corner clubs for appraisal and exchange, among them *Tit Bits*, *Ideas*, *Pearson's Weekly*, *Answers* and the *Police News* with its crude illustrations, but there was little pornography; and this only because we couldn't

---

[4] With a uniform that cost 15*s*, the Scout movement was far beyond the means of most lower-working-class lads; not one in our district, to my knowledge, ever became a member. Once, however, with an older friend, Sydney, and unbeknown to parents, I did try an obscure troop across the town where uniform was not *de rigeur*. Here we soon noted that the leader, a manly type, seemed over fond of looking one straight in the eye and, hand on shoulder, giving what he called 'health chats'. 'We don't go to no camps!' said Syd briefly. One night in autumn our leader did not appear. A curate, taking over, explained he had gone away for a year. 'He's gone for twelve months!' said Sydney. 'Let's join the Lads' Brigade!' But Father wouldn't hear of a bugler in the house.

Many boys in our district sported for a time the pillbox of the Church Lads' Brigade. This movement, at the time paramilitary in intent, had its greatest strength in the Manchester region. Its attraction for boys lay in a very cheap, sketchy uniform and the pleasure of marching through Sunday morning streets (cursed by late sleepers) to the sound of bugle and drum. But our local ranks were continually thinned by the rector's insistence on members' weekly attendance at classes for Bible reading and drill.

get it. In the criticism and arguments which followed, the young, the backward and the unlettered would pick up some new words and concepts. One of the more articulate members might tell a story or amuse with puns, riddles or other word play; two would sing in harmony, an accomplishment much admired; another give a solo or perform tricks with string and matches. A happy air of concord hung over all. And in the heart of the group itself, shielded by lounging bodies, a small card school would sit contentedly gambling for halfpence. Suddenly one hears a shriek of warning. The gang bursts into a scatter of flying figures. From nowhere gallop a couple of 'rozzers', cuffing, hacking, punching, sweeping youngsters into the wall with a swing of heavy folded capes. The street empties, doors bang. Breathing heavily the Law retires, bearing off perhaps a 'hooligan' or two to be made an example of. The club is over for another night, leaving its young members with a fear and hatred of the police that in some perfectly law-abiding citizens lasted through life and helped colour the attitude of a whole working-class generation towards civil authority.

There are historians who write as if Northcliffe and George Newnes with their newspapers and weekly periodicals were responsible, if not for the spread of literacy, at least for exploiting it for the first time. Well before 1890, however, Sunday newspapers and the local evening and weekly gazettes had familiarised the manual worker with written English, though Northcliffe and Newnes certainly went on to simplify the style. Except in periods of national crisis or celebration, industrial labourers, though Tory, royalist and patriotic, remained generally uninterested in any event beyond the local, horse racing excepted. A national morning newspaper had little appeal. Some workers hardly ever went into their own city, and London was a place where royalty lived, that and little more. Having no official connection with national government beyond an occasional election, they did not feel the State as a reality at all. A mid-day racing sheet catered for our punters, and the two evening papers, like the weekly gazette in normal times, dealt almost entirely with city and district affairs. For years after its appearance in 1896 the *Daily Mail* sold its sensational snippets to the lower middle class, shopkeepers and the growing army of city clerks, as did *Tit Bits* and the rest, though rapidly during the first decade of the new century they

began to be taken up by the skilled working class. Many households, however, did not buy a morning paper until after the first
world war. *Tit Bits, Answers*,[5] *Ideas* and similar weeklies were
quick to sense that millions of ordinary people had acquired little
more than the basic reading skills, and before the *Daily Mail*
they dispensed with the polysyllables and solid columns of print
found in staider periodicals and presented information in a short,
easily assimilated form. They found the right formula, too, offering just those innumerable bits of inconsequential fact that simple
readers and the newly literate love. Their vast increases in circulation, however, did not come through literary content: they were
based on the introduction of spectacular competitions which
offered readers dazzling cash prizes or pensions for life.

Betting on horses was about the only way, other than theft, that
the worker knew of to get money without earning it. Racing held
the rabid interest of millions. It bound the labourer with a cap-
touching loyalty to the aristocrat. There were those who would
back only King Edward's, Lord Derby's or Lord Rosebery's
horses. Winning, they felt for a brief moment a glow of unity
with the greatest in the land. There was a flood of cheap print
devoted entirely to racing form and tipsters' views and forecasts.
I had an uncle who spent most of his leisure sprawled on a sofa
with the handicap book. An intelligent man, untaught in other
ways of using his natural skill, he lived like countless others of
the time for petty gambling. Yet the sport of kings drew many
along the road to literacy. When the ability to read offered a
chance of sudden wealth through the mere deciphering of
'Captain Cole's Special Selection', with some the need for basic
education grew urgent. Many a man made the breakthrough to
literacy by studying the pages of the *One o'Clock*. Many a child,
too, would spell out the list of 'Today's Starters and Jockeys' for
unlettered elders, make out their betting slips and so improve
both in handwriting and in vocabulary. Altogether, for the
Edwardian lower orders, not widely interested as yet in other
sport, life without racing would have been stale and flat.

The bookmakers in our district, as in others, usually did
business standing on a chair behind a locked back-yard door.
One handed up the betting slip while he, later in the day, handed

[5] *Answers*, a penny periodical founded in 1888, in less than five years had
a weekly sale of more than a million copies.

down any winnings. At the catwalk end his 'dogger-out' stood watch. This system facilitated the bookie's quick getaway in the event of a police raid. By gentleman's agreement the dogger-out allowed himself to be taken and fined at regular intervals. Old bookmakers, talking of the time, state categorically that they had to bribe the police frequently to stay in business at all.

That small paved area behind each house, the back-yard, had an important role generally in family activities. It held, of course, the water closet, the only place where a member of the household could be assured of a few minutes' privacy—a boon in an over-crowded kitchen. With some boys, however, even this privilege was not allowed: there were parents with a phobia about mastur-bation who insisted that young sons should use the privy only with the door wide open. The yard itself had many uses: it acted as a boudoir for mother and a haven for younger children fearful of rough street life. Father cobbled and mended there, kept a rabbit or two, pigeons (common indeed) or a few hens. Someone was always whitewashing walls, and folk strolled chatting in and out, all in the spirit of good neighbourliness. Some families, how-ever, scoured and brown-stoned their flags, close-bolted the door and held their yard as a piece, almost, of holy ground. Such neighbours were often those who, over a lifetime, permitted no one, adult or child, other than the family to cross their threshold. Near relatives might pay a visit, almost secretly, but everyone else was kept firmly on the other side of the doorstep. 'Folk only want to see what we've got!' said one sour exponent of the practice in the shop. 'We keep 'em all out!' But neighbours knew well enough the number of her total possessions: like theirs, they could all have been pushed away on one hand-cart. What the woman demonstrated in fact was a show of exclusiveness which, she hoped, would give her family an added social standing.

Comic papers in the years before the 1914–18 war had firmly established themselves among the sub-literate, their drawings appealing naturally to those who had little or no reading ability. But the literate adult usually stamped all 'comics' as infantile and quite unworthy of his attention. I still recollect the superior smiles of a group of customers in the shop when a child, daughter of illiterate parents, spoke of her next errand for 'Father's weekly papers—*Chips, Comic Cuts, Merry & Bright* and *Lot o' Fun*'. Yet such material must have played an important part in keeping

K

the printed word at its simplest before the lowest social groups.

Nearly all levels of the working class took Sunday newspapers. Their combined sales until as late as 1947 remained greater than the total circulation of the morning dailies. The 'Sunday' was of far greater social and literary importance than any other newsprint or periodical. (Many newly literate men whom I had taught in prison told me that the heaviest penalty of ignorance had been their previous inability to read the *News of the World*.) Traditionally, many households invested in a copy of *Old Moore's Almanack*; since the eighteenth century the almanack had been a popular means of disseminating knowledge, but beyond this they took in no printed matter save the Sunday newspaper. In the houses of innumerable members of the lower working class one would not find a book of any sort. Indeed, I have heard men say that after leaving school they never opened a book again. Very many among the middle-aged and elderly, continuing a veto of their own parents, forbade all books and periodicals on the grounds that they kept women and children from their proper tasks and developed lazy habits. As far as children were concerned, our local council seems to have concurred in this: from the opening of public libraries half a century earlier until 1906, no one under fourteen years of age was allowed membership. Rules were finally modified to permit children of ten or upwards to take out one book a fortnight. In the trickle of young borrowers that followed, boys outnumbered girls by more than two to one.

One branch library lay well beyond the confines of the village up two flights of stone steps. Its stock of about five hundred volumes—'Fiction; Literature; Science; Art; Music'—stood bound in black beyond a broad high counter, save for a display in two glass 'turrets', one at each end of the bastion. Borrowers pointed through the window at the volume required.

From 1900 the number of people using the borough's eight local libraries had been growing slowly. Even so, for the whole of 1914 only 9,800 adults had borrowed books out of a population of more than 200,000. This, the librarian noted with satisfaction, was an increase of 2,000 over the previous year. It was necessary to admit, though, that the populace had had little time either for the arts or for science: in twelve months only 47,000 'non-fictional book issues' had been made. The new literates, it seemed, had far to go yet. It was perhaps in public libraries that officialdom first dropped that hauteur which until the first world war it had generally reserved for contact with the manual worker: library assistants were usually as courteous and helpful to borrowers of every sort as they are today. But even there children often got short shrift. Borrowing was restricted to two days a week. One hadn't to be too long peering into the bookcase and those who dared to ask for a volume by title were often fobbed off with 'If it's not on show it's not in the library!' 'Much of our stock', the chief librarian complained, 'is long out of date.' To the mass, however, book reading of any kind remained an irrelevancy. Most men struggling for a living knew well enough that for them literacy bought no bread.

Our district voted solidly Conservative except for once in the famous election of 1906, when a fear that the Tories' tariff reform policy might increase the price of food alarmed the humble voter. A Conservative victory, it was widely bruited, would mean the 'little loaf', a Liberal win, the 'big loaf'. These were politics the poor could understand! They threw out the local brewer, their long-standing representative, in favour of a Liberal. Men like my father, who revered Lloyd George, free-trade-minded shop-keepers and the few artisans around were delighted—until the next election! The overwhelming majority of unskilled workers remained politically illiterate still. The less they had to conserve the more conservative in spirit they showed themselves. Wages paid and hours worked might spark off discussion at the pub and street corner, but such things were often talked of like the seasons —as if no one could expect to have any influence on their vagaries. Many were genuinely grateful to an employer for being kind enough to use their services at all. Voting Conservative, they felt at one with him. It was their belief, widely expressed at election times, that the middle and upper classes with their better intelligence and education had a natural right to think and act on behalf of the rest, a right that one should not even question. In Bristol as late as 1909 there were only eight labour representatives on a council of ninety-two. In all, then, before 1914 it is true to say that a poor man knew his place: he wanted that place recognised, however humble, and he required others to keep theirs. To command his class respect, it needed to be shown by means of money, mien, goods or connections that one belonged to a higher social level. Then, and only then, as a free-standing

Englishman, would he doff his cap. Apathy, docility, deference: our village as a whole displayed just those qualities which, sixty years before, Karl Marx had noted, stamped the poor industrial workers—qualities which convinced him that the English proletarian would never revolt of his own accord.

A culture of the streets existed from which the young especially profited: one soaked in information of every kind from posters and advertisements pasted on gable end and massive hoarding. But above all young intelligence learned from a regular scrutiny of newsagents' windows. The picture postcard boom developed more slowly in Britain than on the Continent owing to a General Post Office monopoly on postcards, not abolished until 1894. By the early 1900's German manufacturers had begun to swamp the country with cards in innumerable variety. English traders soon realised that a new craze had arrived. Newsagents' shops became festooned with cards scenic, cards comic, cards topical, but above all with photographs of famous Edwardian actresses looking soulful under rose-covered studio trellises. For this exercise they were paid large sums. Clubs sprang up in every town and people collected and exchanged specimens. A family album filled with a varied selection was not the least item of entertainment in an evening spent at home. To a child avid for experience a newsagent's shop with a good display provided pleasure free and delightful. The picture postcard became a new aid to self-education as effective as any of his school lessons. Every great event of the day was reflected in illustration and explained in simple text. Through cards I remember the loss of the *Titanic* with awful vividness. Coloured photographs of Marie Studholme and later the young Gladys Cooper fixed the child's conception of womanly beauty. The scraps of lush verse that often went with them seemed to one far more 'poetic' than the stuff learned by rote at school. Again, the comic card with its bulging females, leering men and sly caption might suddenly provide the solution to some problem of sex relationship long troubling the young mind, or merely open up avenues for more puzzled surmise.

'Programmed' learning and visual aid, too, came to the child in the shape of cigarette card series. The value of the 'fag' card, from 1900 onwards, as a conveyor of up-to-date information was enormous. First used in plain board to stiffen the paper packet holding cigarettes, it developed into offering a panorama of the world at large. The Ogden tobacco company alone, with its 'Guinea Gold' brand, issued no fewer than eight thousand different pictures, from nature series of all kinds through patriotic sets to 'Statues and Monuments'. In the end all the great tobacco companies took up the gimmick and no field of popular human knowledge seems to have been left unexplored. Before 1914 it would have been hard indeed to have found a boy in the working class without at least a few dog-eared cards about his person, dreaming of making up, by swap and gambling games, that complete set of fifty.

If mother or aunts were readers a child would be sent to the newspaper shop on Sunday evenings after tea to buy copies of *Home Notes* or *Home Chat*, two thin little weeklies containing tales about governesses or the more ladylike servants of the upper classes. Absorbing the stories himself later (one read all print irrespective of its interest), he would widen his knowledge of a world which had no point of contact with his own. Some weekly magazines did produce fiction that had a proletarian background but a class motif almost always ran through the plot. The heroine, who remained chaste throughout, usually worked in a pickle or jam factory, where she was pursued by the owner's sons, called Rupert or Sir Gerald. In the end she married the foreman or a decent skilled mechanic, but never failed to take a clearly defined step up the social scale.

Many houses contained a library made up entirely of books the children had received for regular attendance at Sunday schools. Although sent under durance, most youngsters did not at all mind going to such places: discipline was slack there and the teaching, often by incredibly poor amateurs, made little call upon the attention. By 1900 the great drive which the Sunday school movement had made against mass illiteracy the country over had long ceased and instruction had become purely religious. For adults attendance at church and chapel still gave some cultural returns but in the cities few working-class Protestants went. About one fifth of the inhabitants of our village were Roman Catholic, and nearly all came from the lower ranks of the community: their going to church had no social value among us whatsoever. While one saw little open hostility, except among schoolchildren, religious prejudice was deeply ingrained. Protestants held a series of beliefs about the 'Micks' which for the most part precluded any genuine friendship between them. People assured one another in the shop, I remember, that nearly all Roman Catholics were dirty and ignorant and even the cleaner ones could never be trusted. When a member of that faith new to the district came in to buy, customers in the shop would nod and mouth at one another—'Catholic!' It was widely held that they went in dread of the priesthood, who had beaten obedience into them in childhood and who now exploited their fear of death and mulcted them for the Church, no matter how deep their poverty. Neighbours watched a priest's passing along the pavement with a cold eye and left his 'good day' unanswered. Working-class Roman Catholics, it was said loudly in pub and workshop, were forbidden by the Pope to discuss their faith or even touch a Bible; yet we suspected them all the time of seeking to make converts. Of all the sects Catholicism was undoubtedly the one most criticised and disliked.

One 'papist' family, I remember, set the district a pretty prob-lem in social assessment. The mother had been a teacher and a headmistress to boot. This should have placed her way above anyone else. Unfortunately she had been head of a Catholic school. Moreover, her husband, once a drunkard, was now a permanent invalid. They lived in considerable poverty. All this called for realistic evaluation. The woman spoke in an educated way (good) but with a brogue (bad). She kept her house clean and her two daughters from any contact with the other girls in the neighbourhood (very good), but they could not prevent the younger son from consorting with all the rapscallions of the village (very bad). In due time the girls became shorthand typists and went to 'business' in hat, coat and shoes (excellent, since their contemporaries were mill girls in clogs and shawls) and out of all assessment when one became the wife of a solicitor (Catholic, true, but still a solicitor). Balance was restored, however, after the son married into a labouring family, Irish Catholic, from a 'low' street. The old lady herself, ignorant of all the social anomalies her family had caused, or indifferent anyway, went on treating everyone with the same simple courtesy and goodwill. The whole affair puzzled our class fixers, who never quite succeeded in slotting Mrs O'T. and her family into any agreed social niche.

The Jews, twenty thousand strong, dwelt in an area adjacent to ours on the north side, some in a poverty so appalling that it shocked even us. Our own poor grew hostile. They sensed the menace of a horde of hungry foreigners seeking to share in charities which, they felt, as true-born Britons belonged to them alone. Odd Jews who strayed into the village were driven out at once. Very early in the century one did venture to set up a small second-hand clothing store. Ignored by the police, thugs arrived, carried his stock into the road and set fire to it. From then on we were saved from further contamination. In 1905 a new 'Aliens Immigration Act' barred the entry of the destitute altogether. No more 'Sheenies' came our way save one. Our elders tolerated a tall, bearded glazier who padded along the pavements clutching glass in a wooden frame and called diffidently, 'Vinders!' The young trailed behind, jeering, and mocking him with that same awful question howled down the centuries by anti-semites. Once, when he carried it on his back, the boys threw stones and broke his glass. Grown-ups lolled, amused, in doorways. (At police courts and elsewhere 'Sheenies' were always 'comic'.)

'You don't shout after the glazier, do you?' my mother asked us sternly.

'Never!' we lied.

Once a winter, on sight of him, she would break a small scullery window with the end of a scrubbing brush (it cost ninepence to repair) because she hated to 'offer charity'. 'Go and tell the gentleman,' she would say, 'there's a job for him.'

'Gentleman?'—the word seemed ill-chosen. He came to the back kitchen one afternoon out of a wind full of frozen sleet, wearing broken shoes and a frock-coat past his knees. He stood, big-eyed, beard frozen, and looked embarrassed. I watched too curiously till a nod from my mother sent me from the room. But going no further than the small ventilator outside, I climbed a box to peep in on what was now an odd sight. The Jew still stood gripping glass and wooden frame to his side, and my mother, close to him, was trying to remove that which, somehow, he seemed unwilling to give up. At last I understood: after hours of his wandering in the cold, cramp had locked one arm rigid to the body. She loosened his frock-coat. It swung open. The man was naked from the waist up. Then my mother did a shocking thing—she placed a hand in the folds of the garment and, standing very close now, began to rub life into his body and arm. Soon he relaxed and gently they removed the frame and the coat. I gazed, then stepped down—frightened at his emaciation. The tap ran. She was drawing hot water—bringing heat to his rod-like arm. Later when I looked again the window had been mended. They were standing drinking tea from cups without saucers. The Jew offered her food from a newspaper. And she took and ate it! They talked smiling together like friends. I turned away disgusted. She seemed sullied.

In the evening my mother looked up at me, cool and un-repentant from the sewing machine. 'The gentleman left a ball of putty,' she said. 'He thought you might like to do some modelling.'

'Don't want it,' I grunted.

'You take it,' she told me a little grimly, 'and let me have no nonsense!' But in the way of mothers, then, to eight-year-old sons, she didn't deign to make any explanation. From that time on whenever the glazier was in the district he called upon her and they chatted over the shop counter, but with the war he came no more.

In the decade before 1914 whilst organised religion still kept a hold on some from the upper working class (the undermass had defected generations before) a drift towards secularism was already well on the way, though backsliders salved their conscience by strict insistence on their children's attending Sunday school.[6] Very few people would, in fact, admit to not being Christians: one merely 'disliked' the church, the parson or the congregation. In pub and workshop outright atheists were looked upon as tempters of Providence, very odd fish indeed. The *Freethinker* was banned from the public library. Every denomination had of course its own social cachet; each knew its position, with the Church of England out in front and the Primitive Methodists bringing up the rear. Roman Catholics didn't count. Around 1912 there was much sad fluttering in our local chapel when its leading (and richest) member, a grocer, felt a call to join the established Church, and much surprise, too, that after fifty years of loyalty he could so easily abandon the principle of dissent. Yet shrewder observers knew only too well that its late superintendent had merely conformed to a practice common for generations

---

[6] Half a century earlier St Paul's Sunday School, in Bennett Street, Manchester, had a regular attendance of 2,600 scholars—'the largest in the county'. But everywhere, now, those palmy days were over.

among the newly opulent; money followed money out of chapel
into church.

In the Church of England the social barrier that existed between 'possessors' and poor mirrored itself in the Sunday school,
where a plain division showed between those children who
wore their 'best' and those who attended in weekday clothes.
Fortunately all who came to the Ragged schools in whatever
condition were made welcome. Everywhere Sunday clothes stood
as a powerful emblem of status. Roman Catholic mothers who
were to be seen in clogs and shawls with their ill-clad children
going to Mass on Sunday morning were thought by this only
to emphasise their known low breeding.

The 'riff-raff' had naturally no clothes complex and, given
social weather, not too freezing, some would attend free concert,
lantern lecture or treat given by any denomination, with broad-
minded eclecticism. Such contacts, though, appeared to have little
effect upon conduct, and cultural gains seemed slight. Children
and adolescents by regular attendance at some place of worship
could acquire a series of illustrated text cards, negotiable in lots
of fifty for a 'good' book, the same trick that got Thomas Sawyer
a Bible being common practice. *Uncle Tom's Cabin, The Old
Curiosity Shop, Black Beauty, Heroes of the United Services* and
A Basket of Flowers were among the most popular prizes. Many
of our sub-literates treasured these books, but, I discovered,
seldom read them. They stood on the chiffonier as ornaments
and were not looked upon as objects to be handled. Children
were forbidden even to touch them. Our local chapels appeared
to take no great interest in music, the same dozen or so hymns
being served up year after year to each succeeding generation
of attenders, but at least songs sacred helped to eke out the self-
entertainers' scanty repertoire when they amused themselves, as
they often did, by harmonising together in the home. Compulsive
singers of a single hymn tune were known in shop and factory
and heartily damned.

All in all, however, it seemed that by the early years of the
twentieth century churches and chapels had little to offer that
would attract much longer those from the lower multitudes who
still stayed loyal. The class structure of English society remained
as intact as ever, but the moral authority of religious establishment, though still not openly questioned, was at least being

quietly ignored by more and more members of the manual working class. Those diversions aimed at the weaker vessels to temper the rigours of religion—Pleasant Sunday Afternoons, Bright Hours, Band of Hope concerts—were growing stale. Faced with the music hall in its hey-day, they seemed to represent all that was feeblest in entertainment. More and more pews stood empty: people stayed at home. But not for long!

Cinema in the early years of the century burst like a vision into the underman's existence and, rapidly displacing both concert and theatre, became both his chief source of enjoyment and one of the greatest factors in his cultural development. For us in the village the world suddenly expanded. Many women who had lived in a kind of purdah since marriage (few respectable wives visited public houses) were to be noted now, escorted by their husbands, *en route* for the 'pictures', a strange sight indeed and one that led to much comment at the shop. Street corner gossip groups for a time grew thin and publicans complained angrily that the new fad was ruining trade: men were going to the films and merely calling in at the tavern for an hour before closing time. The disloyalty of it! Children begged, laboured and even thieved for the odd copper that would give them two hours of magic, crushed on a bench before the enchanting screen.[7]

Moralists were not long in condemning cinema as the tap-root of every kind of delinquency. Cinema owners protested virtue: one kept an eight-foot-long poster across his box office: 'CLEAN AND MORAL PICTURES. Prices—2*d*. and 4*d*.' In our district the Primitive Methodist chapel, recently bankrupt and closed, blossomed almost overnight into the 'Kinema'. There during the first weeks would-be patrons of its twopenny seats literally fought each night for entrance and tales of crushed ribs and at least two broken limbs shocked the neighbourhood. In the beginning cinema managers, following the social custom of the theatre, made the error of grading seats, with the most expensive near the screen and the cheapest at the back of the house. For a short time the rabble lolled in comfort along the rear rows while their betters, paying three times as much, suffered cricked necks and eye strain in front. Caste and culture forbade mixing. A sudden

---

[7] In 1912 the governor of Durham gaol was struck by the number of boys in prison who confessed to stealing in order to get money to go to picture palaces.

change-over one evening, without warning, at all the local cinemas caused much bitterness and class recrimination. By 1913 our borough still retained its four theatres, but already thirteen premises had been licensed under the Cinematograph Act.

Yet silent films for all their joys presented the unlettered with a problem unknown in theatres—the printed word. Often in the early days of cinema, captions broke into the picture with explanations long, sententious and stage-ridden. To bypass this difficulty the short-sighted and illiterate would take children along to act as readers. In this capacity I saw my own first film. When picture gave place to print on the screen a muddled Greek chorus of children's voices rose from the benches, piping above the piano music. To hear them crash in unison on a polysyllable became for literate elders an entertainment in itself. At the cinema many an ill-educated adult received cheap and regular instruction with his pleasure, and some eventually picked up enough to dispense with their tutors. Yet in spite of all the aids to culture and learning, unknown fifty years before—compulsory education, free libraries, the spate of cheap print, the miles of postered hoarding, and then cinema, the brightest lure of all—among the lower working class a mass of illiterates, solid and sizeable, still remained.

Before 1914 the proletariat contained, far more than it does today, many men and women of personality, character and high intelligence, who were chained socially and economically within their own society. Such people in a more equitable system would, of course, have found a place far more fitted to their abilities: but only a very few, aided by luck and determination, succeeded in breaking through their environment. The vast majority, half conscious often of talents wasted, felt a frustration they could hardly have explained. These were not Richard Hoggart's 'scholars'[8] of the '20's and '30's, or the odd queer customer seeking to get on by attending trade classes at night school; they were an integral part of the working community. They talked more, read more and possessed a much larger vocabulary than their neighbours in general. True, many of their words, having been picked up from print only, were mispronounced; but such error was a sign of intelligence struggling for self-expression. They showed impatience with the many stale saws and clichés that peppered working-class talk: 'witticisms' out of the 'oral tradition'

[8] *The Uses of Literacy.*

as Hoggart admiringly calls it. These expressions, in fact, brilliant at birth, had been worn to vacuity through over-use and met condign ridicule from the more intelligent. A natural leadership within the community gave pith and purpose to tavern talk, trade union branch meeting and factory dinner-hour break. Especially during this free time at work did skilled men in discussion benefit from the only 'adult education' that came their way. The Great Debate concerned itself for the most part with the need for economic betterment through trade union action, a debate that began to take on bitter urgency in the four years previous to 1914. In spite of propaganda, the growing strength of the Labour Party, the splendid idealism of the Clarion movement, the million copies of *Merrie England* sold, socialism continued to make little appeal to the lower working class. Its adherents were dubbed 'agitators' or 'red rags'. *The Times'* labour correspondent, always deeply sympathetic to the aspirations of the workers so long as they did nothing to realise them, felt that the common man was much too sensible to be taken in by socialism. Yet though the 'agitators' met with small political success, their influence in the industrial field grew steadily. Typical, I remember, was the admiration for these proselytisers felt by one of my elderly workmates, member of the ILP himself, who spoke of a 'couple of ordinary brass-finishers—around 1907. They had sense enough on the job', he said, 'to keep mum about their Marxist views. In six months, after getting work at —— [naming an engineering shop] they persuaded forty-three men in ones and twos to join the "Brassfounders and Finishers" —before they got sacked!' Only to start, no doubt, the Great Debate elsewhere. From such men, and women too, came the cream of working-class society. In factory and workshop they were very often the most skilful and knowledgeable hands, doing work to the highest standards, not to suit an employer but to satisfy their own integrity. They wanted nothing but what was earned: that they demanded and would fight for. Active in their 'society' or 'trades club', as the union was commonly called, members of choirs, cycling and walking groups, socialist Sunday schools or Methodist chapels, readers of Ruskin, Dickens, Kingsley, Carlyle and Scott, teetotallers often, straitlaced, idealistic, naïve, they troubled and disturbed the Liberal voting artisan, made him feel that his preoccupation with mere party issues of the day was pitifully inadequate when a whole new society waited to be born. Obscure men enough then, forgotten now, innocent perhaps in their hopes, they fought not only for self- or sectional interest but for the betterment, as they saw it, of a whole community. Many a young factory worker and apprentice who later went into politics to help change the social structure of Britain had cause to be grateful for their teaching and example, and so today has the whole working class.

Yet it must be remembered that these pioneers with their egalitarian dreams formed only a very small part of the working-class intelligentsia. The Liberal-voting skilled worker, his demigod Lloyd George, easily maintained ascendancy as the purveyor of progressive ideas, ideas in which there was, in fact, little place for true equality with those beneath him. Until 1914 the members of this élite generally, as far as class values were concerned, stayed almost as conformist and establishment-minded as their Tory counterparts. Together they stood, the great bulwark against revolution of any kind.

The lower working class, Victorian in spirit still, long after the rest of the workers had moved into the twentieth century, clung to the jingoism of its fathers. The *Daily Mail*, established in 1896, had from the beginning adopted a grossly chauvinistic policy, whipping up hatred first against France, giving frenzied backing to Kitchener's Omdurman adventures and then, a year later, supporting the London imperialistic mobs in their clamour for war against the Boers. With the South African hostilities hardly over, it began a belligerent campaign against the Germans which lasted with a few intervals until the outbreak of the first world war. Many of the nationalistic ideas plugged in the *Daily Mail* and similar newspapers filtered into lower-working-class minds, already imbued with the imperialistic teachings of school days, and found enthusiastic welcome there.

For nearly half a century before 1914 the newly literate millions were provided with an increasing flow of fiction based on war and the idea of its imminence. 'The constant fact behind the development of these imaginary wars', writes I. F. Clarke,[9] 'was the customary consideration of war as normal and romantic.' Popular fiction and mass journalism now combined to condition the minds of the nation's new readers to a degree never possible

[9] *Voices Prophesying War.*

before the advent of general literacy. In France and Germany, too, writings in the same genre were equally successful in stimulating romantic conceptions about the carnage to come. When the final cataclysm did arrive, response to such ideas set the masses cheering wildly through the capitals of Europe. Der Tag!—The Day—was here at last! they could hardly wait!

Most people at the time felt that no war between nations could last for long, a view backed by expert opinion. The French General Bonnal stated, 'It will be decided in less than a month after the opening of hostilities.' His confrère, Commandant Mordacq, thought it would last 'about a year'. Up to 1904 the English fiction writers on warfare had always cast France as the enemy, but after the *entente cordiale* they turned their pens as one against Germany. In return German authors poured out stories about the defeat and conquest of England. *The Riddle of the Sands* (1903), Erskine Childers' tale of a Teutonic plan to invade Britain, ran to several hundred thousand copies in the cheap edition. Guy du Maurier's melodrama *An Englishman's Home* (1909), again about German invasion, played to packed houses in London and stirred audiences so deeply that an office was opened in the theatre to recruit men for the Territorial Army. In 1913 Saki, with his story 'When William came', uttered still another 'warning'. From lesser-known authors came a flood of fiction, all pursuing the same obsession. Many wrote, not primarily to entertain, but to force the government to increase the strength of the army and navy. Admirals and generals did not scruple to lend their names to such endeavours.

The arch-propagandist was William Le Queux. Notorious already from 1899 for his story against the French, *England's Peril*, he had, by 1906, in line with government policy, made peace with Gaul and turned his oracular powers against the Teutons. His story *The Invasion of 1910*, first serialised in the *Daily Mail*, then published in book form (it sold over one million copies), made a profound impression on the ordinary public in Great Britain and did much to consolidate the belief that a war against Germany must and should take place. Omitting the introduction by Field Marshal Earl Roberts, the Germans paid Le Queux the compliment of translating his book; but the end, of course, was changed to give their nation victory. It was then distributed widely among a people already conditioned into arrogant consciousness of their military might and played its part in making war inevitable.

Spy stories abounded. Germans who came here to 'work', we were assured, could be spotted by a special button worn in the lapel. Each man had, we believed, sworn to serve Germany as a secret agent. With this, and innumerable myths of the same sort, the seeds of suspicion and hatred were sown, not only in Great Britain but all over Europe.

'During the ten years before the first world war', says I. F. Clarke in his excellent book, 'the growing antagonism between Britain and Germany was responsible for the largest and most sustained development of the most alarmist and aggressive stories of future warfare ever seen at any time in European history.' Conversely it should be said that all these stories acted, not only as an effect, but as one of the basic causes of that mutual antagonism.

Our district, like all industrial ghettoes, showed itself immensely patriotic, and that in the late-nineteenth-century manner, since we remained ignorant still of the shock that the Boer war had given the more thoughtful of the middle classes in Great Britain. Nationalistic ditties learnt in school and music hall were widely popular. 'In the fight for England's glory, lads,' we chorused, 'of its world-wide glory let us sing! And when they say we've always won, and when they ask us how it's done, we proudly point to every one of England's soldiers of the King!' That, and scores of similar songs lauded the makers and defenders of the empire. Yet, strangely enough, neither victory nor national pride could alter the common soldier's social status one iota. With us, as with the rest of the working class, 'regulars', ex-regulars and their families stayed unquestionably 'low'. One eldest son, I remember, who after a row at home walked out and joined the Fusiliers was considered by his father (a joiner) to have brought 'shame and disgrace on all the family'. Yet the same parent, stolid Conservative like the ex-soldiers he despised, drank himself into insensibility to celebrate the accession of George V.

The two coronations before 1914 each gave occasion among us for a wild and drunken display of fealty. Several neighbours lime-washed the fronts of their houses in royal blue. To honour Edward VII's crowning the local coal dealer's mother (having died of heart failure putting up decorations) was buried in a red,

white and blue shroud. In all high days and holiday times, coronation days stood supreme.

Not all the gaiety and excitement, however, can be said to have
been a reflection solely of loyal sentiment. Earlier in the century
every national holiday gave a feeling of release. One felt the
coming together of a whole country for a day of contentment
and freedom. Easter, Whit week, August bank holiday, Yuletide,
New Year's Eve and the following day, each had its peculiar
aura to be savoured and enjoyed. Now almost all, with the
exception of Christmas, are banished, with a consequent loss in
human bond.

Many members of the working class, following a habit of their
nineteenth-century parents, had an obsessional interest in the life
and pedigree of the royal family and aristocracy and took joy
in retailing snippets to any who would listen. Others gained
prestige through claiming special knowledge of King Edward's
private life and loves. One old lady in our neighbourhood had
been a kitchen maid in the great Yorkshire house from which,
she alleged, the King, as Prince of Wales, had been expelled for
cheating at baccarat. Her graphic account of the affair on Saturday
evenings in the 'snug' of the 'Craven Heifer' kept listeners en-
thralled and the narrator in milk stout for many a year. There
were others who hinted darkly at knowing the physical reason
which compelled Queen Alexandra always to wear a broad band
of pearls around her neck. When drunk enough they would
crudely reveal the 'secret' to hearers who might have been shocked
had they not heard the legend countless times before. Similar
wearisome stories, true or fanciful, about court and society were
retailed *ad nauseam* until, among the young, the tellers and the
tales became subjects for secret ridicule.

In home, street group, pub and trades club people, using a much
smaller vocabulary, conversed more in groups than they do today.
Opinion in this narrow, integrated society still continued to be
created and moulded far more by word of mouth than by any
other medium. Here was the true oral tradition. The top-class
natural leaders of the workers—the good, intelligent talkers—
acted above all else as assessors, arbiters and makers of the
common conscience, most, although having abandoned church
and chapel, still espousing a Christian ethic. The pressure of
their beliefs, prejudices and errors seeped slowly through the

social layers of working-class life and conditioned the minds of all. Though a man might fear the law he feared too the disapproval of his neighbours and especially the condemnation of those who through articulateness, intelligence, economic and social standing acted as moral exemplars within the community. It is, perhaps, the almost complete disappearance of this élite from the manual working class of the present day that has caused such a shift in conduct and morals.

Yet in pre-1914 Britain the industrial undermass, though harshly punished for individual crime, could at times transgress in the mob with impunity. On abnormal occasions, with sanctions temporarily in abeyance, it was the 'no class' and the 'low class' who externalised common emotional upsurge with illegal deeds their superiors acquiesced in, but which propriety forbade them perform for themselves. The assaults on 'pro-Boers', the attacks on Jewish traders and Roman Catholics, excesses during strike riots, the sacking of small German-owned shops during the first world war, stand typical examples of what could happen when the upper working class withdrew its stern moral hand.

In all it may be said that during the first years of this century the cream of the working class still remained coldly respectable, very conscious of its position and much concerned with keeping those judged socially inferior to the levels which, it was believed, a natural order had allotted them. The upper classes, it was said, 'despised' the manual worker and the bourgeoisie 'feared' him; but it is certain that they both cherished basic beliefs about him which did much to cement their common self-assurance. At bottom, they felt, the working man was 'sensible'. Generally he knew his place and deeply respected his social superiors. He could be amusing too: his ignorance, broad talk and dropped aitches gave cause for endless fun. It had to be admitted, though, that he was rather stupid and given to discontent. If, however, one had any secret fear that the working classes might yet rise in 'unvanquishable number' it was overlain by the conviction that, put to patriotic test, they would do precisely what their masters ordered—a belief that the first world war fully bore out.

Despite poverty, discontent and social unrest, by 1913 the Labour Party was represented in Parliament by a mere thirty-eight members—four fewer than in December 1910—and most of these held their seats by leave of the Liberal voter. Whenever a

L

candidate fought as a socialist alone he found himself at the bottom of the poll, often enough with a derisory number of votes. Whatever the working man wanted, it wasn't socialism. The Liberal government, with its budget of 1909, its Old Age Pension and National Employment and Insurance Acts, had made the first tentative steps towards the principle that the community as a whole has some responsibility for its unfortunates; but well before the war its reforming zeal ran out. In our own constituency the Liberal intellectual MP had come and gone and the Tory brewer was back in the saddle, fighting, among other causes, for the right of every British working man to 'get drunk'. Things, felt our local publicans, were moving again in their natural grooves.

In spite of sporadic disorders up and down the land, the strikes and lock-outs, the syndicalist talk and 'revolutionary situations', the undermass remained stable. Ignorant, unorganised, schooled in humility, they had neither the wit nor the will to revolt. Like the working class as a whole they went on gazing up still to the ineffable reaches of the middle and upper orders and felt that there stood wealth, wisdom and an ordained capacity for command far beyond a simple man's knowing, and that leadership they would follow. It took the worst war in history to disenchant them.

Chapter 9

The Great Release

There's a good time coming
Song

The first world war cracked the form of English lower-class life and began an erosion of its socio-economic layers that has continued to this day. In our own community, well before the war was over, we began to see basic alterations in certain habits and customs. Similar changes were taking place in every industrial corner of the land. 'Things', people repeatedly told one another, 'will never be the same again.'

The fourth of August 1914 caused no great burst of patriotic fervour among us. Little groups, men and women together (unusual, this), stood talking earnestly in the shop or at the street corner, stunned a little by the enormity of events. But soon public concern yielded to private self-interest. A rush of customers to the shop gave us the first alarm—sugar,[1] flour, bread, butter, margarine, cheese, people began frantically to buy all the food they could find the money for. 'Serve no strangers!' my mother ordered after the first hour. 'Only "regulars" from now on.' At once she despatched us children in relays to join queues already formed outside Lipton's and Maypole Dairy and other multiple grocers on the high road. One day of our foraging, I remember, brought in 28 lbs of margarine and 20 lbs of sugar, which my mother promptly sold off in small lots at a penny a pound profit.

Soon we heard loud protests from people returning laden from the large shops—'stuck-up folk', they reported (the middle class), were coming from the suburbs with horse and trap, bassinettes and even go-carts, buying up sugar and flour by the half-sack. Near-riots took place: shop windows were broken and the police called in. Within two days both sugar and flour had doubled in price. And many in the upper classes showed no more patriotic

[1] Before 1914 two-thirds of the country's sugar was imported from Central Europe, hence the shortage of sweetstuffs throughout the war.

restraint than the foragers from suburbia. In Parliament Mr Runciman, President of the Board of Trade, complained that, though he had no evidence of the massive cornering of foodstuffs, there had been 'practices in many parts of the country that have led to great hardship, especially among the poorer classes, caused by the panic and greed of the better-to-do people, who have disgraced themselves by taking long queues of motor cars to stores and carrying away as many provisions as they could persuade the stores to part with'. Newspapers denounced the 'selfish rich'. But soon came the *détente*—no need to panic: there was enough food for all. And anyway, people had had it 'official' (a most impressive word)—the war would be over by Christmas.

The *Daily Mail* was heartily damned in Parliament for issuing one of the first of the many phoney 'special' editions that some newspapers, exploiting little more than rumour, put out to whip up circulation. The report in the *Daily Mail* of a great naval battle off the coast of Holland, said Mr Reginald McKenna, was 'untrue in every detail' and had no foundation whatever. On the same day the *Manchester Guardian* gave a list of eight such canards, all of which had appeared in the press as fact.

On 5 August in our village we saw Mr Bickham, a veteran of the Boer war, returning from an attempt to join up. He stopped by my mother as she hung washing across the street. 'Turned down!' he said disgustedly—'Bad teeth! They must want blokes to bite the damned Germans!'

She laughed, sympathising.

Mr Bickham went on his way. 'They'll be pulling me in, though,' he called over his shoulder, 'before this lot's done!'

By 5 August 1915 he had been lying dead three months in France.

All 'aliens'—a new word—had come forward 'eagerly', the local paper said, to register at the town hall: more than 600—Germans and Austrians. A Kurt Wurtheimer somewhere on the outskirts had been fined for keeping carrier pigeons in his back yard. There was no hatred of the Germans yet. The earliest atrocity stories appeared in the second week. Soon we had other things to alarm us: unemployment was increasing at a remarkable rate. Five hundred children usually had free dinners on the town: the number soared now to three thousand, our own school providing places for 532 of these.

'Some estate agents', the weekly press reported, 'are very agitated at the prospects of getting rents from cottage property. There are cases where the rent man is met with a pitiful "I can't give you anything today. The war has lost my master his place. I don't know how to get food, never mind money for rent." '

The editor went on to ask rent men to be 'lenient' to those they knew to be 'respectable and worthy'.

By early September prospects looked grim and the war became a mere side issue. The mayor opened a relief fund that almost immediately brought in £8,000. Unemployment leaped again, and now the local newspaper became really alarmed. Not only were the poor suffering (after all, they were used to it) but 'scores of warehouses have closed in the city and many are out of work in respectable areas. There must have been a great loss of wages and it is too horrible to contemplate the dire consequences if there is a prolongation of hostilities.'

'Shopkeepers can give no more credit. The outlook for the winter appears gloomy indeed. The need for relief grows daily. With many families it may soon be a fight for sheer existence.'

This plainly was not the martial spirit. But the editor went on: 'It cannot be too strongly impressed, that never was there a time when patriotism demanded of one and all the exercise of the most careful thrift.'

Some of the humblest by now, however, had nothing to be thrifty with.

The local drill hall was taking recruits at the rate of eighty a day. Officials stressed that many more had applied, only to be found unfit, though the standards fixed by some medical officers do not seem to have been too rigorous. The clerk to our own board of guardians reported, for instance, that 'two phthisics' had left the workhouse hospital without permission and gone to join up, and that one of them, an 'absolute consumptive, has been accepted and sent off to Winchester Barracks'.

There was no suggestion that he might be called back.

Some men after joining the forces were delighted to find that it meant a full stomach—'meat every day!' as the recruiting sergeants had truly said. 'The nation which went to war in 1914', wrote Burnett in *Plenty and Want*, 'was (still) so chronically undernourished that for millions of soldiers and civilians war-time rations represented a higher standard of feeding than they had ever known before.'

In the first few months of hostilities many local recruits returning on their first 'furlough' (leave was a later term) astonished us all. Pounds—sometimes stones—heavier, taller, confident, clean and straight, they were hardly recognisable as the men who went away. Others, seeing the transformation, hurried off to the barracks.

Some men seem to have volunteered in haste and absconded at leisure. While the front pages of our press gave long lists, parish by parish, of those who had joined up, the back columns never showed fewer than a dozen names a week of men being prosecuted for desertion: Jim Parris, for instance, a local drayman. Jim had marched away at Christmas 1914 with the RASC and marched back again in May, his ardour so wilted that he packed up his uniform at once and sent it back to headquarters. In late August, according to evidence in court, P. C. Jackson had 'apprehended the defendant down a coal hole in South Street'. 'Prisoner was detained to await escort', the constable being presented with five shillings by the court. Money prizes to the police for capturing deserters were common. Awards varied considerably; five shillings seems low, even for an RASC private, though, the class system being what it was, prize money might well have reached as much as £5 for catching, say, an absconding colonel in a coal hole.

Our first recruiting drive packed the Sunday school, and folk overflowed into the street. On the platform we had a baronet, a canon, a councillor, a reverend and the magistrates' clerk. 'Great enthusiasm prevailed.' Some attempt was made to explain the causes of the war. Again nobody denigrated the Germans. Our councillor merely said that the Kaiser was suffering from a 'hot swelled head', and that evening he wanted men to come forward 'to help cool it for him'. 'At this there was laughter in the audience.'

The baronet told us that the British army was doing splendidly, but more men were needed and he had every confidence that those present that night would do their duty. They didn't breed cowards in that part of the North. 'Cheers and applause.'

The magistrates' clerk said that there were no rich and no poor now, no Protestants and Catholics, no Conservatives and Liberals; we were all Britishers! ('Applause.')

The canon stated that every man who was able to take his position in defending the honour of his country and did not do so was a 'poltroon and a coward and not worthy of the name of Englishman'.

The reverend announced that he agreed with every word the canon had said.

That week the first general casualty list appeared in the press. Twelve thousand men had been killed, wounded, or were missing. The numbers shocked: such slaughter in so short a time. Already among us one heard of a young man 'killed in action' from this street, another missing from that. The more thoughtful in the shop looked grave. 'This is something,' they said, 'you can't see the end of.'

'We'll all have a holiday in the summer-time,' folk were singing in the street, 'but it won't be beside the sea! Left! Left! I had a good home and I left . . .' By Christmas the first horror of what the war was really like came drifting down to us from men returned. This was no holiday. Casualties had soared to more than 104,000.

By the end of the year doubts were widely expressed that the voluntary system of recruitment would ever provide Britain with enough fighting men for her needs. Earlier, authority had solemnly promised that married men would not be called upon to serve. This started a run on the registry office that vied with the rush to the colours: 1915 held the palm for the highest number taking to matrimony ever recorded in Great Britain. But all to no avail; in May 1916 the government conscripted the married too: the bottom of the voluntary barrel had been scraped. Some time before this, however, appeals of the heartier type for 'gallant lads' to come forward had grown fewer; the call now took on a stern, even a vituperative note. Thus wrote an anonymous contributor to our weekly newspaper in April 1915:

To Shirkers of National Duty
By a Candid Friend.

Gentlemen,

It is a good thing to be polite, even to a mean contemptible creature. I call you gentlemen, which, I trust, some of you may yet become. But at present there does not seem much reason for the hope and therefore it may not do you any harm to see yourselves in the mirror this letter provides.

In a time of unexampled national danger when the lives of the children, women and your fellow-countrymen are in peril, you stand aside and leave the task of defence to the married men, for nearly 75 per cent of Lord Kitchener's Army have family burdens to carry.

Granted that many of you are not able to bear arms, by reason of your culpable neglect of the laws of physical development, and there are some who through domestic circumstances can present a valid excuse for not joining the Army, there are still too many single men without serious responsibilities skulking in this supreme hour of trial.

This much, however, may be said by way of palliating your despicable conduct. Some of you have not been taught what patriotism really means. You have been brought up in schools where the national flag (until last August, at all events) was seldom, or never seen and almost tabooed. To speak of the flag, to praise what it stood for, to know it, would have been regarded by the power in authority as an insidious attempt to introduce militarism. So would physical exercises bearing even a remote likeness to military drill.

You have unfortunately in too many cases been guided and controlled—some might call it educated—by cranks and faddists and ignorant, hare-brained chatterers of the peace-at-any-price fantasy. Thus you lost one chance of learning what a vigorous manhood means. You have had drummed into your ears from infancy the alluring doctrine of 'getting on'. You have been told a thousand times what an admirable thing it is to rise above others without descending to manual labour; in short you have been encouraged to think narrowly, live selfishly and to do nothing for your neighbours and country that would not bring speedy and visible returns.

In no other country in the world would you be tolerated as you are here. You would be dragged from your holes like rats and held up to the execution [*sic*; execration?] of an outraged people with a very certain prospect of interviewing the enemy in the hottest part of the trenches.

But seeing that the dragging process has not yet begun—though I trust it will not be long delayed—we must rely upon other means. You could be told that the resources of civilization are not exhausted when we mark our reprobation of your meanness and cowardice by shunning you as creatures without honour or courage and branding you as traitors to the land of your birth, deserving not less, but more ignominy than so many German spies.

You have been appealed to for your help since this terrible struggle began, graciously, forcibly, beseechingly and you have turned down every entreaty. It now remains for the State to make you realise what power it possesses to compel you to recognise and discharge the first of all great national duties.

Was there a whiff of the canon behind all this? After its appearance we saw no great stampede of creatures to the colours; most men still preferred to await compulsion. As it was, the size of Britain's forces before the introduction of compulsory military service—nearly one million men—remained the wonder of conscripted Europe. Strangely enough, statistics show that, altogether, fewer conscripts absconded, in proportion, than volunteers. It is hard to know what the canon would have made of this, except perhaps that it requires courage both to join an army and to desert it.

By early 1915 the rapidly rising casualty figures, the appearance of thousands of Belgian refugees, the many atrocity stories, together with innumerable letters the like of that cited from our local press finally turned simple patriotism into something much more grim and ugly. The 'people' demanded 'reprisals'. These came immediately after the torpedoing of the *Lusitania* in the form of attacks on premises bearing foreign names in the larger cities. Our local vengeance was typical.

Incensed by the sinking of the *Lusitania* on Friday last [the District Press announced], crowds of young people and women congregated in the vicinity of shops owned by persons with German names and attacked them with some degree of violence. The crowd in the early morning numbered several thousand and began by jeering outside the shop and house of Mr Herman Pratt, pork butcher, of New Road. Then the more daring spirits threw stones. By the time every window had been smashed the police had lost control of the crowd. Receiving no reply to their jeers, the rioters, surging forward, broke down the shop door or scrambled through the window and tossed pork cuttings and everything they could find into the street. While some smashed the kitchen widows and hurled the crockery and furniture into the street, others mounted the stairs and began to throw ornaments from the first floor into the street. Chairs followed and couches, bedding and stair rods were all treated in the same way. The waiting crowd, in which there were many women, seized upon the wreckage and the greater part of it was burned on an adjoining croft.

The premises were completely wrecked. 'I have never seen anything like it before,' said a constable who took part in an attempt to check the rioting. There would be many a breakfast table set better this morning than it has ever been. Folk went off with sides of bacon, brass curbs and fire irons. One woman complained to the police that she had only been able to procure a pot of dripping.

Finally when a piano was dropped from the window a man rushed forward and to the singing of the crowd he played, 'Rule Britannia', 'It's a Long Way to Tipperary', and other popular ditties before the instrument was completely wrecked.

The fact that the owner of the premises had lived there for twenty years, well liked and respected, had not saved him from complete ruin. Warned of the danger, he had escaped earlier to Blackpool with his family, where, in the guise of 'Belgian refugees', they were kindly treated.

During the next few days thirty other shops were despoiled in the same way, including several which bore Russian and Jewish names. After this the police grew alarmed and put down further disorders seemingly without difficulty at all. Views expressed by our own customers on the raids left one in no doubt about communal feeling. The 'squareheads', it was considered, had got just what they deserved, but those who had profited materially from justice done were no better than 'bloody thieves!'

Towards the end of 1914 unemployment figures had begun to fall; but in spite of increased production for the needs of war, economic conditions in many parts of the country remained surprisingly bad. In 1915 an official study on the state of working-class households in four industrial towns showed that 32 per cent of all adult wage-earners still received less than 24s a week, and that 16 per cent of the working classes were living in 'primary poverty'. 'Prices in June 1915', wrote one historian of the period,[2] 'were only 32 per cent above pre-war level,' but for the masses of industrial workers trying to keep a family on less than 24s a week such a rise was nothing short of disastrous. We had our local difficulties with 'primary poverty'. There was Mrs Mary Munro, among others, from a few streets away. Mary, unable to pay what she owed, took what the magistrates were apt to call the coward's way out: she tried to drown herself.

A witness, Thomas Danson [said the report], saw the prisoner take off her shawl and jump into the canal. He raised an alarm and Sergeant Bradshaw, who was on duty, dived in to rescue the woman. He brought her to the towing path. She was still quite conscious, said the Sergeant,

---

[2] L. Woodward, *Great Britain and the War of 1914–18.*

and asked, 'Why don't you let me drown? It will be over in a minute.'

The Inspector said the case was a very sad one. The prisoner's husband was a chronic invalid suffering from consumption of the throat. He had done no work for months. The prisoner had done very little work during the past month owing to slackness of employment. She had got about £2 behind with the rent and was also in debt for household goods. At 5.50 p.m. last Monday when she returned from work her husband told her that the bailiffs had left word that they were going to take the furniture away. This so upset her that she went and jumped into the canal.

The Stipendiary said that the case appeared to be one for relief. The prisoner would be remanded in custody. In the meantime something would be done to help her over her difficulties.

Among the very poor only patriotic calls to 'support the nation' stifled open discontent. But the new demands for goods and the prospects of quick profits soon had employers crying out for labour to replace those workers, many of them skilled, who had rushed off to the forces. Thousands of men and women, drawn by higher rates of pay, flocked from the less important industries into engineering and allied trades. For these semi-skilled and un-skilled workers embarking hopefully on the jobs of craftsmen some master of languages coined the word 'dilutees'. The trades-man, aristocrat of the working classes, looked upon this influx with the gravest misgivings, and not without reason. In the name of patriotism he saw himself called upon to teach the mysteries of his craft to hordes of newcomers who in due time, he feared, could easily be used by employers to force down wages and ruin his trade and living standards. And the engineer had another dread, unspoken, perhaps even unconscious at the time, which added impetus to the bitter struggle which was to follow.

Among craftsmen there had always been much argument about which trade called out the greatest kind and number of skills; but all the élite were as one in scouting the impudent pretensions of certain manual groups who had set themselves up as skilled workers without the necessary seven years' apprenticeship. When the National Union of Railwaymen, the first industrial union of size, was founded in 1912, the engine drivers (ASLEF) had refused to join, basically for fear of losing caste. This brought some withering comment from certain locomotive makers, mem-bers of a craft society. Men in ASLEF, they said, had no cause at all to give themselves airs: engine driving required little skill;

after a few weeks' training anyone with good eyes and common sense could do it. Doubtless the image of the locomotive driver in the nineteenth century and after was as much overblown as the airline pilot's is today. Yet what of the proud tradesman in war-time? Just how long, he wondered now, would it take the tiros with 'common sense' to master his own craft? The Jacks-of-no-trade might pick up all that was necessary to get by, and that in a period far less than the hallowed seven years. There was solid justification for his fears.

Well before 1914 many engineering firms, especially the so-called jobbing shops, had abandoned bound apprenticeship schemes, or had never subscribed to any. 'Sweat' shops abounded. The system of one learner to so many journeymen was very often disregarded and 'apprentices'—unindentured teenagers—were used as a source of cheap labour. With repetition work now long established, these youths moved from one simple, monotonous task to another, often staying at a drilling machine, say, or at the same kind of repair work for as long as three years out of the supposed seven in training. They learned little indeed. Very few attended a technical college or received explicit instruction on the job, except perhaps for the odd tricks learned from a kindly senior anxious for a lad to learn his trade. But if a man was on piece work, that scourge of the trades, he had little time for teaching. On coming out of their time, untold thousands of apprentices, supposedly fully fledged, possessed no more than a few basic skills of a kind that any lad could have acquired after only a few months' practice. Many 'improvers' on reaching full pay at twenty-one were promptly sacked and had to compete on the labour market with experienced men. Some failed and were compelled eventually to take labouring jobs, so that seven years on low apprentice wages had availed them nothing. And what of the journeyman? In expertise the vast majority were little better equipped than the fully served apprentice, except that experience had given them greater speed in turning out the repetition work needed. The best workmen, however, were either those who, through natural ability, had been given the difficult (and interesting) jobs in a shop, or had gained skill and knowledge by moving from firm to firm. Some of the younger men had attended technical institutes. They, the true craftsmen, numbering perhaps not more than one tenth of the whole, had nothing to fear. As for the rest, many had spent a working lifetime at one or two firms, terrified of moving, and doing the same uncomplicated tasks with little variation. Yet always they held the assumption that such work lay far beyond the abilities of a common labourer. And now the challenge!

But a far greater danger threatened, and this in the open—'mass production', as men called it then, might yet go far to eliminate hand skills altogether. For a generation already, in certain sections of the trade, the spread of new American machines had been checked only by stern union restriction. Now the demands of war could sweep away every safeguard. In a nightmare the tradesman saw himself, at best, as a mere troubleshooter looking after rows of 'automatics' run by women and common labourers, all doing his old tasks with a speed and efficiency he had never approached. And when peace came and with it a return to normal production—what then? Against the 'dilution of labour' skilled men felt they must fight to the death, war or no war.

The first serious clash of interests occurred at an engineering works in Essex shortly after the outbreak of war, when mechanics objected to setting up machines to be operated by women. This turned out to be merely the forerunner of a complex series of acrimonious disputes that lasted throughout the whole war. From the start union resistance to dilution was damned as grossly unpatriotic by government spokesmen, employers and cheap press[3] alike, but the engineers held their ground. After months of wrangling the unions agreed to accept the new labour and relax their regulations; but only on condition that immediately after the war the 'previous rules' should be restored 'in every case'. In the meantime the employers promised not to use semi-skilled and unskilled labour as a means of reducing wages. There would also be some limitation on profits. Dispute after dispute broke out still; but the gates of change stood open wide and the new workers poured through, to the dismay of many a conservative tradesman who saw the 'dummies' acquiring some of his own skills with

---

[3] Lieutenant-Colonel W. H. Maxwell, in an article in *London Outlook*, felt that 'Trade unionism, that shelter of slinking shirkers, is imperilling our existence, and by its action a rot of our national soul has set in. One remedy, and one remedy alone, can eradicate this state of rot—martial law.' —David Boulton, *Objection Overruled*.

disturbing ease. My father was typical. In his cups he was wont
to boast that, at the lathe, he had to manipulate a micrometer
and work to limits of one thousandth of an inch. We were much
impressed, until one evening in 1917 a teenage sister running a
capstan in the iron works remarked indifferently that she, too,
used a 'mike' to even finer limits. There was, she said, 'nothing
to it'. The old man fell silent. Thus did status crumble! Before
the end of the war more than 642,000 women had gone into
government factories and engineering works of some sort, with
millions more, men and women, doing manual work of almost
every kind and developing new skills and new self-confidence on
the way. The awe that many simpler souls had felt before the
mystery of craft began to evaporate, to be replaced by at least
some rational understanding.

And some of the poorest in the land started to prosper as never
before. In spite of war, slum grocers managed to get hold of
different and better varieties of foodstuffs of a kind sold before
only in middle-class shops, and the once deprived began to savour
strange delights. This brought the usual charge of 'extravagance'
from their social superiors. 'But why shouldn't folk eat their
fancy?' my mother said. 'They work for what they get.'

One of our customers, wife of a former foundry labourer, both
making big money now on munitions, airily inquired one Christmas time as to when we were going to stock 'summat worth
chewin''.

'Such as what?' asked my father, sour-faced.

'Tins o' lobster!' she suggested, 'or them big jars o' pickled
gherkins!'

Furious, the old man damned her from the shop. 'Before the
war,' he fumed, 'that one was grateful for a bit o' bread and
scrape!' He, like thousands of skilled engineers throughout the
country, was filled with rage. The dilution of labour had brought
with it an agreement which guaranteed that any increase in out-
put caused by the introduction of new machinery or simplified
processes should not lead to a cut in piece work rates. Soon production increased, then soared as the great influx of American
machine tools made itself felt.[4] The wages of machine-minding
tiros, men and women, often rose well beyond those of their

---

[4] This contribution of the United States towards winning the war has
hardly yet received its due.

mentors, the skilled tradesmen (on fixed time rates) who were there to set up the mechanism and repair machines when they broke down under clumsy hands. It was the skilled men, too, who often inaugurated the simpler methods that brought even heavier wage packets to their social and, until very recently, economic inferiors. Despite the efforts of 'dilution officers' who stamped the land settling local disputes, the problem remained acute: in fact a commission appointed in 1917 to probe industrial unrest found it one of the major grievances. Happily, the lowest orders, fast forgetting their stations and growing in economic stature each day, went on the make while the making was good.

With the return of peace the great mass of regulations safeguarding the status of the artisan were certainly restored, but where unionism was weak some employers did not scruple to use a war-taught labour in order to drive down standard rates of pay. Nevertheless, the dilution of labour and the employment of women brought communal gains of immense value, not only in engineering but in many other fields. Socially, the barriers of caste that had previously existed between the skilled worker and his family and the lower industrial grades was permanently lowered; the artisan felt less superiority, the labourer and semi-skilled man more self-assurance. Of the semi-skilled, several categories were now accepted in certain craft unions: the once exclusive 'Amalgamated Society of Engineers' became, with syndicalist Tom Mann as secretary, the 'Amalgamated Engineering Union'. Women grew in social stature and gained an authority they have never lost since.[5] Many without home ties, and often against parents' wishes, had joined one of the auxiliary forces, and here class reared its head: the Women's Auxiliary Army Corps, we soon gathered, was for working-class females,

[5] In the north-west of England and in the West Riding, with their long tradition of married female labour in mills, giving partial economic independence, working-class women were not as subservient to the male as were those elsewhere, especially in the North-east. The belief that 'very few' women at this time were aware how much their husbands earned won't stand examination. The standard wages for various jobs were only too well known. As for overtime rates, it was simple enough for a wife in doubt about her spouse's pay to go quizzing among other women with husbands in the same trade. Quarrels generally arose not over the amount of wages but over how much of it the husband should retain for his 'beer money'.

whereas the 'Wrens' and the WRAF catered for the nicer girls. But whatever war did to women in home, field, service or factory, it undoubtedly snapped strings that had bound them in so many ways to the Victorian age. Even we, the young, noticed their new self-confidence. Wives in the shop no longer talked about 'my boss', or 'my master'. Master had gone to war and Missis ruled the household, or he worked close to her in a factory, turning out shell cases on a lathe and earning little more than she did herself. Housewives left their homes and immediate neighbourhood more frequently, and with money in their purses went foraging for goods even into the city shops, each trip being an exercise in self-education. She discovered her own rights. The pre-1914 movements for her political emancipation, bourgeois in origin and function, meant very little to the lower-working-class woman. In the end the consequences of war, not the legal acquisition of female rights, released her from bondage.

Yet too much should not be made of war as the agent of woman's emancipation generally: in the twenty years which preceded it enormous new social forces had been developing, powered by economic pressure. The census showed that by 1914 women, for the first time, had moved not only into the industries of the North and Midlands, but into commerce and the professions as well. About one quarter of all commercial clerks were female—an increase in a decade of 110 per cent. Local authorities now employed 176,000 and the civil service 34,000. There were more than 200,000 women teachers and 350,000 in professional occupations and subordinate services. In fact, by August 1914, 3·2 million women were employed in industry and commerce, which was nearly half the number of wage-earning men. Such economic might must inevitably have brought more social freedom. And their ranks were to make startling increase. By July 1918 the number of women at work had reached nearly five million; more than 400,000 working in agriculture alone. The events of 1914–18, then, did not start, but they accelerated significantly, a movement already well developed, one which would go some way to release that other great social undermass of the time—the working-class women of Britain. After it all, the males, warriors or not, returned to peace-time life somehow diminished. As for the lowest orders, no longer quite so humble and acquiescent, they jockeyed vigorously for a place on the social scale more in

keeping, they felt, with the new riches and knowledge that turmoil had brought with it.

A whole nation at war threw up anomalies that no one had
dreamed of. While it is certain, for instance, that the education
of school children from 1914 to 1919 suffered considerably,
evidence shows that during that period the incidence of illiteracy
and sub-literacy among adults might well have decreased. The
avid need for information from battle fronts, the frequent issue
of 'special' news sheets, cried with wild excitement along the
streets to proclaim real or specious victories, all meant wider dis-
tribution of newspapers and periodicals and a greater attention
to print. As more and more joined the forces and anxiety rose
with casualties, as others went working away from home, the
need for personal communication grew even more urgent.
Thousands of adults who perhaps had never before penned a
single letter now felt the strongest desire to put words on paper.
Then began the run in army canteens and every corner shop in
the country for 'equipment': threepence bought the lot—a bottle
of Stephens' ink, a packet of writing paper and envelopes and a
pen. One cleared a space, sat four-square before the menacing
blank page and began!

Daily newspapers, magazines, periodicals (*John Bull* in particular), comics and, as people grew richer, even books made their
appearance in homes almost bare of print before the war. Com-
munications from husbands and sons, official forms and, later,
ration books all made hitherto unknown demands upon the unlettered or near-illiterate, and the younger and more intelligent,
confronted with an even more frequent problem, made shift to
solve it by acquiring, or developing again, skills in simple reading and writing. In ships, trenches, camps, barracks, hospitals,
men finding themselves often with hours of enforced leisure took
to reading and some, without perhaps realising it, completed a
course in self-education. In our own world of the early '20's, my
mother often noted with relief that requests for her services as
local scribe, while still not uncommon, fell far below the pre-
1914 level. Whatever the cause, it is certain that the literacy
standards of our adult neighbours had much improved.

But well before the end of hostilities observers noted other unusual changes among us. Nearly all the 'unemployables' had got
jobs of some sort, taking over mostly part-time and casual tasks,

M

whilst the former 'casuals' found regular work. All thereby acquired new abilities and status. For the first time ever they had money in their pockets all week. Many wives of fighting men discovered that they could manage far better on government allowances than they ever did on their breadwinners' meagre wage. Mrs Cassidy with a young brood in a house near the shop now drew nearly three times the amount her usually drunken husband had brought home. 'They can keep Mick for ever!' she said, delighted. Pawnbrokers began to complain about the falling off in the number of pledged goods, though their sales of trinkets for cash shot up.

By late 1916 abject poverty began to disappear from the neighbourhood. Children looked better fed. There were far fewer prosecutions for child neglect. Well before the end of the war the number of pupils taking free dinners at our school fell to one fifth of the pre-1914 figures. In spite of shortages women appeared less unkempt and better dressed. Slowly clogs and shawls generally began to give way to coats and hats, an undoubted sign of increasing affluence and status. To the shocked stares of the respectable, housewives with husbands away or on night work could now be seen going off in pairs to the pictures or sitting with a glass of stout in the Best Room at the pub.

Two of our neighbours, having taken overmuch drink one night, were brought up next day before the court. The stipendiary, who seldom passed a sentence without a moral, thought it 'perfectly disgraceful' that women whose husbands had to fight and die for king and country should spend the allowance given to them on drink. Two other women called as witnesses were, it transpired, unable to read and write, a disability they both attributed when questioned to being 'too delicate' to go to school as children. At this the justice waxed sarcastic: 'There appear', he said, 'to have been a lot of delicate children in this town to judge from the number of illiterates who come before my court! Defendants are fined ten shillings or fourteen days!'

In the shop one heard endless talk about visits to photographers —having one's 'likeness' taken—'half a dozen in sepia', and sending them off to loved ones away from home. And artificial dentures! It seemed the ambition of every other woman to get a mouthful of flashing 'pots' before her husband came home from the war.[6] Bold teenage girls, a type never encountered before (folk were scandalised), earning plenty of money, and foot-loose young housewives began to use face creams—'Icilma', 'Silver Foam'—even powder and dabs of rouge. My eldest sister, gone early in the war out of a cotton mill into the rich pickings of engineering, used cosmetics surreptitiously until one evening the old man caught her with a whole 'dorothy' bag full of the stuff. He threw the lot into the fire. The house, we understood, had been defiled. Hadn't Joe Devine (a neighbour), he thundered, 'turned his daughters into the street for using this muck?' Never again must she dare . . .

Jenny stood unperturbed, 'I either go on using it', she said, 'or you can turn me out too.'

Shocked beyond measure, my father threw up his hands. This could only lead to one end—sexual looseness, moral decay. And authority, the upright thought, had not helped much. Noting after the outbreak of war a rise in illegitimacy rates and an increase in venereal disease, it had boldly arranged lectures to the troops on hygiene and contraceptive methods, of which knowledge many coming on leave appeared to be making full use. In opposition to this policy, I remember, we saw several films put out by moral welfare agencies, all of which seemed to show the same young officer biting his lips and making a certain proposal to the same virginal-looking blonde. This, to a screenful of words, she tremulously rejected. In the end, after considerable tedium,

---

[6] T. S. Eliot's poem in *The Waste Land* captures the feeling of the time with marvellous accuracy:

> When Lil's husband got demobbed, I said—
> I didn't mince my words, I said to her myself,
> HURRY UP PLEASE ITS TIME
> Now Albert's coming back, make yourself a bit smart.
> He'll want to know what you done with that money he gave you
> To get yourself some teeth. He did, I was there.
> You have them all out, Lil, and get a nice set,
> He said, I swear, I can't bear to look at you.
> And no more can't I, I said, and think of poor Albert,
> He's been in the army four years, he wants a good time,
> And if you don't give it him, there's other will, I said.
> Oh, is there, she said. Something o' that, I said.
> Then I'll know who to thank, she said, and give me a straight look.
> HURRY UP PLEASE ITS TIME

we viewed them coming radiantly down the aisle, he with his right
arm in a sling. 'They were so glad they had waited!'

Such salutary tales may have checked promiscuity among
young officers, but they failed with many in our own rank and
file. The district bore a whole crop of war babies, one lady pro-
ducing no less than three, each with a father, it was said, in a
different regiment. Local prostitutes, well aware that they were
known and marked, had always gone about their business with
decorum. Now a deal of circumspection went by the board. Two
henna-haired girls from Cardiff, people said, who openly established themselves in a hovel not ten yards from our back door,
scandalised the whole matriarchy. Much befrilled, yet wearing
serge jackets with brass buttons which gave them the nautical
touch, they set out most evenings for the 'Barbary Coast', a lane
that ran from dockland, and returned, when the pubs closed,
singing with sailors. On Sunday mornings one of the girls, hair
on her shoulders and looking strangely deflated in a long rain-
coat, would slip into the shop and with some diffidence buy
breakfast food for four. My mother served her pleasantly and
made no comment afterwards, but often enough the old man
would raise his head from the *News of the World* to damn all
such 'trollops'.

'A bloody disgrace to the neighbourhood! I wouldn't have 'em
in the shop!'

'They've got to eat,' my mother snapped, 'like anyone else.'

By the end of 1917 there had been a rapid fall in nearly all
forms of petty crime, including a great decline in the number of
women imprisoned for prostitution, but it is unlikely that this
meant an improvement in the nation's sexual morals. Some
prostitutes, it is true, had abandoned the profession for war work,
but depleted police forces, manned mostly by elderly officers and
'specials' and burdened with new regulations every week, had
little time or desire to scour darkened streets seeking those who
remained. Much was winked at and women who got arrested
were usually let off lightly indeed. 'The sentences on the girls
charged with prostitution or accosting,' said the chaplain at Manchester prison, voicing a general complaint, 'seem absolutely
trivial. Girls look upon the charge as a joke. There is a girl here
at the present; she has three previous convictions of 7, 13 and 25
days respectively.'

Over the country as a whole the number of those under the age of twenty-one committed for prostitution rose by 54 per cent. At Liverpool prison, one of the major centres for the reception of prostitutes, the governor reported that a large proportion of the convicted were 'mere children'. The chaplain at Holloway in 1918 saw a 'great deterioration in the type of prostitute received there'. The girls for the most part are very young and very ignorant, very vicious and very corrupt. Frequently they come from the provincial towns and country districts. They are distinctly a war product.'

There was of course no fall in committals for this offence in those towns where the fighting men were stationed, but according to one military policeman of the time, 'they had to be real cheeky with it before they got taken up'. The chaplain at Plymouth gaol noted a 'substantial increase' in prostitution. 'Out of 132 women who came in, 81 were first offenders. There were 23 first offender prostitutes in our prison last year whose sentences did not exceed a fortnight.'

By 1917 even the more moderate citizens spoke of a recklessness and indifference among people of a kind they had never known before. Moralists condemned those who, they claimed, were living it rich at home, oblivious of the vast slaughter across the Channel; yet the plain fact was that, up to the end of 1916, only the young, the very poor and the profiteers of business had substantially improved their living standards. Foodstuffs rising steadily in price could still be bought regularly, except for sugar—the first food to be rationed. In scarcity, as always, the poor suffered first.

For two weeks before Christmas 1916 there was sugar famine in the district; at our shop we had none at all. Then with excitement my mother heard forty-eight hours before the Eve that a small consignment had arrived at the wholesaler's. Her share would be 12 lbs in half-pound packets. 'Put them,' she said to me, 'in this leather hold-all, and away you go!'

'I *was* thinking,' I told her, 'of going to the library.'

'Think again!' she said. 'Now off you go to that wholesaler's and back like lightning. I've twenty-four customers—promised and waiting.'

At the street corner I met Eddie, a friend, standing with *The Last of the Mohicans* in his hands. 'It's got to be in today,' he warned, 'else there's a fine. If you don't come now you'll miss it.'

At that time I yearned for the printed word like a toper for his tipple. Eddie went on tempting—'We could rush there, get it swopped over, then away across town. You could get to the sugar place before six. Your mother would never know.'

I went, and fifteen minutes later Fenimore Cooper's master-piece was mine. Brisk with intent, I ran for a while and had eased into a trot when the book slithered from my jersey, fell and bounced open. I picked it up, glanced at the frontispiece, read the first sentence, the second . . . and was trapped! Steps slowed into a dawdle, I wandered through the streets, near-sighted eyes pinned to the page, then wild over the prairies rang the evening hoots of a dozen cotton mills. Gripped with panic, I began to run: the warehouse lay still a mile away across the city. I arrived two minutes before closing. A surly counterhand with his rain-coat on pushed a parcel at me. 'And tell her,' he growled, 'that's your lot till February!'

Sugar! I picked up my precious load and bore it reverently into the dusk. Two miles of the toughest slums in England lay between me and home. In such areas a boy's aggressive powers stood in inverse proportion to the distance from his own door-step. Unconfidently I entered now.

Quite without warning a bold shower burst out of the evening. I scurried for shelter, but already the brown paper covering the sugar was darkened with wet. And the bag? Somewhere in that lovely browsing between library and warehouse I had lost it. It grew darker. In between showers I hurried along, anxiety fast turning into fear. Now the top of my parcel gaped wide. Then came heavier rain, slapping viciously into the sugar. I ran into the doorway of an empty shop and stood gasping. Then I felt it— the gentle granular pouring: the parcel was disintegrating. I bent and it slid from my clutch on to the ground. Kneeling, I tried foolishly to scrape sugar into the folds of my jersey, stopped and wept in despair. One inkling of this and the street lads would be down like vultures. My chin fell on a pigeon chest—*The Last of the Mohicans*! Sadly I transferred this to the seat of my trousers, sat on it and wished I was dead.

Succour came in the shape of an Irish lady making her way home from a spinning mill to a street behind the shop. Together we scooped damp sugar and wrappings from a filthy floor into her apron and set off home. Outside the shop stood a considerable queue gathered in hope, or the happy certainty, of sweetness for Christmas. As we appeared a ragged cheer ran along the line. Sugar!

The shop was full, two helpers serving hard. My mother looked up from slicing bacon, suddenly anxious. We went into the small storeroom behind the shop and the Irish woman explained all, shooting as she did so a wet, grey mass on to the kitchen table. My mother gazed stunned, then, recovering enough to bid adieu to Mrs O'Shea with many thanks and a pot of strawberry jam, she demanded an account from me. And for the first time I lied to her—a bold and graphic story of attack by half a dozen lads outside the warehouse; how I had fought them off; how they stole the bag. Then the rain. She believed me and sighed: 'All that sugar ruined! Sugar above everything else—in war-time! And those poor folk disappointed for Christmas. And I promised! But you did your best.'

I turned to go. Her sharp eyes noticed the bulge in my corduroys. She stooped and drew out *The Last of the Mohicans*. 'Now the truth!' she said.

I spent a poor Christmas.

Soon there were graver shortages than sugar. During 1916 the Germans, for propaganda and tactical reasons, had ceased to sink shipping without inspection. The country had plenty to eat, but owing to maldistribution and the cornering of scarcer foods the poor began to find basic needs harder to come by each week. Then, in January 1917, U-boats received orders to sink at sight all ships using British ports. Within a few weeks queues grew longer outside foodshops: the battle for very existence was on.

1917! The year when the twentieth century really began. New ideas ran abroad in the world: men were making blueprints for the future. Away beyond the western lands of Europe something very strange seemed afoot. At home people remarked continually on the change among the undermass: regular wages and the absence of class pressure from above had wrought in many a peculiar quality which looked uncommonly like self-respect. Yet during the early summer months of the year in our obscure corner all seemed wrapped in gloom. Bread, like the weekly newspaper, grew greyer each week. What the local editor captioned, and everybody called, the 'casuality[7] list' lengthened steadily, extending one Friday to two and a half columns of small obituaries. Everyone knew a neighbour who had been killed. The deserters' 'roll of dishonour' on the back page of the local press increased in proportion. One of our reluctants, Mike Riordan, discharged himself from the Royal Artillery on no fewer than four occasions—and this was an expensive business, since deserters, when caught, had to buy their own railway ticket back and pay besides the fares of their escort. By 1917, though, more than a quarter of a million Irishmen were fighting for Britain: perhaps Michael felt that was enough.

One evening in that year my eldest sister came home, placed a page of sheet music on the piano and began to play and sing, 'Oh, oh, oh, it's a lovely war!' The old man sat much amused; but at about the third rendering, with the whole family gathered round intent on learning the words and tune of this rollicking new song, my mother, who had not joined in, got up, took the sheet from the stand, rolled it into a cylinder and returned it to my sister. We stood astonished . . .

'I won't have it,' she said quietly, 'not in this house—such carnage! And people sing "it's a lovely war!" '

'Don't you see?' said my father. 'It's skitting! It's ridicule! "Up to the waist in water!" ' he sang. ' "Up to the eyes in slush!". . .'

'I see well enough,' she said, 'but some things are too terrible for ridicule.'

My sister got up, tossed the music on top of the piano and flounced out.

As 1917 wore on, ordinary folk, feeling a deepening weariness of war but not daring to show it too openly, became boldly critical of things about them and especially of those who, they believed, were making huge profits[8] at the country's expense. Our town council grew captious and ill-tempered too, going on about

[7] The war, of course, introduced a whole flux of new ideas which served to widen the common culture, and for a time some words suffered in the process. Casualty became casuality; admiralty, admirality. 'Outdacious', often used, seemed in meaning to be a combination of audacious and outrageous. Incredible was commonly pronounced with an extra syllable—'incredible'.

[8] In November 1917 Ben Tillett, standing in the constituency next to ours as an 'anti-profiteer', easily won the seat against a government rubber-stamp nominee sent up from London.

'waste' and people not pulling their weight. In line with government direction they moved to set up a committee to teach people economy and the nutritional values of food. One wholesale baker appeared a little over-ready to exploit the new terms involved. 'Groves Bread', he advertised, 'contains twice as much protein and calories as any chop, steak or fish. If Groves Bread is eaten instead of chops, steaks, or fish, you will keep down the cost of living!' We strove in our turn to keep down Groves' bread, eating more and more of the darkening pulp, but only because each day now chop, steak and fish were growing harder to come by.

Those engaged on what the council considered useless work got short shrift indeed. The supervisor of our 'Juvenile Employment Bureau', having the impudence to ask for a rise in salary from £200 a year to £225 to meet the increased cost of living, was publicly reprimanded in the press and his request sternly rejected. Councillor Gunn thought the man was engaged on 'wholly unnecessary work'. 'The bureau,' he said, 'should have been closed two years ago and the supervisor transferred. He might have gone into the army!'

Nationally the gloom deepened, too, though the Ministry of Food, at least, was taking what looked like vigorous action. Lord Davenport, a master grocer, who knew a great deal about business but less, it seemed, about new-fangled dietetics, had been appointed Food Minister. In April 1917, a month in which a million tons of shipping was to be sunk and with only six weeks' supply of wheat left in the country, he introduced the 'meatless' day. Imported cereals were fast running out and home livestock was increasing. Food experts responded with shocked protests: to feed grain to animals, they pointed out, merely to obtain meat was a scandalously wasteful process. Land now given over to cattle could be used far more profitably for the production of grains, vegetables and fruits. But in spite of the experts' opposition we had our little Lent each week, the comics singing about it on the music halls until their ditty died of inanity—'My meatless day, my meatless day! I do not want to eat, any any sort of meat, meat, meat!' . . .

At the end of that same month of April our sitting Member, a knight, arrived from London, bent on scattering despondency. He addressed the Conservative Association's annual meeting, the mayor presiding. 'The war,' he assured them, 'is undoubtedly going well. There is no question about it!' (Applause.) And, coming from the heart of the empire, he hinted, he knew more than most of his listeners concerning what was what. (Applause.) Soon the Americans would be coming. As for the rest of it, discussion in the House had been much as usual. Women's suffrage, now—they knew he supported that—'in a modified way'. And education—he favoured that, too, even compulsory schooling up to the age of fourteen: always provided, of course, that any wages lost by parents through its introduction could be made up. (Applause.) There was a hope indeed! Everyone, however—mayor, councillors and meeting—seemed buoyed by his descent among them.

Meanwhile, in a less salubrious ward, a peculiar gathering was taking place. The British Socialist Party,[9] having just held its sixth annual conference in the town, was meeting again for a unique purpose—'the commemoration of the Russian Revolution'. 'Some ladies were present,' reported the weekly press sourly, 'but speakers were chiefly members of the Russian Jewish Social Democratic League from London.' Local leaders were, as it happened, prisoners of conscience in Dartmoor. In commemorating, speakers noted with no satisfaction at all that the British capitalist press had welcomed the overthrow of the Czar, not for its heralding of the dawn of democracy in Russia but only because the triumphant revolutionaries, they believed, would now attack Germany with rejuvenated vigour. The purpose of revolution, however, one socialist declaimed, was in no wise to win wars for capitalism but to usher in the new age. A telegram was then approved and dispatched—'This meeting sends its cordial fraternal greetings to the revolutionary Russian working class and expresses its unity with them in their struggle for international solidarity.'

The British press as a whole showed little understanding of the implication of events in Russia, but they knew enough soon to turn support into vituperative opposition. Equally, too, among

---

[9] The British Socialist Party was founded in 1911 by a union of the old Social Democratic Federation with a number of ILP branches and supporters of the Clarion movement. All were dissatisfied with the 'supine' policy of the Labour bloc in Parliament and demanded militant action. The BSP faltered on until 1920, when it joined with other small Marxist bodies to form the British Communist Party.

many democratic idealists in movements like the Independent Labour Party, high hope gradually changed into acrid disillusionment. Nevertheless, the long socialist dream had taken on, however distortedly, some kind of reality at last.

In our small grey purlieu of the industrial North we heard indifferently about a Russian revolution, only perking up interest at the news of 'cannibalism among the "reds" '. A few strange un-English names lodged for a time in our consciousness. Among a litter of pups, Mrs Woods, the butcher's wife, had a pair which she called Lenin and Trotsky. We laughed. Russia was no concern of ours.

And the Americans did come! One sunny evening, to our wild astonishment, the cattle sidings were suddenly alive with soldiers, thousands of tall, clean, upstanding men—from the 'Middle West', they said—in boy scout hats and spick and span uniforms —all dumped in the heart of a northern English slum. They marched with a band, friendly and smiling, along our main way —and sang, too: 'Over there, over there. We won't get back till it's over over there!' Everyone who could move poured from the slits of streets onto the high road to see them pass, screaming with joy: for so long now we had had so little to cheer. What denizens of a dark world we must have seemed to these men from the American prairies! Mrs Harbin, a tousled scrap of a woman, unwashed, a shawl about her shoulders, ran from a fish and chip shop to hold a grey basin to the shoulder of one of the marching men. 'Thank you, ma'am!' he said. He took a chipped potato, put it to his lips, chewed and swallowed. 'God bless yer!' she called after him. He raised a hand. I trotted by his side and twenty yards on saw him drop the food to the ground and flick his fingers. We followed them far into the dusk until they turned into one of those great barracks built a hundred years before to intimidate the half-starved workers of the North. In the shop for days after people repeated the same things—'Did you see them? Wonderful fellers! They'll show the Germans! It won't be long now.'

Chapter 10

High Days and After

Over my shoulder goes one care,
Over my shoulder goes two cares!
Song

By the end of the war working-class women, as we have seen, had gained far more than a limited right to vote. For years now, in their menfolk's absence, many had reared a family, and found in the responsibility a new freedom. Women were more alert, more worldly-wise. Yet the liberty won, some felt they would have to fight hard to retain once the warriors returned. But with surprise they discovered that husbands, home again, were far less the lords and masters of old, but more comrades to be lived with on something like level terms. Women customers in the shop commented on this change time and again. Life had broadened in scope; a certain parochialism had gone for ever. Food illiterates—husbands who had left home the bane of a wife's existence over what they could and could not eat—came back permanently cured; their taste, often enough, widened by army food. Customers remarked on it with amusement and relief—'They'll try anything now!' Boys in their war-time waywardness warned by mothers of what would happen when the ruler of the house returned were often surprised to find father good-humoured, indifferent to minor misdeed, understanding, even; a human being, not a tin god. Grown children, remembering the authority that clothed him in pre-war years, felt indignant at the liberties now bestowed upon the 'spoiled' younger end. Disciplines steadily eased all round. The gulf that had stood so long between parent and child began to narrow at last.

From mid-1917 to the end of 1920 the times boomed. In a period of soaring profits trade unions gained considerable advantages for their members. By 1921 wages on average had increased by 170 per cent above the 1914 level, though of course many prices had risen almost as steeply. Our little shop prospered as never before. At the beginning of 1918, when general food rationing was introduced, my mother felt again that this might be the finish for us; customers, she feared, would register at the big multiple grocers with all the advantages to be had there. Instead women once the poorest amongst us remembered her help in days past and brought in their registrations by the score. We were saved again! Soon, for the first time in more than twenty years of married life, she opened an account at the local bank. The shop was taking more than £45 a week—a true reflection of the neighbourhood's prosperity. Not opening now until eight o'clock in the morning and closing by law twelve hours later, with Sunday after mid-day free, my mother happily contrasted the times with those around the turn of the century with its sixteen-hour day (7 a.m. till 11 p.m.), 400 customers a week and a gross weekly taking of about £7! For the very poor this was a changed world indeed. On armistice day she announced that the family now possessed £100 cash in the bank. We were staggered. Her yearning, long cherished, to get us out of Zinc Street seemed at last on the edge of fulfilment. Father, after a heart attack and a doctor's warning, had mellowed more and was drinking less, confining himself strictly to a quart of beer a day. Again he had solemnly agreed to leave. With another £100 in the bank, she told us, and perhaps £450 from the shop (in selling, one asked £10 for every £1 of takings) we should all be away at last. We knew her 'dream' house, of course—near a park it had to be, and a good library; quiet—with a parlour and a back garden: not much, but that was all she wanted. 'After this,' she said, 'we'll have a few decent years together. It gives me courage to go on.'

Immense poverty and wretchedness could be observed still in every part of industrial Britain, yet, the war over, a gaiety never experienced before swept the land. It stemmed naturally from a feeling of enormous relief that the slaughter had ended and showed itself among the common folk in innumerable family jollifications, as serving men returned home with anything from £4 to £40 gratuities in their pockets. Night after night in our village and countless others like it the pubs, the cinemas, the dance halls were filled to overflowing, and well into 1919 the euphoria continued; nobody quite knew why. Only one thing was certain, though, as letter writers to *The Times* pointed out— we would have to pay for it! Morality had gone to the dogs!

In the year 1919–20 the number of people committed to prison fell to 35,439: a decline from 1913 of 74 per cent. War-time prosperity and the introduction in 1914 of the Criminal Justice Administration Act had ended for many an economic and physical servitude. This remarkable reduction alone, I think, did much to establish a new dignity among the emergent poor. In our district, and doubtless in other similar areas, a sub-class appeared consisting of those known to have been in the 'Stone Jug' before the war, but to whom time and affluence had given a sheen of respectability. Only a street row or a neighbour's malicious tongue would reveal to surprised newcomers to the village that the eminently conformist Jud Hamson and his missis 'used to go "inside" reg'lar before the war'. Even in the slump years after 1920 the prison population increased only slowly. The authorities of prisons, who liked to keep a finger on the moral and social pulse of the times, were 'unanimous in ascribing so small an increase during this exceptional year [1921] principally to the effect of Unemployment Pay, which has prevented acute distress'.

Other causes named by Governors, apart from Unemployment Pay, as being the cause of this reduction are: improved education; fuller information is obtained by Courts as to offenders' antecedents, which often results in committal being avoided; higher wages and better conditions of the working classes, who now have more reserves in the form of invested savings, *the extreme destitution of pre-war days having now disappeared* [author's italics]; war pensions; restricted drinking facilities; the provision of juvenile courts; the effects of the Borstal system.

But most of all, they felt, what kept people out of prison was the new 'privilege' which for the first time permitted an offender to pay an imposed fine by instalments. Between 1914 and 1920 every sort of common, non-indictable offence fell to remarkably low levels. In 1913–14, 15,000 people were sent to prison for prostitution. After the war prosecutions began to rise again steadily, but at no time did they approach the figure registered in 1913–14. Yet it would be dangerous, I feel, to assume from this that as the century grew older the country in some way became more sexually conformist.

Rising prosperity among the poorest is best shown perhaps in the committal figures for 'begging and sleeping out'. During 1908 more than 27,000 went to prison for the offence: in 1912, the 'prosperous' year, nearly 16,000; but in the first year after the war fewer than 2,500 offenders were committed. The new Criminal Justice Administration Act gave all, where necessary, time to pay. Yet this privilege was allowed only if the prisoner could supply the police with a checkable 'permanent address'. Few vagrants could do this, or pay their fine on the spot either; so they went where they had always gone, but in greatly diminished numbers: all over Britain the rest had moved up, socially and economically, into the working community.

The national decline in 'drunkenness and assaults' was most impressive of all: from 62,882 committals in 1908, war, weak beer,[1] licensing restriction and changing social habit reduced the incidence in 1918–19 to a mere 1,670! But the brewers pressed hard for and soon gained an extension in opening hours. The prison population began to grow again. In 1920–21 there were 8,752 committals for drunkenness and assault. Just as the brewing trade before 1914 had been perturbed by the impact of the cinema on their sales, so they worried in the early '20's about a new and sinister influence that was tending to keep good men away from their beer—the 'wireless set'. Several publicans in our neighbourhood, following a national trend, tried to scotch the menace by installing what they called a 'listening-in apparatus' in their Best Rooms. This brought a flurry of protest letters in the weekly press from 'T.T.', 'Abstainer' and others who looked upon the device as no more than a vicious trick to lure the unwary into pubs. But our local man replied to his critics with dignity. 'People', he wrote, 'sitting in comfort, listening to a Covent Garden opera, or a speech by Mr Lloyd George, or possibly a sermon by the Archbishop of York, would not get drunk—they would sup their beer, slowly, moderately and with deliberation.' The listening-in apparatus would make for sobriety. Sadly, however, the figures for drunkenness continued to rise.

By 1921, with the first ominous trade slump and major strikes, the working class began to settle into what, the following year, was considered a 'return to normal'. But there was to be no going back for the young; a more confident and restless race than their fathers, they turned their faces to the twentieth century and went

---

[1] The quality of war-time beer was a subject of acrid complaint among all hardened drinkers. By 1917 the acreage of land given over to hops had been reduced by half; but there was no shortage of water.

dancing almost to the end of the decade. In factory, mine and workshop, however, a new and graver spirit moved. Men were changing their minds. From 1918 to 1920 the ILP had increased its membership by a half. We noted change, too, in the little streets about the shop. Poor families, dyed-in-the-wool Tories, who had voted Conservative since getting the franchise, were talking now not 'Liberal'² but 'Labour'. In the machine shop and foundry discussion among men took on a common drift. 'Afore the war,' I well remember an elderly fitter grumbling, 'there were talk on trade unionism, and fair enough; but very little o' that claptrap about profit an' t' bosses an' socialism an' there bein' no God!—talk not fit for my ears, never mind youngsters like you! Now everyone's at it!' But in all the 'claptrap' some among the awakened went on busily making reassessments of old social values, and not a few found in it all cause for a glorious new hope. Old deference died; no longer did the lower orders believe *en masse* that 'class' came as natural 'as knots in wood'. Not, it should be said, that all the workers were now avid in seeking theoretic Marxist backing for their economic demands. I recall a course which opened with fanfare and fifty-four students in a room over the bar at the local trades club, to study (under a man with a large red beard) the 'first nine chapters of *Das Kapital*'. After a month only three of us remained, and one was a girl whose father (standing guard in the bar below) insisted on her attendance. This class was the prototype of innumerable similar fiascos which occurred right through the '20's. Of Marxism the proletariat wanted not even the 'first nine chapters'.

Ever since the Russian revolution in 1917 those behind the scenes in Britain with real power had shown themselves mortally afraid of any attempt at a proletarian uprising. First, like the successful Russian revolutionaries themselves, they completely over-estimated the ability of those war-time leaders of the shop stewards' movement to turn a local messianic fervour in Glasgow into a national upheaval of the proletariat.³ Emissaries went, it is

² Before the first world war manual workers in general were only socially class-conscious; after 1918 they became more or less politically class-conscious, hence the massive switch from the Liberals to the 'party of the workers by hand and brain'.

³ Equally unrealistic were the many Marxists among some eleven hundred 'United Socialists' meeting at the famous Leeds conference in June

true, among the deeply disgruntled workers of the industrial North preaching the word; yet, as before the war, at no time was the working class ready to be led into revolution. But the government feared otherwise. Remembering pre-war labour troubles and uncertain of the mood of the returning forces after several mutinies, they made an attempt to establish what the Home Secretary called a 'Citizen Guard', manned by 'members of the public'. An appeal for volunteers was made to employers and through the press. But the government knew neither the mood nor the temper of its common folk: they looked for revolutionaries and found ratepayers! The indignant reaction of one trade union branch was typical: 'The 1,200 members of this Branch,' they protested, 'all resident ratepayers of the Borough, strongly resent the strike-breaking circular sent out to employers by the Chief Constable and demand its immediate withdrawal.' Failing this they would take the 'ultimate step' and call a 'town's meeting'!

The government, perhaps moved by this, and innumerable other dire menaces of the same kind, soon decided that the 'need for such an organisation is now considered past'.

But the workers went on talking, and talk it was, above all else, that swept the Labour Party to its first victory, of sorts, in 1924. On the night of that triumph, our constituency returning its first Labour MP, simple socialists like my mother wept for joy and we, the young, felt ourselves the heralds of a new age.

In those early post-war years one observed a growing maturity in mass attitudes towards strangers and a decrease in that xenophobia rife before and (of course) during the war. Italians, Indian seamen, the so-called Lascars, with small groups of coloured people—to all the first decade after the war brought toleration. A certain kind of ignorance had vanished and many old bigotries, though still inlaid deep, remained dormant. Jewish traders came among us now undisturbed, opened shops and moved freely in a social atmosphere unknown before. The war-time travel and experience of so many men, the upheaval in the lives of so many

---

1917 who believed they had come together to arrange the Revolution. All delegates congratulated the Russians on their achievement and some returned home to set up 'workers' councils' on the Russian model. For a short time we even had a 'Manchester soviet' (David Boulton, *Objection Overruled*): our local general staff stood ready; but where were the troops?

women had acted in the end as a form of liberal education: the house, the street, the district, the town even, all somehow mattered less; a new sophistication was abroad.

Great fissures continued to appear in the structure of our village life, filling the older inhabitants with dismay. During the later war years matrons in the streets had seen the first WAACs (women soldiers) swagger by with their bobbed hair, and gazed shocked at the impropriety. By 1922 bobbed, and later even shingled, themselves, powdered and rouged a little, and with a mouthful of pot-white teeth, some of the younger wives had joined their husbands in the pubs and sat drinking with them in the Best Room—'bitter for bitter'. Smoking, however, among working-class women was not, I believe, 'general', as one writer has claimed; indeed, they bought very few cigarettes for themselves, still considering the habit much too brazen for decent women. The young, as always, especially independent teenage girls of the poor working class, gave cause for concern: they were flatly rejecting, whenever possible, any kind of domestic service. In 1900 that occupation provided work for more men and women than any other, and even in 1914 it still employed, at 1,261,000, by far the largest number of wage-earning women. Only five years later the age-old supply was drying up for good. English working-class girls preferred any kind of job in mill or factory, or even a place with rock-bottom wages at Woolworth's, and freedom—above all, freedom to meet men easily—to the best that domestic service could offer. Reluctantly, after relying for ages on cheap native muscle, the middle and upper classes had to turn for aid to the labour-saving mechanical device, or to the Irish and foreign poor.

And nowhere did young emancipation flash itself more openly than in dress. Evening found teenage girls massed round the new-laid dance floors in their knee-length skirts, silk stockings and vee-necked blouses. A man these days, complained one shocked pensioner in the shop, '—a *decent* man—doesn't know where to put his eyes'.

The short skirt sent a kind of seismic shock through the nation. Female erogenous zones had of course been displayed before, according to the behests of fashion; but never had women shown their legs so wantonly. Many social historians have offered explanations of the phenomenon and especially of the 'immature male' air that women assumed with it. Dr Willett Cunnington[4] suggests that the massive loss of young men during war-time had destroyed the balance of the sexes, causing a 'wave of psychological homosexuality which glorified the boyish ideal. The schoolboy figure became the structure on which fashions were built and young women sought by every physical means to obliterate their feminine outline and assume that of the immature male.' Youth of the time, he believes, was glorified. 'The glorification of youth was, at root, a lament for those who had gone. So much was gone, we had to make the most of what was left.'

This theory has been received with much respect and it may truly have reflected the feelings of many in the middle and upper social reaches. After long inquiry, however, among working-class men and women, young in the early '20's, I have yet to find any who thought that the short hair and schoolboy look of the time represented anything more than a superficial fashion, soon to be replaced by the 'schoolgirl' look. What undoubtedly attracted young men of the period was legs! Far from looking male, girls, with that daring length of limb on show, appeared not less but more delightfully feminine than ever. Young men grouped in dance halls talked 'legs'—ankles, calves, shapes. Other female curves, it is true, had vanished and, with breasts bound to a flatness, all lay concealed within the de-sexed, sack-like dress—a severe emotional loss to the young male; yet this, we felt vaguely, was a sacrifice, the price one had to pay for all this sensual flaunting of the lower limbs. Female legs, scandalised society seemed to be telling us, are now regretfully permitted, but not legs, breasts and buttocks too! It is merely coincidence that when women, the battle won, took to slacks at the end of the '20's they curved boldly again in their natural places? But whatever else the rising and falling skirt of that decade did, for common wear it never swept the ground again. Social freedom brought physical liberty.

Creamed, perfumed and powdered like the 'immoral' actress of 1910, the post-war daughter of the common labourer certainly gloried in the new permissiveness. Our ageing matriarchy, still a mighty power in the land, threw up their hands in horror and blamed it all on the war and the modern lack of parental discipline. Clothes grew lighter in colour and weight. The young men in their ever-widening 'bags' and double-breasted jackets,

[4] C. W. Cunnington, *Women's Clothing in the Present Century.*

slicked and fresh, a different race from their fathers, 'jazzed' with the shameless females in those dance halls and they became together, almost incidentally, the first 'moderns' of the twentieth century. For youth Queen Victoria was indubitably dead. A feeling of release filled the air: impossible to say whence it came; but dumbly one felt that the millions lying lately dead in Flanders had somehow made a contribution.

Yet the newly emergent society had, it seemed, a price to pay, after all. Changing habit brought altered ethical values. In our own community the shop, ever a reactor to local shifts, social and economic, began to register alarming trends. Some old-established credit customers, for instance, became more and more lax in settling up, leaving bills partly unpaid week after week, to allow them cash for leisure spending. Married sons and daughters, recommended by parents of integrity as suitable clients, 'blued' the shop for considerable sums; and this, often, not through poverty. A few, hitherto honest customers, attempted to falsify their tick books. Others began to indulge themselves with 'luxury' foods—best butter, boiled ham, salmon, tongue, cream biscuits—publicans' fare!—on a weekly wage that allowed little more than saveloys and bread and margarine, leaving the shop to suffer for their gourmandise: all practices, my mother indignantly affirmed, almost unknown in the district before the war. The more blatant of our debtors—families earning good money, who had eaten well at our expense and then refused to pay—the old man sued. He would take a half-day off work to go and 'put them in the county court', returning finally to announce in triumph that he had 'show-caused the bloody lot!' The indicted had then to 'show cause' why they should not be sent to prison. This tactic invariably brought a settlement of the debt. But honesty, it seemed, as a social virtue was beginning to fall steadily in general esteem. One reason for its decline was heard loudly espoused, and it may have had some substance. During the war 'winning' and 'scrounging' government property had been a common enough activity of men in the services, often in circumstances which they considered ethically justified. Many perhaps who did not engage in the practice themselves fell into condoning it with a good-humoured cynicism that coloured their attitude in civilian life later. Whatever the reason, property, with those who owned it, after several years of warfare had somehow lost a certain sanctity.

Undoubtedly, from 1918 on, the lives and anti-social practices of the 'low' were looked upon with a far less jaundiced eye than previously. Labourers and even the 'no class' who only a few years before had 'known their place' and kept to it, after military service, perhaps in the trenches (prisons were combed for recruits), seemed no longer willing to return to the ranks of servility. 'Hard faced' now, in street, pub and club, they began to confront their 'superiors', mingling in a way unheard of in pre-1914 England. Against much opposition still, they joined in to profit from the laxer moral code and the easier social climate already being enjoyed by the young of the great dance halls and elsewhere. An increase in the crime rate followed, with a rising incidence of lawlessness[5] among the more 'respectable' working class.

This perturbed the authorities. Already by 1921 the governor of Durham gaol had noted the 'changed character' of some of his inmates. 'A new stamp of offender', he reported, 'has sprung into existence. Men and women of respectable antecedents and parentage, in regular employment and in no respects associated with the criminal class, are taking to serious crime (embezzlement, fraud, false pretences, housebreaking and robbery) with astounding facility.'

Some people, he said, put all this down to the 'spirit of lawlessness acquired by men whilst serving in the forces', but he did not think so: it was rather to be found in the fact that

high wages, once easily earned, more easily spent, are now no longer obtainable. Men and women, boys and girls have all got used to 'big' money out of all proportion to the slight effort necessary to obtain it. The slow but sure economic readjustment of the past year has created a number of disconsolate, feckless people who do not realise that they have been living in an artificial wage market, and unconsciously resent the changed conditions of supply and demand, work and pay. Money they must have to provide the luxuries and amusements to which they have grown accustomed. So they steal, pilfer and loaf.

---

[5] 'The Pools not having been invented, football was free from gambling.' —L. Bailey, *Scrapbook for the Twenties*. This is incorrect. Football pools 'nationalised' a local form of gambling. Before their introduction bookmakers supplied men in factory and workshop with fixed odds football coupons weekly. This kind of illegal betting was very common indeed. Football pools merely made lawful what could not be prevented.

The governor of Shrewsbury gaol noted that

many men are now received into prison whom, in the years before the war, it would have been quite the exception to receive, e.g. railway guards and engine drivers, men with excellent records of long service and in receipt of high rates of pay. Unfortunately pilfering on the railway and elsewhere is very prevalent, and further is done by men who receive good wages and who ordinarily would be classed as very respectable.

The governor of Wandsworth stated that the 'experience and knowledge gained in the Army of motor mechanics has led to a large increase in garage breaking and motor thieving; the type of man affected is usually intelligent and of fairly good education'.

Inside prison and out the working classes were beginning to mix. Nevertheless, the fact remained that the very poor no longer went there either so often or in such large numbers as they had done before the war: by 1921 'general admissions' had fallen by 62 per cent. There was, however, in early post-war years a large increase in the number of people committed for debt[6] and in default of wife maintenance and bastardy payments. This the authorities ascribed to hasty war-time marriages and to 'domestic unfaithfulness during a soldier's separation whilst on active service'. To the fury, no doubt, of many serving sentence, but not before it was time, in 1921 the weekly bastardy payment was raised from five shillings to ten.

Blurring of the social layers continued everywhere throughout the '20's, and the trend became even more marked when thousands of newly unemployed from the upper working class found themselves compelled to share the same economic misery with those they had always looked upon as their social inferiors. Parity in wretchedness bred mutual sympathy. Unquestionably many younger members of the undermass profited culturally and intellectually, too, from this weakening of class distinction and some, through marriage or the rewards of better paid jobs, left the lower stratum behind.

During the first ten years after the war, in our neighbourhood and districts similar, shopkeeping relatives all agreed, rather grudgingly, that in spite of a decline in integrity people appeared

---

[6] In 1918–19 only 1,830 went to prison for debt; in 1922–23 the number had risen to 12,995.

healthier and happier: parents were less authoritarian and closer to their children, who were cleaner and better fed. In spite of the massive unemployment of 1921 and of the slump years later, poverty was never again of the same depth and magnitude that we knew in Edwardian Britain. Repeatedly our old neighbours remarked, 'Times are bad now, but nothing like before the war.' The worst cripples, the imbeciles, the openly destitute had begun to disappear into institutions. Less conventionally moral, less censorious and self-righteous, our community had somehow grown in knowledge, confidence and sophistication. One felt the new awareness that men had brought back with them from war. Not only the poor but the working class as a whole had somehow grown far bolder and more articulate. A street discussion took progressively a more intelligent political turn; labourers were no longer grateful to their masters. At intervals ILP speakers gathered attentive audiences not five yards from our shop doorway, where the old SDF speakers had preached in vain. Labour Party candidates easily gained places now on the local council. Many more books, periodicals, newspapers were to be seen in ordinary homes. My mother recalled the plaint of our burial club collector. 'Some of 'em are reading mad!' he grumbled. 'They buy paper after paper, but won't pay the weekly penny these days, to bury their dead!' The *Daily Herald*, a powerful left-wing voice now, had reached a circulation of nearly 300,000. Certainly our two newsagents' shops, poor strugglers before the war, flourished now, dealing with printed words in a quantity and variety unprecedented; though let it be admitted that the racing novels of Nat Gould and the exploits of Sexton Blake and Nelson Lee stood easily first in popular taste. Many more people in the district owned small musical instruments, especially banjos and ukeleles. Gramophones had long since grown commonplace and pianos, with the developing hire-purchase system, ceased to remain the preserve of shopkeeper, publican and rich artisan. After 1922 the wireless crystal set spread with phenomenal speed into the lower ranges of the working class, its parts being so cheap to buy and easy to assemble. Radio even more than cinema brought tremendous gains, cultural and social, which are probably unassessable. A new literacy was on the march and with it a change in morals.

After the war, writes one modern historian, 'sexual morality was alleged to have become laxer. There is little serious evidence for this and some against it.'⁷ He gives no support to either view. If, however, laxer sexual morality means an increase in copulation outside marriage, his statement will surprise only those—in the working class, at least—who lived through the times with their young eyes open. The 'gay' '20's, the 'crazy' '20's, were not so called for nothing.⁸ But the staid facts first.

Save for the cracks about its base, the British social structure stood essentially the same as it did before 1914. The post-war activities of a small section of middle- and upper-class nonentities, publicised by the popular press, gave rise to much talk about 'sex mad' youth but little proof of a wholesale decline in sexual morality. The social effects of 'Noel Cowardism' were never widespread. It would have taken more than four years of external warfare to undermine the stolidity of an English bourgeoisie set in a mould at least seventy years old. Only major defeat, and foreign occupation perhaps, could have accomplished that. By 1920 men and women who had lived forty years under Queen Victoria were only sixty years of age. They held the reins of political and social power still. After 1918 men poured back into civilian life. To judge from the literature of the time and the free talk of those who served, especially married men, it is striking to find how many attested to strict fidelity to their wives; this either through fear, embarrassment, a belief in the sanctity of the marriage vows, or through a mixture of all three. Many of the celibate, afraid of both copulation and disease, claimed an equal chastity. Despite all these assertions, however, and the assurances from high places about the 'honour' of Britain's fighting men, the plain fact remains that by 1917, when sheaths were officially issued, approximately twenty per cent of the forces had contracted venereal disease. How many of the rest, and in what proportion, had been 'honourable', cautious or lucky, no one can ever know. In 1914 Lord Kitchener, fully aware, as was every decent Englishman, of the erotic nature of the French, allies though they might be, warned the British Expeditionary Force *en masse*: each man received a personal printed message from the Field Marshal himself. 'In this new experience', he said, 'you may find

⁷ A. J. P. Taylor, *English History, 1914–45.*

⁸ From 1918 onwards the USA, roaring through a mindless euphoria of its own, poured into Britain a flood of new films, new fashions, new songs and dances, all replacing or invigorating primmer native productions.

temptations . . . and while treating all women with courtesy, you should avoid any intimacy. Do your duty. Fear God. Honour the King.' Later in the war the French authorities (who perhaps never got the message) kindly provided the British troops with brothels; but the queues outside were never as long, maybe, as some shocked observers reported. The alarming increase in both venereal disease and illegitimacy had compelled the education of the Forces in the use of contraceptives. This later went a long way to dispel the furtiveness which in past years had always attached to their sale.

Altogether, though, it is surely inadmissible to suggest that the aftermath of war led to no laxity in sexual morals and even to greater restrictions. In 1920 the divorce rate alone was at least twice as great as it had been in 1913–14. Very soon after the war, it is true, the 'flaunting women' amateurs giving soldiers a good time on leave had vanished in a storm of neighbourhood disapproval. Some returned to home and husband with a badly dented reputation; but two, at least, in our village, like others probably, went on to professional prostitution. Beyond doubt, in the working class, signals were flying which left the discerning in no two minds at all about moral shifts in the times. The possession of a rubber sheath succeeded in giving to thousands of young men a new-found self-assurance in their relationships with women, which, after leaving the forces, they lost no time in proving. This led to something unique in the working class. From 1919 onwards every workshop and factory of any size sported a new type of employee—the male in his twenties, demobbed after years in the army or navy, unattached and obviously out to get some 'joy'. A sex education, crude but effective, was promptly passed on to apprentices, improvers and other teenagers, who, of course, looked up to their tutors as sophisticated men of the world. For these Lotharios, to display French letters (a commonplace) was merely to show passports to manhood. Some older workmen frowned on the practice, but, save for a few strait-laced exceptions, they enjoyed well enough the constant flow of obscene joke and story that accompanied talk about sex. This, though, did not at all prevent their complaining that in prewar days there had been much less lasciviousness in workshops, though, they admitted, more drunkenness.

One young journeyman of the new type, an ex-sailor, passed on to our astonished ears a legend now grown hoary. On account, he gave us to understand, of ecclesiastical and government pressure, the makers of sheaths were compelled, secretly, to manufacture one in every half-dozen specially fragile: this to prevent the possible extinction of the human race. He, himself, though, careless of posterity, foiled both Church and State by testing every new packet of his own sheaths on the compressed air blower in the foundry, and, sure enough, found the weakling. No girl, he assured us, at the 'Crown', our dance hall, needed to fear the consequences of his manly ardour, and he wanted the fact generally known.

Early in 1918 Marie Stopes published her *Married Love*, a book, selling in vast quantities over the next decade, that made an enormous impact on working-class consciousness. The young apprentice saw it in the 'dirty rubber goods shop' snuggling between the works of Paul de Kock and Balzac's *Droll Tales*: he marked it with a knowing grin, believing the author to be some sort of notorious female who had taken to pornography. Wherever labouring men gathered, the name of this astonishing woman, who in 1921 had opened the first birth control clinic in Britain, was always good for a mindless guffaw. Yet we had the few journeymen, too, and the odd woman in the mill and sewing shop, who would quietly lend out their own copy of *Married Love* or *Wise Parenthood* to anyone genuinely seeking enlightenment. The libel action in 1923 which Marie Stopes brought, and finally lost, against the Roman Catholic Dr Halliday Sutherland, focused nation-wide attention on the question of birth control and the use of contraceptives. Out of it all, youth did not fail to gain some positive information and many women and girls a knowledge that led to more sexual freedom, both inside and outside marriage.

In the explosive dancing boom after the war, the young from sixteen to twenty-five flocked into the dance halls by the hundred thousand: some went 'jigging' as often as six times a week. The great 'barn' we patronised as apprentices held at least a thousand. Almost every evening except Friday (cleaning night at home) it was jammed with a mass of young men and women, class de-segregated for the first time. At 6*d* per head (1*s* on Saturdays) youth at every level of the manual working class, from the bound apprentice to the 'scum of the slum', fox-trotted through the new bliss in each other's arms.

About the interior of our paradise there hung a faint Moorish air, given off perhaps by the wallpaper, with its minarets, and a narrow gazebo attached high in the angle of an upper wall. From this an excellent band dispensed rhythm almost without cease. Beneath it stood an arc of a dozen chairs in an area known as the 'whores' parlour'. Round the rest of the walls ranged wooden forms. An MC, relict of pre-war days, still presided. He lingered on, in fact, until the '30's, when, in those seedier days, he turned into a 'manager'. Our major domo stood five feet one—a pocket Valentino in evening dress. He had, however, a fearsome reputation as a Don Juan and was alleged to have fathered no fewer than seven bastards on the hall's lady patrons. Dances were still announced (a practice that soon disappeared with the lees of other formalities), the band struck up, the great hall dimmed and a searchlight hit a huge ball of coloured mirrors turning at the ceiling, setting a myriad bright dabs of spectrum gambolling along the walls. At a signal from 'Rudolph' a dozen bold 'stewardesses', superb dancers, rose, quitted the 'parlour', picked off the benches any callow, presentable youth, in for the first time, and swirled him on to the floor, there to taste the sweets of motion and, later, to add substance to the belief that no stewardesses wore corsets. This in itself was highly educational in a milieu where one's own dancing girl friend, encased from waist to shoulder blades, had all the resilience of a pillar box.

Generally, men lined one side of the hall, women the other. A male made his choice, crossed over, took a girl with the minimum of ceremony from in among and slid into rhythm. The floor lay a perfect gloss, spoiled only by a canting towards the north-west. Nowhere in the land were Great Britain's $1\frac{3}{4}$ million surplus women more in evidence than at the dance halls. There, when every available male had found a partner, blocs of girls either still flowered the walls or had paired themselves off in resignation to dance with each other—though in this last there was yet hope. At all 'common' halls men danced together too. For the most part, this in no way indicated homosexual inclination: a couple of males on the move could mean that they were still too shy to ask girls; but more often their mobility would give them a better chance to judge a female pair's dancing ability and charms. Having made selection, one sailed up in mid-foxtrot and 'split' the couple.

In his way our MC (backed by two large chuckers-out) was a stickler for decorum. All dancers had to perform in a seemly manner; the standard of the *habitués* was high indeed. He made no objection to the effeminate few who danced together all evening, but came down heavily on any males gyrating as they smoked, or with their hats on. That, he felt, lowered the tone. Most of us went to the 'Crown' to dance and to find a girl to dally with on Sunday evening—sex night Number One—down some local lovers' lane. The country over, this sabbath activity, of course, meant nothing new. What shocked the staid was the vast increase in its incidence and the youthfulness of some of those participating. Most youngsters naturally fell in love, courted and wedded in the conventional way, an artisan's daughter in the now highly competitive marriage field being only too happy to tie herself to a labourer's son. Some wily males, conditioned by evidence of the dance halls, soon gauged soundly enough the state of the marriage mart and the anxiety of many in the opposite sex to quit spinsterhood. The young uncommitted male time and again saw fine attractive girls 'throw themselves away'—sometimes with a great sigh of relief, it must be said, that their days of freedom were over. 'They'll wed anyone in trousers now,' said our matrons, talking sadly in the shop.

Many girls assumed a personality role to suit the men they picked up with an expertise that it was a pleasure to witness. Did the male appear to like a respectable, homely type, like his mother, who wouldn't let any man touch her (except him—just a little)? That's what he got! Or did he seem to prefer more accessible charms, with the promise of further delights as soon as the pact was sealed and *publicised*? That, too, was available. And there were others still who would take a chance without promise beyond a 'gentleman's' word. Many and varied were the anxious subterfuges used, and heard of, on the over-stocked female market, and all, in the context of the times, were understandable. In any society, where one sex greatly exceeds the other in number, the accepted marriage form tends to the polygamous or polyandrous. Is it not likely, then, that in post-war Britain monogamy came under some pressure and that the young unmarried woman in her anxiety grew less sexually moral? That, at least, is how it seemed to the young male on the scene at the time. In the new airs that certainly blew during the early '20's, plenty of working class girls, in their efforts to 'beat the market', went well beyond the tenets laid down by mothers. Some, we knew, dared all and failed: others got their man with a pregnancy. 'I would have married her, anyway,' crestfallen friends told us—for not all, unfortunately, learned a lesson from the Lotharios. And the wise boys with their 'self-protectors' went on happily dancing in a city littered with 'common' halls. If only a few of their triumphs, boasted of later at lathe and bench, were true, the new men had great cause for satisfaction.

Again, in the early '20's, more young people began to frequent public houses. Young men bragged of having had a drink with father: a real breakthrough, though some seniors would not countenance this at all. My own father professed himself shocked to the core by the sight of his nineteen-year-old son standing in a public house. Walking the countryside became for the first time a widespread attraction among the manual working class. Young men and women in pairs, groups and droves went 'rambling'. Market Street, Manchester, on a Sunday morning was typical of many another city street—one saw what looked like a marching army of youth *en route* for London Road station and the Derbyshire hills. There was less parental supervision. Adolescent boys and girls started to stay out later in the evening, defying home rule. This was still hazardous and led in many homes to curtailment of leisure and even beatings. *And the pattern of it all was repeated in every corner of industrial Britain.* A dancing craze continued through the land; every hall where a few couples could meet and shuffle round a candle-waxed floor rang to syncopated music. Religious bodies, except the narrowest, after much troubled thought, let their rooms for decorous little hops; the Roman Catholics even allowed dancing after church on Sunday evenings. 'Momma goes here,' we sang, 'and Momma goes there, Momma goes jazzing everywhere, But poor Poppa!'—Many a poor poppa of the old school sat at home angry, puzzled, frustrated, slowly unclenching his authority. 'Disgusted' went on writing to the newspapers. And the young sons and daughters of the common herd danced night after night, bodies close in an ecstasy of rhythm. Never before had the children of the people tasted such freedom, and didn't they take some advantage of it? There may be statistics to show that the times were more moral sexually than ever, but I for one must take leave to doubt them.

Very soon in the '20's one heard much savage criticism about a 'frivolous, dance-mad, sex-crazy nation' bent on 'betraying all those things for which men had made the supreme sacrifice in war'. Preachers, playwrights, politicians, novelists all spoke as if the men who died had fought, as one, for some newer, purer, nobler Britain which they themselves now held in ideal. This myth has persisted ever since. Yet it is doubtful if any man joined the forces through the politicians' lures of a 'better world' to come. Indeed, that much-quoted promise of a 'land fit for heroes to live in' was not made until November 1918. Men enlisted for other reasons, some spurred on in mid-war, perhaps by promises that never materialised. Yet how many expected social miracles or in fact even wished for basic change? In the 'victory' election of 1918 the country returned an overwhelming mass of Conservatives to a coalition government; Labour representatives increased from a pre-war fifty at best to sixty-three. The prime of British manhood lay dead in foreign fields, that we all too tragically knew. Had they lived, people said, what a different land Great Britain would have been! But one is forced to ask—how different? The great majority of those who never returned, like the men who survived, were products of a class structure which conditioned them to defend, with all its faults and virtues, the country *they knew*, not to fight for some idealised land of the future. The lost ones, with all their courage, had been cast in the same mould as those who came back. Would they not, returning too, have gone on to act out their lives within the same traditions and class patterns as the rest? To talk, then, of their being 'betrayed' is surely meaningless. The post-war decade, for all its great social shortcomings, was a far more humane and civilised time than the twenty years which preceded it. One major example of the stirring of social sense was to be seen in the terms of the Unemployment Insurance Act of 1920.

By the end of the war the wage gap between skilled and unskilled workers had narrowed considerably, causing a commensurate change in all kinds of social attitudes. In 1920 unemployment insurance was extended to cover virtually all those who earned less than £5 a week. A scheme which at its inception in 1911 had insured only 3 million in building, engineering and shipbuilding, now took in 12 million—nearly the whole of the working population. The skilled and unskilled, on falling out of work, were entitled to draw unemployment pay *at the same rate*. This one Act alone undermined an age-long class barrier that had divided artisan from labourer. More than any other single factor it might well have stifled revolution.

By the mid-'20's a few children in our village were beginning to attend technical and 'Central' schools: something entirely new in the culture pattern. Several local apprentices went to night classes and one saw more acquaintances in the public library; though even here, by 1926 the whole of the Lancashire library service had only 8,000 readers and a book stock of a mere 20,000. This rose within the next ten years to a readership of 167,000 and a stock of 297,000 books. Men went on changing their minds. Steadily, in the innumerable industrial ghettos of which our village has been the example, the old pre-war élite, arbiter of public conduct, manners and morals, began to lose its influence and power. A new generation was establishing itself, less sure perhaps of dogmatic moralities but more aware, better educated and growing more certain of its rights and needs. Above all, the children of the pre-war poor lived in a world better than their fathers had ever known. When unemployment struck, with a new authority, men no longer begged, as their elders had done, for the 'right to work'; they insisted on the right to be maintained with a voice and vigour unheard of before, and maintenance of a sort the State grudgingly allowed. The children of the undermass were mute no more.

And the small shop at the corner? One day in the late '20's my mother had started packing. After thirty-two years she was leaving it all at last! I came home late one evening. The house was still, Father in bed; pictures from the walls leaned the length of the Welsh dresser. My mother stood in the back kitchen, her face grey.

'What happened?' I asked.

She didn't answer at once, then: 'He won't go,' she said quietly.

'But he promised!—again and again!'

She shook her head: 'He calls the shop his little bank now, his second pension,' she said bitterly. 'He changed his mind: he won't go.'

So she left him. But after thirty-four years together neither could live apart from the other, he in a sort of pride, she in sorrow, and they soon died, both victims, like countless others, of the industrial Moloch, hardly catching a glimpse of what the good life could have been.

That little world between the railway lines, with many another of its kind, has now been swept away. Except for a factory here and there, desolation remains. Perhaps the next generation will landscape it and there will be fields again, trees, flowers, a stream maybe—much as it must have been two centuries ago. And all that dark excrescence of an industrial age, like the poor folk who lived and toiled there, will have vanished like a lost medieval village.

Conducted Tour

The first field he saw was the property of the city ratepayers. A notice said so, and added succinctly, 'Keep Off'. 'Come on,' said his sister, 'there's some grass up 'ere they'll let yer walk on.' But he bent down, pressed his face against the railings and full in view of an approaching ratepayer he ripped up a handful by the roots. His sister registered horror. 'You wicked, awful boy!' she shrilled. 'Put it back this very minute! If t' parky sees yer 'e'll chuck us both out, an' quite right an' all.' Primly she began to press the clod back into position, then, noticing his injured look and the ratepayer's receding back, she changed her mind and dropped it into her carpet bag. 'P'raps it'll do for t' winder box edgin'. But listen, stupid, we don't want no grass—grass is nowt; it grows between t' nicks in t' flags. It's flowers we're after.' Her eye fell on a rectangle of daffodils some thirty yards beyond the railing. She stopped, and gazed like a lover across the sward. 'That lot, now,' she whispered, 'them's beauties!'

'It's a grave,' he said, 'don't pinch off a grave!'

'Garn',' she answered scornfully, 'this is a park—a public park, they don't bury 'em in 'ere. Now 'old this bag, will yer, an' listen. If yer see a bloke with a long coat, flat cap, whistle an' stick—that's 'im! Give us a shout an' 'op it.'

Fascinated, he watched her clear the barrier like a hurdler and skim over the grass on her bare feet. She had gathered no more than half a dozen when agonised whistle blasts shrieked detection. Two park keepers were galloping towards her over the green. Petrified, he stayed long enough to see her, still clasping the flowers, describe a flying circle round her pursuers and disappear with swift grace into the rhododendrons, then he fled in a blubbering panic.

She found him half an hour later, snivelling to himself, in between sips from his bottle of sugar and water. She stepped gaily up the twisting path with an early rhododendron nodding from

o

her bosom. 'Oh, 'ere y' are,' she said. 'Can't yer read a notice? This is t' females.'

'I didn't know if I was a male or a female. Did—did they catch yer?'

'Them!' she said contemptuously. 'They couldn't catch cold. But there's a long thin 'un, though,' she added reflectively, 'an' 'e's pretty 'ot. Come on now, stop weeping, an' we'll go an' 'ave us dinner on the 'ill, among all them lovely statues.'

'Don't,' she said, as they finished their bread and she screwed up the wrapping, 'don't ever leave paper about in the park. It makes an awful mess. Allus put it in a basket.' Suiting her action to the words, she tossed the paper into a receptacle and, in exchange, retrieved a piece of orange peel, which she shared with scrupulous exactness between them. He nibbled meditatively and considered the statuary. 'They're all niggers,' he said at last.

'They look like niggers,' she corrected. 'But they're not. Scrat 'em with a nail, an' they come up lovely an' white.'

'I 'aven't got a nail,' he said regretfully. 'What's that lot with all snakes round 'em?'

'Them,' she explained, 'is called "Laycoons"—snake charmers.'

'An' 'im wi' t' stone trouzis on?'

'Oh 'im,' she said, 'that's a bloke called John Smart Esq., though,' she added, eyeing with some distaste a favourite perch for pigeons, ' 'e doesn't look so smart from 'ere.'

'An' 'er with a crown on?' he inquired. But there was no answer. She stood silent, transfixed.

' 'Er with a crown on?' he said again. He followed her gaze to where the late John Smart reared in filthy stone out of a triangle of tulips.

'Jus' look at 'em!' she breathed softly. 'Jus' look! I could love 'em!'

Fear fluttered like a little bird in his stomach. 'Not again,' he whispered.

' 'Old that bag,' she said quietly.

Then, with astonishment, he felt himself whipped round on his heels, and they were hurrying down the avenue. 'Come on,' she said, 'we goin' in t' public museum.' Cursing his carelessness, a long, thin park keeper strolled from behind the statue.

In the vestibule she wiped his nose, pulled up a stocking from round his ankle and fastened a loose clog. 'An' walk on yer tiptoes in 'ere,' she said. 'Clogs make such a clatter on marble. First,' she advised, 'we're going ter see a man what's been dead ten thousand years. All wrap up in bandages 'e is.' 'E must 'ave 'ad a terrible accident, she thought.

They pushed open a glazed door into a dim world of naked men and women, standing about on little stone tables. His nostrils sensed a familiar disinfectant. ' "Klensit Kleaner" they're using,' she remarked knowledgeably. 'Good for insects too.'

At the far end of the stone bodyguard, beyond the turnstile, they saw a figure slumped in repose across a bentwood chair. 'We're laughin',' she said, ' 'e's asleep.' Stealthily they inched down the hall, the girl a good yard in front. With soft care she negotiated the turnstile, when suddenly it kicked her viciously in the back and cast her forth again.

The official rose and rubbed his eyes. ' 'Op it,' he said.

'It's for the public, isn't it?' she asked.

'You and 'im,' he remarked heavily, pointing down at the boy as if he were sixpence, 'you an' 'im is not the public. Now 'op it, afore I put me foot in yer.'

'I could,' she said, with great distinctness, 'bring a policeman to make yer.'

'What!'

They were through the door again with the swiftness of a dream, blinking in the over-brilliant sunshine. Behind them the echoes from the turnstile still chattered indignantly among the naked gods.

Sitting at the knees of Discobulus they recovered their composure. There, in response to his earnest pleading, she consented magnanimously not to call the police forthwith.

'But it's not fair at all,' she told him, as if he now were partly responsible for the humiliation. 'Last time I walked straight through an' saw every single thing, an' I got a lovely little jug an' all.'

Her eye settled on a grimy Greek temple, skulking behind some shabby sycamores. The museum was forgotten. 'Public Reading Room an' Library,' she announced. 'Now, stop 'ere this time an' wait.'

'Will I 'ave ter go to that—that place again?' he quavered. She considered the question.

'No,' she said, 'not if I come out walking.'

He watched her go, trembling at her courage. She crossed the path and disappeared down a flight of cavernous steps into the cellar that housed the public library. With his heart thumping, he prepared for flight. Soon, however, he saw her returning quite sedately. Her carpet bag seemed weighted now against oscillation.

'He's a nice ol' cock down there,' she said. 'I allus call. I'll get a book off 'im one o' these days, you'll see. 'E says 'e'll let me join when I'm eleven.' She dived into her bag and took out a large black volume. 'Hum! *Better Badminton*,' she sniffed. 'No pictures, neither. Do yer want it?' He shook his head. She was about to punt it into the shrubbery when she noticed Queen Victoria athwart a lump of granite, perusing the city's charter with deep indifference. She climbed the podium and slipped the volume onto her grimy lap. 'There,' she said, ' 'ave a go at that— it'll be a change for yer.'

By a charmingly direct route, across another holy plot, the shallow end of the duck pond, two tennis courts and a crown bowling green, they reached the swings. At the entrance they fell in with two park keepers. His heart leapt in his chest and he started to bolt.

' 'S all right,' she said. 'They're busy.' Between them the keepers were dragging, half carrying, a terrified little man in a yellow raincoat.

'Where are they takin' 'im?' he asked.

'Prison,' she said briefly. ' 'E's a nasty ole man.'

All the swings in the ground were occupied. She chose one tenanted by a red, bullet-headed lad, and tried direct action. 'Come off it!' she ordered. 'It's 'is birthday, an' 'e wants a swing.'

'Birthday is it?' said the boy. 'Well, 'ere's a present for 'im.' The iron-bound swing cleaved the air and, in the ascending arc, hit him full across the stomach. He collapsed without comment, his forehead in the warm sand, and lay quiescent. His sister, spitting fury, flew into the chase. Two bigger lads carried him to a wall, sympathetically took possession of the swing and forgot him. After an age the pain in his stomach dissolved into a dull ache. He opened one eye and, without interest, watched a sand beetle scuttle across his line of vision. Then, quite gently, he vomited. She returned in triumph, flicking her long hair from her shoulders with a sharp jerk of the head.

'I pasted 'im all right,' she said, 'an' ripped 'is shirt too. Are yer satisfied?'

'Lemme go 'ome,' he said dully.

'Oh, not yet,' she cried. 'There's t' paddlin' yet.'

With his clogs on a string round his neck, he stood knee-deep in the pool and waited. The water was alive with children and smelled of 'Klensit Kleaner'. Dully he watched his sister filling his stocking with water and wielding it on all about her like a soft bludgeon. Once she came across and shook him by the arm.

'We're 'aving a lovely time, aren't we?' she yelled.

'Yes,' he said, 'a lovely time.'

He remained standing in one place until his feet throbbed with cold. The noise surged up against him, beating on his eardrums. He felt tired, very tired. His sister came across once more and flicked a spray of water towards him.

'Splash yer!' she screamed. 'Splash yer!' He smiled and cupped his fingers towards the pool. Quite suddenly he vomited again.

'Come on,' she said. 'You've 'ad enough.'

They made their way up the hill as the keepers' whistles, in long, melancholy blasts, moaned out lock-up time. Children dribbled in hundreds along the paths for home. The park stood waiting, like a weary mother, for the brood to be gone.

At the top of the hill the girl turned and gazed over the few fields to the great sullen vale that lay behind. ' 'Undred and twenty chimbleys,' she said. 'I've counted 'em. 'Undred an' twenty big black fingers!'

'Come on 'ome,' he whimpered. 'I wanner go 'ome.'

She stared beyond the smoke, far beyond, to where the Pennines, green and aloof in the day's last sunshine, were breaking the horizon.

'Them's 'ills,' she said.

He began to whimper again. She placed a thin arm round his shoulders. 'Now don't cry, son,' she said, 'not now. Yer've been such a good boy all day.' The whimper took on volume.

'Listen!' she said eagerly, 'I'm goin' ter let yer throw this bottle at a statue.' She took the empty water bottle from her bag and handed it to him. 'There! Now, take yer pick.' He chose an imposing figure that stood upon a pedestal smiling benignly at the dark city. 'Sir Joshua Grimes,' she read doubtfully. 'Mayor, 1897–1900—"Ars et Industria".' The bottle hit him behind the right ear and tinkled down his toga. 'That's catched 'im a beauty,' she said.

Then she took his hand in hers and together they passed through the gates and into the darkening city road.

'Well,' she said, 'it's been a lovely day, though *I didn't* get you a birthday present after all. But never mind,' she added. 'Next time, if you're a *very* good boy, I'll try an' get yer a real live duck!'

Snuffy

The public library which Snuffy patronised in the early years of this century was housed in a commodious cellar. All its contents were bound in black, toning, often enough, with the borrowers' hands. Mr Shadlock, the 'Lib'arian', as he called himself, had been a policeman until one evening during the dockers' strike of 1899, when two stevedores borrowed his truncheon and invalided him permanently from the Force. Through the good offices of his uncle, however, Alderman Ben Shadlock, he had been grafted on to the public library service. Fortunately he could read.

Joining the library sixty years back was, for a child, an essay in adventure. Snuffy went, nerves tensed, cap in hand, down the long, dark ramp, eased himself through the swing doors and tiptoed to the counter. Beyond, on a stool, bathed like a priest in holy calm, sat Mr Shadlock himself, deep in the racing handicap book. The boy stood for a time in respectful silence, then he sighed, sniffed, shuffled twice, coughed politely through his hot fingers, and at last, his heart pounding, he dared to put the question. 'P-please, sir, could I 'ave a joinin' form, sir?' Mr Shadlock pursued his studies. The minutes trod softly by. A gas jet belched delicately behind its frosted globe. The wall-clock tittered. Snuffy drew breath and tried again, but the words stuck in his gullet; a thin, foolish bleat threaded the silence. He blushed scarlet, licked his dried lips and turned to go. Then Mr Shadlock spoke, suddenly, violently. 'Eh?' Panic-stricken, the boy stuttered into speech. 'P-please, sir, could I—could——' Like a bomb the Librarian burst among the faltering syllables. 'Out of it!' he roared.

'Didn't yer tell 'im it was for the vicar?' asked his elder sister later. Snuffy admitted the error. 'You should allus say it's for the vicar,' Em' counselled, 'or for Mr Arnott at the "Duke of York", or some nob like that. It's terrible 'ard to get a form off yer own bat.' After five attempts, however, Snuffy succeeded.

' ''Ow old are yer?' asked Mr Shadlock suspiciously.

' ''Leven an' 'alf, sir,' he lied.

'Yer on the small side for eleven an' 'alf.'

'All our family's on the small side,' pleaded the boy.

'Mm. We like 'em,' said the Librarian, 'at least, to come with their 'eads up to the counter.' Grumbling, he flicked him a long, pink form. 'Get one alderman or two burgesses to go bail for yer.'

Snuffy's acquaintance with either aldermen or burgesses being limited, he provided the signatures himself, and appended that of 'one (male) parent', feeling, in his father's case, that a mere cross might prejudice his entry into the literary world. Mr Shadlock, to his surprise, viewed the result with black suspicion. 'These 'ere names, now,' he said, after a long inspection, 'if you ask me, was all the work of the same 'and.' He paused, studied again and launched into calligraphical detail. 'Just look at them s's now! An' them F's!—Forbes, an' Forster —the dead spitten image o' one another.' He paused once more, flicked his glasses up his forehead, glared down at the boy from a tremendous height and repeated slowly, accusingly, '—the dead, spitten ruddy image! You could be 'ad up for this.'

Snuffy got his chin on the counter, gripped the chamfered edge to control his trembling, and reproved the Librarian coldly. 'I am not,' he said, 'in the 'abit of forgin' people's names.'

'No, I can see that,' said Mr Shadlock. 'An' don't give me none o' yer lip, neither.' Suddenly he crushed the form into a ball and bounced it off Snuffy's skull. All hope blasted, the boy turned away. He had reached the swing doors when, quite surprisingly, the Librarian called him back and spun another form across the counter. 'Now go an' get two proper burgesses.'

'No book?' asked his sister when he reached home. Snuffy explained the bitter injustice. Em' went and got pen and ink. 'Gimme that form,' she said wearily . . .

'Now that's somethink like!' approved Mr Shadlock when Snuffy appeared again. 'Now why didn't you act like a straight-forward, decent, honest boy before—eh?' Snuffy hung his head in repentance. 'Go an' take yer pick.'

Books for circulation stood in two glass cases about four feet square, one at either end of the counter. One case was labelled 'Fiction', the other 'General'. Mr Shadlock, feeling no doubt that the distinction was merely academic, mixed both categories with brisk abandon. Snuffy pressed a finger against the dusty pane. 'This one, mister.' The Librarian jerked a book out, stamped it, then flicked over a page or two.

'See there!' he said, pointing. 'That's a list o' pictures in this 'ere book. Let there be one missing, just one, when yer bring it back, an' you'll be 'ad up.'

Snuffy began to read as he left the library counter. He read eagerly, lovingly, soaking up the words that fell like water on a dry place, his short-sighted eyes close to the page, his lips moving in concentration. And slowly, as he drifted through the streets, his mind took flight, 'winging its way' into a world of sunlit forests and incredible adventure. Three hours later, sitting on the edge of his bed, he returned to reality. For a time he stared in front of him, drugged, stupid with words, then with a delicious sigh he turned to the frontispiece, gazed long upon its garish brilliance, and then, carefully, tenderly, he tore it out.

Mr Shadlock, let it be said, was not a man to interfere with his young readers' freedom of choice. He never, for instance, tried to force his own selection upon their notice. All he asked was reciprocal treatment. Any child who requested a book by title he at once designated as 'forward' or 'lippy'. 'If it's not in the case,' he would announce briskly, 'it's not in the Liberry. Go take yer pick, an' sharp about it!'

Once Snuffy, seized with a longing for *The Last of the Mohicans* and desperate from a diet of improving works, pointed to the towering racks beyond the counter. 'Maybe it's one o' them, mister?'

The Librarian pursed his lips, shook his head and looked grave. 'Oh, we mustn't disturb them, boy, not them,' he said, 'them's 'oldin' up the roof.'

In despair Snuffy went to the case, peered closely through the glass and his heart leapt. It was there! there! the letters twinkling gold upon the dirty spine. 'This one, mister!' he called, 'this one!'

Mr Shadlock snatched at the case, stamped the book with a bang, pushed it across and turned his attention to a stoutish adult. Snuffy dived between the covers and recoiled in horror. *Work*, said the title, *and Prayer*. Agonised, he turned again to the counter.

'I don't want this, mister, please, not this.'

'No?' said Mr Shadlock pleasantly. 'No? Sorry if 'is lordship's not satisfied. 'And it back, then.'

Snuffy returned the volume and hurried once more to the case. 'It's this one I want, mister, this one,' he called.

'Card suspended for one month,' announced the Librarian, to the nodding approval of the stout gentleman. 'Young devils!—run the feet off yer if you'd let 'em.'

Of all Mr Shadlock's juvenile readers Snuffy's elder sister bloomed for a term his prime favourite, a state of grace due partly to her frank, open countenance and partly to a mere accident of geography.

'Lemme see, now,' said the Librarian, as Em', a most assiduous reader, returned him a gutted copy of *What Katy Did*, 'lemme see, yer pass Baker's Yard on yer way 'ome, don't yer, missy?'

'Oh yes, sir, certainly, sir. Anythink I can do?'

Mr Shadlock stared at her hard. 'Yer a careful girl?'

'Allus careful, sir.'

'An' honest?'

'I'm top in Miss Abel's Bible class,' she said.

The Librarian passed her a sealed envelope. 'Baker's Yard—you'll see a tall gentleman in a muffler. Give 'im this.'

Outside, Em' slit the envelope, considered the contents and sneered. 'Shillin' win, Boston Boy. If cash, all on 2nd Favourite, 4.30 Kempton,' she read. 'Did you ever see the like of it! Not a cat in 'ell's chance—Boston Boy!' She dropped the shilling in her purse and the envelope, a little later, over the canal bridge. Snuffy, with a regard enhanced for his sister's worldly knowledge, watched in silence as it fluttered onto the water and lay still. 'Ask me for threepence,' she said, 'when I get change.'

Mr Shadlock's judgment of form continued faulty until the Epsom meeting, when he had the good fortune to find the nicely priced winner of the Oaks. Em' had made no provision for such a contingency. Coolly she calculated the odds on the kitchen wallpaper, patterned with similar data worked out on her father's behalf. 'We are,' she said at last, 'seventeen and ninepence shy.'

The enormity of the sum horrified Snuffy. 'An' what about yer liberry book?' he whispered. 'Yer can't never face 'im, yer can't never go back!'

'You take it,' she said indifferently.

'Me! But what can I tell 'im?' he quavered.

She considered a moment. 'Tell 'im,' she said, 'I'm dead.' Then she added as an afterthought, 'Tell 'im I died sudden.'

Snuffy, overwhelmed, put off the dreaded interview as long as possible, but his sister's threats, the fear of a fine and the passionate craving to read another book, all combined to drive him to seek the awful presence. Hare-eyed with fright, he went down the ramp and pushed his head through the doors, then a peace, a blessed joy swept over him. Mr Shadlock was gone, and in his place stood a tall, sour-looking female wearing pince-nez. At once, from the depths of fear his mind swung high in hope. He approached the counter boldly, handing over Em's book.

'' 'Ave yer got a story, please, Miss, that's called *Last o' the Mohicans?*' and added, anxious to assist her in any research she may have to undertake, 'By Dickens.'

'If it's not in the case,' she said distantly, 'it's not in the Library. And,' she went on in acid tones, 'don't you come here again with those hands!'

'It's the only pair I got,' said Snuffy, feeling that the cause was lost.

'No impudence now!' she warned. 'Go and make your choice.' Ignoring his selecting finger, she took a volume, stamped it with a regal gesture and slid it towards him. 'Now be off!' Outside he sat upon the Library steps, opened the book and peered with watery eyes at the title page. *Work*, it said again, *and Prayer*.

With the summer-time Snuffy lived in the streets from early morning until the edge of darkness, his longing for the printed word half forgotten. One day, however, in late August he received an impressive blue document, which, after quoting certain bye-laws, went on to inform him that 'your sponsors, Alderman Thomas Hines and the Rev. Theodore Clarke, B.D., have been apprised of your having unlawfully retained a Public Library volume 53 days beyond the permitted period for perusal'. The penalties, he gathered from the ruck of words that followed, were appalling. Panic seized him. He began a frantic search for *Work and Prayer*, snivelling the while in deepest sympathy for himself. He found it at last under the sofa. Without knowing why, he wrapped the volume in the grey garments of a *Sporting Echo* and, carrying it like a platter, set off at half a run. Suddenly a new, a terrible thought jerked him to a standstill—henceforth the doors of the Library would be closed to him, inevitably and for ever. Barely had he sipped before the sweet waters had run dry. He stared, then began to weep again, softly, to himself. At last, when he was done he sighed and wiped his eyes with the base of his thumb. 'I should of remembered,' he said.

The Library was empty except for Mr Shadlock's successor, who, her back towards the counter, sat knitting by a distant window. Snuffy edged his way across the floor, freezing with fear as she stopped once, but only for a moment, to push a needle under her hair-net and scratch vigorously. Then inch by inch he stole his way forward until at last he reached his goal. And there, as one who lays flowers on a hope that has lately died, he placed his book upon the table and crept away.

Bronze Mushrooms

He made the first at five past six one Monday morning in January 1885. Promotion it was, a step up from brewing tea, sweeping floors and fetching beer for the journeymen brass-finishers. With a skill nonchalant and contemptuous the foreman showed him how. 'Now get thee belly well set against t' lathe bed,' he said, 'feet planted solid on t' floor, an' rip into 'em.' Jockey ripped into them. Golden dross spurted under cold steel. Soon the first bronze mushroom valve jerked away from the headstock and bounced into the box beneath.

'That's the style,' commented his tutor. 'It'll be right after polishin'.'

' 'Ow many will I 'ave to do?' he asked innocently.

' 'Ow many stars in 'eaven?' asked the foreman, and walked away.

Jockey was fifteen then. He was made for the job—neat, compact, big in the forearm. He never did anything else for sixty-one years. As the firm grew, he grew with it. By the start of the new century there was hardly a city on the face of the earth that hadn't, somewhere in it, a 'Sligon' steam chest, and Jockey had made the valves, every single one. He was unique—mushroom maker to mankind.

When he came out of his time, though, there was none of the usual hullabaloo, no rhythmic clouting of spanner on steel to herald the full-blown brass-finisher. ' 'E's doin' a little lad's job,' they said. ' 'E's no tradesman!'

Jockey worked on apologetically. The first twenty thousand valves were behind him. Reluctantly they took him in the union. When he was twenty-five his feet went through the floorboards. A joiner came from the pattern shop and fixed in some new strips. Jockey excused himself: 'I gotta press down, yer see—it wears.'

'Don't apologise,' said the joiner. 'It's not my bleedin' floor.'

P

In 1905 Sligon Steam Chests became a limited company. The owner went round the brass shop shaking hands with his journeymen. 'I started up in 'ere,' he said, 'me an' a little lad. An' look at it now—nine acres of it!'

Jockey felt proud. He was well on the way to his first half million. 'Dullish,' he told himself, 'but steady. They sack 'em an' start 'em—good times an' bad: but all the while they gotter 'ave mushrooms.'

His feet broke through the boards again in 1907 and again in 1916. 'There's no keepin' up wi' thee,' said the old joiner. Jockey smiled sheepishly. It was in 1916 when pressed for labour that they moved to change his job. The new task required the use of templates and a knowledge of the micrometer. Patiently they tried to teach him but, left to himself, Jockey abandoned his lathe and hurried away down the aisle. Curious, the foreman followed. He found him in the shadows behind a giant shaping machine. He was crying to himself.

'I'm past it,' he sobbed.

'All right,' said the foreman wearily, 'get back to thee mushrooms.'

In 1918 Jockey had three days off—'Spanish 'flu,' he apologised, 'couldn't 'old my 'ead up'—and two in 1935, when his wife died; he didn't say anything then—five days in sixty-one years. He was never late. When he was seventy-six, a week after making his millionth valve, the worn-out floor caved under him for the last time. 'That's all I was waiting for,' he said. He flicked off his lathe and went across to the foreman, a man young enough to be his grandson. 'I'm finishin' up at week end, George!' he called over the rattle of machinery.

The foreman looked sympathetic. 'Eh, now fancy! And we was just thinking of makin' you permanent! Well, we'll miss yer, Jockey.'

Together they went back to the lathe and the foreman picked up a valve between finger and thumb and spun it into the air. 'Eh, you must have made a forever of 'em,' he said. 'I'd bet they'd stretch from 'ere to 'ell!'

'Aye,' said Jockey, 'and back.'

The men bought him an armchair. That pleased him. 'An' when you've worn t' seat out o' that,' they said, 'we'll send the joiner to put some boards in!'

Late Friday afternoon the foreman came along with a small bespectacled apprentice. 'Just put him in the way of it, will yer?' he asked.

Jockey smiled down gently at the apprentice: 'Sithee,' he said, 'there's not much to it. Get thee belly well set against t' lathe bed now, feet solid on t' floor, an' rip into 'em!'

Select Bibliography

Unless otherwise stated, the place of publication is London

Angell, N., *The Great Illusion*. Heinemann, 1910.

Arnold, M., *Culture and Anarchy*. Smith Elder, 1869.

Bailey, L., *Scrapbook for the Twenties*. Muller, 1959.

Beer, M., *A History of British Socialism*. Bell, 1919.

Bellamy, E., *Looking backward, 2000–1887*. Ticknor (Boston, Mass.), 1888.

Bennett, A., *Clayhanger*. Methuen, 1910.

— 'Middle class' in *Selected Essays*. Harrap, 1926.

Blatchford, R., *Merrie England*. Scott, 1894.

Booth, C., *Life and Labour of the People in London*. Macmillan, 1902.

Boulton, D., *Objection overruled*. MacGibbon & Kee, 1967.

Box, M., *The Trial of Marie Stopes*. Macdonald, 1967.

Briggs, A., *Victorian Cities*. Odhams, 1963.

Bruce, M., *The Coming of the Welfare State*. Batsford, 1961.

Buckley, J. H., *The Victorian Temper*. Allen & Unwin, 1952.

Bullock, A., *The Life and Times of Ernest Bevin*. Heinemann, 1960.

Burn, W. L., *The Age of Equipoise*. Allen & Unwin, 1964.

Burnett, J., *Plenty and Want*. Nelson, 1966.

Canning, J. (ed.), *Living History: 1914*. Odhams, 1967.

Carr-Saunders, A. M., and Caradog Jones, D. A., *A Survey of the Social Structure of England and Wales as illustrated by statistics*. Oxford University Press, 1927.

Chorley, K., *Manchester made them*. Faber, 1950.

Clapham, J., *An Economic History of Modern Britain*. Cambridge University Press, 1930.

Clarke, I. F., *Voices Prophesying War, 1763–1984*. Oxford University Press, 1966.

Cole, G. D. H., *British Working-class Politics, 1832–1914*. Routledge, 1941.

— *Studies in Class Structure*. Routledge, 1955.

— and Postgate, R. W., *The Common People, 1746–1946*. Methuen, revised edition 1946.

Court, W. H. B., *British Economic History, 1870–1914*. Cambridge University Press, 1965.

Critchley, T. A., *A History of the Police in England and Wales, 1900–1966*. Constable, 1967.

Cunnington, C. W., *Women's Clothing in the Present Century*. Faber, 1952.

Dangerfield, G., *The Strange Death of Liberal England*. Constable, 1936.

Engels, F., *Condition of the Working Class in England in 1844* (trans. Henderson and Chalenor). Blackwell (Oxford), 1958.

Ensor, R. C. K., *England, 1870–1914*. Clarendon Press (Oxford), 1936.

Farnie, D. A., *The Establishment of the New Poor Law in Salford, 1835–50*. MS, Salford Central Library.

Faucher, L. J., *Etudes sur l'Angleterre*. Paris, 1845.

Frazer, P., *Joseph Chamberlain*. Cassell, 1966.

George, H., *Progress and Poverty*. Appleton (New York), 1880.

Gorer, G., *Exploring English Character*. Cresset Press, 1955.

Grossmith, G. and W., *The Diary of a Nobody*. Arrowsmith (Bristol), 1892.

Halevy, E., *History of the English People in the Nineteenth Century*. Unwin, 1924–34.

Hammond, J. L. and L. B., *The Town Labourer, 1760–1832*. Longmans, 1917.

— *The Skilled Labourer, 1760–1832*. Longmans, 1919.

Hannington, W., *Never on our knees*. Lawrence & Wishart, 1967.

Harrison, J. F. C., *Learning and Living, 1790–1960*. Routledge, 1961.

The History of 'The Times', vol. 3: *1884–1912*; vol. 4: *1912–48*. The Times, 1952.

Hobhouse, L. T., *Democracy and Reaction*. Unwin, 1904.

Hobson, J. A., *Imperialism*. Nisbet, 1902.

Hoggart, R., *The Uses of Literacy*. Chatto & Windus, 1957.

Housden, L. G., *The Prevention of Cruelty to Children*. Constable, 1955.

Inglis, K. S., *Churches and the Working Classes in Victorian England*. Routledge, 1963.

Keynes, J. M., *The Economic Consequences of the Peace*. Macmillan, 1919.

Kingsley, C., *Alton Locke*. 1850.

Kitson Clarke, G., *An Expanding Society*. Cambridge University Press, 1967.

Klapper, C., *The Golden Age of Tramways*. Routledge, 1961.

Klein, J., *Samples from English Culture*. Routledge, 1965.

Lansbury, G., *My Life*. Constable, 1928.

Leavis, Q. D., *Fiction and the Reading Public*. Chatto & Windus, 1932.

Lenin, V. I., *On Britain* (trans. Kvitko). Lawrence, 1934.

Lewis, M. M., *The Importance of Illiteracy*. Harrap, 1953.

Longmate, N., *The Water Drinkers*. Hamilton, 1968.

Lowe, C. J., *The Reluctant Imperialists*. Routledge, 1967.

Mann, T., *Tom Mann's Memoirs*. Labour Publishing Company, 1923.

Marcus, S., *The Other Victorians*. Weidenfeld & Nicolson, 1960.

Masterman, C. F. G., *The Condition of England*. Methuen, 1909.

— *England after War*. Hodder & Stoughton, 1922.

Masur, G., *Prophets of Yesterday*. Weidenfeld & Nicolson, 1963.

McManners, J., *Lectures on European History, 1889–1914*: 'Men, machines and freedom'. Blackwell (Oxford), 1966.

Money, L. G. C., *Riches and Poverty*. Methuen, 1905.

Morris, J., *Pax Britannica*. Faber, 1968.

Mumford, L., *The Culture of Cities*. Secker, 1940.

— *Technics and Civilization*. Routledge, 1946.

Neal, S., *Special report on the state of juvenile education and delinquency in the borough of Salford, 1851*. (Figures quoted from G. R. Porter's *Progress of the Nation*.)

Nichols, B., *The Sweet and Twenties*. Weidenfeld & Nicolson, 1958.

Pelling, H., *A Short History of the Labour Party*. Macmillan, 1961.

— *The Social Geography of British Elections, 1885–1910*. Macmillan, 1967.

Perkin, H., *The Origins of Modern English Society, 1780–1880*. Routledge, 1969.

Petrie, C., *The Victorians*. Eyre & Spottiswoode, 1960.

— *Scenes of Edwardian Life*. Eyre & Spottiswoode, 1965.

Pike, E. Royston, *Human Documents of the Industrial Revolution in Britain*. Allen & Unwin, 1966.

Porter, G. R., *The Progress of the Nation*. Knight, 1836–38.

Quennell, M. and C. H. B., *A History of Everyday Things in England*, vol. 4: *1851–1942*. Batsford, 1942.

Quennell, P. (ed.), *Mayhew's London*. Spring Books, undated.

Raynor, J., *The Middle Class*. Longmans, 1969.

Roberts, R., *Imprisoned Tongues*. Manchester University Press (Manchester), 1968.

Rowntree, B. S., *Poverty*. Macmillan, 1901.

Seeley, J. R., *The Expansion of England*. Macmillan, 1883.

Sims, G. R., *How the poor lived*. Chatto & Windus, 1883.

Smith-Nowell, S. (ed.), *Edwardian England, 1901–14*. Oxford University Press, 1964.

Sturt, M., *The Education of the People*. Routledge, 1967.

Tawney, R. H., *The Acquisitive Society*. Murray, 1922.

— *Religion and the Rise of Capitalism*. Murray, 1936.

Taylor, A. J. P., *English History, 1914–45*. Oxford University Press, 1965.

Thompson, E. P., *The Making of the English Working Class*. Gollancz, 1963.

Thornton, A. P., *The Imperial Idea and its Enemies*. Macmillan, 1959.

Tressell, R. [Robert Noonan], *The Ragged Trousered Philanthropists.* Richards, 1914; first unabridged edition, Lawrence & Wishart, 1955.

Tuchman, B., *The Proud Tower.* Hamilton, 1966.

Ullman, R. L., *Britain and the Russian Civil War.* Oxford University Press, 1968.

Veblen, T., *The Theory of the Leisure Class.* Macmillan (New York), 1899.

Webb, B., *My Apprenticeship.* Longmans, 1926.

Webb, R. K., *Modern England from the Eighteenth Century to the Present Day.* Allen & Unwin, 1969.

Webb, S. and B., *The History of Trade Unionism.* Longmans, 1894; revised edition, 1920.

— *English Poor Law History.* Longmans, 1906–29.

Wells, H. G., *Mr Britling sees it through.* Cassell, 1916.

Williams, R., *Culture and Society, 1780–1950.* Chatto & Windus, 1958.

— *The Long Revolution.* Chatto & Windus, 1961.

Woodward, E. L., *Great Britain and the War of 1914–18.* Oxford University Press, 1967.

Woolf, L., *After the Deluge.* Hogarth Press, 1931–39.

Reports

Prison Commissioners' annual reports, 1895–1925.

Reports of the Royal Commission on the Poor Laws and the Relief of Distress (majority and minority reports, 1909).

Index

1. *General*

2. *Index of Persons*